**Mind**

# Mind

Introduction to Cognitive Science

second edition

Paul Thagard

A Bradford Book
The MIT Press
Cambridge, Massachusetts
London, England

MIT Press books may be purchased at special quantity discounts for business or sales promotional use. For information, please email special_sales@mitpress.mit.edu or write to Special Sales Department, The MIT Press, 5 Cambridge Center, Cambridge, MA 02142.

This book was set in Stone sans and Stone serif by SNP Best-set Typesetter Ltd., Hong Kong. Printed and bound in the United States of America.

Library of Congress Cataloging-in-Publication Data

Thagard, Paul.
  Mind: introduction to cognitive science/Paul Thagard.—2nd ed.
    p.   cm.
  "A Bradford book."
  Includes bibliographical references and index.
  ISBN 0-262-20154-2 (hc : alk. paper)—ISBN 0-262-70109-X (pbk. : alk. paper)
  1. Cognitive science—Textbooks. I. Title.
BF311.T42   2005
153—dc22

                                                                  2004053091

10  9  8  7  6  5  4  3  2  1

For Adam, megamind

# Contents

# Preface

Cognitive science is the interdisciplinary study of mind and intelligence, embracing philosophy, psychology, artificial intelligence, neuroscience, linguistics, and anthropology. Its intellectual origins are in the mid-1950s when researchers in several fields began to develop theories of mind based on complex representations and computational procedures. Its organizational origins are in the mid-1970s when the Cognitive Science Society was formed and the journal *Cognitive Science* began. Since then, more than sixty universities in North America and Europe have established cognitive science programs and many others have instituted courses in cognitive science.

Teaching an interdisciplinary course in cognitive science is difficult because students come to it with very different backgrounds. Since 1993, I have been teaching a popular course at the University of Waterloo called Introduction to Cognitive Science. On the one hand, the course attracts computationally sophisticated students from computer science and engineering who know little psychology or philosophy; on the other, it attracts students with good backgrounds in psychology or philosophy but who know little about computation. This text is part of an attempt to construct a course that presupposes no special preparation in any of the fields of cognitive science. It is intended to enable students with an interest in mind and intelligence to see that there are many complementary approaches to the investigation of mind.

There are at least three different ways to introduce cognitive science to a multidisciplinary audience. The first is to concentrate on the different fields of psychology, artificial intelligence, and so on. The second is to organize the discussion by different functions of mind, such as problem solving, memory, learning, and language. I have chosen a third approach, systematically describing and evaluating the main theories of mental representation that have been advocated by cognitive scientists, including logic, rules, concepts, analogies, images, and connections (artificial neural networks). Discussing these fundamental theoretical approaches provides a unified way of presenting the accomplishments of the different fields of cognitive science to understanding various important mental functions.

My goal in writing this book is to make it accessible to all students likely to enroll in an introduction to cognitive science. Accomplishing this goal requires, for example, explaining logic in a way accessible to psychology students, computer algorithms in a way accessible to English students, and philosophical controversies in a way accessible to computer science students.

Although this book is intended for undergraduates, it should also be useful for graduate students and faculty who want to see how their own fields fit into the general enterprise of cognitive science. I have not written an encyclopedia. Since the whole point of this exercise is to provide an integrated introduction, I have kept the book relatively short and to the point, highlighting the forest rather than the trees. Viewing cognitive science as the intersection rather than as the union of all the relevant fields, I have omitted many topics that are standard in introductions to artificial intelligence, cognitive psychology, philosophy of mind, and so on. Each chapter concludes with a summary and suggestions for further reading.

The book is written with great enthusiasm for what theories of mental representation and computation have contributed to the understanding of mind, but also with awareness that cognitive science has a long way to go. The second part of the book discusses extensions to the basic assumptions of cognitive science and suggests directions for future interdisciplinary work.

I have been grateful for the reception of the first edition of this book, especially its translation into Italian, German, Czech, Portuguese, Japanese, Korean, and two variants of Chinese. For this second edition, I have brought part I up to date and substantially revised part II, adding new chapters on brains, emotions, and consciousness. Other additions include a list of relevant Web sites at the end of each chapter, and a glossary at the end of the book. My anthology, *Mind Readings: Introductory Selections on Cognitive Science* (MIT Press, 1998) remains a useful accompaniment.

# Acknowledgments

I am grateful to the students at the University of Waterloo who participated in several courses in which this material was first developed. For suggestions to the first edition, I owe thanks to Andrew Brook, Chris Eliasmith, Kim Honeyford, Janet Kolodner, Amy Pierce, Michael Ranney, and Eric Steinhart. For suggestions that contributed to the second edition, I am grateful to Chris Eliasmith, Ashok Goel, Michael Ranney, and Ethan Toombs. Thanks to Tom Stone at MIT Press for encouragement and suggestions. While I was writing and revising this text, my research was supported by the Natural Sciences and Engineering Research Council of Canada. Thanks to Abninder Litt for help with proofreading.

# I   Approaches to Cognitive Science

# 1 Representation and Computation

## Studying the Mind

Have you ever wondered how your mind works? Every day, people accomplish a wide range of mental tasks: solving problems at their work or school, making decisions about their personal life, explaining the actions of people they know, and acquiring new concepts like *cell phone* and *Internet*. The main aim of cognitive science is to explain how people accomplish these various kinds of thinking. We want not only to describe different kinds of problem solving and learning, but also to explain how the mind carries out these operations. Moreover, cognitive science aims to explain cases where thinking works poorly—for example, when people make bad decisions.

Understanding how the mind works is important for many practical activities. Educators need to know the nature of students' thinking in order to devise better ways of teaching them. Engineers and other designers need to know what potential users of their products are likely to be thinking when they use their products effectively or ineffectively. Computers can be made more intelligent by reflecting on what makes people intelligent. Politicians and other decision makers can become more successful if they understand the mental processes of people with whom they interact.

But studying the mind is not easy, since we cannot just pop one open to see how it works. Over the centuries, philosophers and psychologists have used a variety of metaphors for the mind, comparing it, for example, to a blank sheet on which impressions are made, to a hydraulic device with various forces operating in it, and to a telephone switchboard. In the last fifty years, suggestive new metaphors for thinking have become available through the development of new kinds of computers. Many but not all cognitive scientists view thinking as a kind of computation and use computational metaphors to describe and explain how people solve problems and learn.

## What Do You Know?

When students begin studying at a college or university, they have much more to learn than course material. Undergraduates in different programs will have to deal with very different subject matters, but they all need to acquire some basic knowledge about how the university works. How do you register for courses? What time do the classes begin? What courses are good and which are to be avoided? What are the requirements for a degree? What is the best route from one building to another? What are the other students on campus like? Where is the best place to have fun on Friday night?

Answers to these questions become part of the minds of most students, but what sort of part? Most cognitive scientists agree that knowledge in the mind consists of *mental representations*. Everyone is familiar with non-mental representations, such as the words on this page. I have just used the words "this page" to represent the page that you are now seeing. Students often also use pictorial representations such as maps of their campuses and buildings. To account for many kinds of knowledge, such as what students know about the university, cognitive scientists have proposed various kinds of mental representation including rules, concepts, images, and analogies. Students acquire rules such as *If I want to graduate, then I need to take ten courses in my major.* They also acquire concepts involving new terms such as "bird" or "Mickey Mouse" or "gut," all used to describe a particularly easy course. For getting from building to building, a mental image or picture of the layout of the campus might be very useful. After taking a course that they particularly like, students may try to find another similar course to take. Having interacted with numerous students from different programs on campus, students may form stereotypes of the different kinds of undergraduates, although it may be difficult for them to say exactly what constitutes those stereotypes.

The knowledge that students acquire about college life is not acquired just for the sake of accumulating information. Students face numerous problems, such as how to do well in their courses, how to have a decent social life, and how to get a job after graduation. Solving such problems requires doing things with mental representations, such as reasoning that you still need five more courses to graduate, or deciding never to take another course from Professor Tedium. Cognitive science proposes that people have mental *procedures* that operate on mental representations to produce thought and action. Different kinds of mental representations such as rules and concepts foster different kinds of mental procedures. Consider different ways of representing numbers. Most people are familiar with the Arabic numeral representation of numbers (1, 2, 3, 10, 100, etc.) and with the standard procedures for doing addition, multiplication, and so on. Roman numerals can also represent numbers (I, II, III, X, C), but they require different procedures for carrying out arithmetic operations. Try dividing CIV (104) by XXVI (26).

Part I of this book surveys the different approaches to mental representations and procedures that have developed in the last four decades of cognitive science research. There has been much controversy about the merits of different approaches, and many of the leading cognitive science theorists have argued vehemently for the primacy of the approach they prefer. My approach is more eclectic, since I believe that the different theories of mental representation now available are more complementary than competitive. The human mind is astonishingly complex, and our understanding of it can gain from considering its use of rules such as those described above as well as many other kinds of representations including some not at all familiar. The latter include "connectionist" or "neural network" representations that are discussed in chapter 7.

## Beginnings

Attempts to understand the mind and its operation go back at least to the ancient Greeks, when philosophers such as Plato and Aristotle tried to explain the nature of human knowledge. Plato thought that the most important knowledge comes from concepts such as *virtue* that people know innately, independently of sense experience. Other philosophers such as Descartes and Leibniz also believed that knowledge can be gained just by thinking and reasoning, a position known as *rationalism*. In contrast, Aristotle discussed knowledge in terms of rules such as *All humans are mortal* that are learned from experience. This philosophical position, defended by Locke, Hume, and others, is known as *empiricism*. In the eighteenth century, Kant attempted to combine rationalism and empiricism by arguing that human knowledge depends on both sense experience and the innate capacities of the mind.

The study of mind remained the province of philosophy until the nineteenth century, when experimental psychology developed. Wilhelm Wundt and his students initiated laboratory methods for studying mental operations more systematically. Within a few decades, however, experimental psychology became dominated by *behaviorism*, a view that virtually denied the existence of mind. According to behaviorists such as J. B. Watson (1913), psychology should restrict itself to examining the relation between observable stimuli and observable behavioral responses. Talk of consciousness and mental representations was banished from respectable scientific discussion. Especially in North America, behaviorism dominated the psychological scene through the 1950s.

Around 1956, the intellectual landscape began to change dramatically. George Miller (1956) summarized numerous studies that showed that the capacity of human thinking is limited, with short-term memory, for example, limited to around seven items. (This is why it is hard to remember long phone or social security numbers.) He proposed that memory limitations can be overcome by recoding information into chunks, mental representations that require mental procedures for encoding and decoding the information. At this time, primitive computers had been around for only a few years, but pioneers such as John McCarthy, Marvin Minsky, Allen Newell, and Herbert Simon were founding the field of artificial intelligence. In addition, Noam Chomsky (1957, 1959) rejected behaviorist assumptions about language as a learned habit and proposed instead to explain people's ability to understand language in terms of mental grammars consisting of rules. The six thinkers mentioned in this paragraph can justly be viewed as the founders of cognitive science.

The subsequent history of cognitive science is sketched in later chapters in connection with different theories of mental representation. McCarthy became one of the leaders of the approach to artificial intelligence based on formal logic, which we will discuss in chapter 2. During the 1960s, Newell and Simon showed the power of rules for accounting for aspects of human intelligence, and chapter 3 describes considerable subsequent work in this tradition. During the 1970s, Minsky proposed that conceptlike frames are the central form of knowledge representations, and other researchers in artificial intelligence and psychology discussed similar structures called schemas and scripts (chapter 4). Also at this time, psychologists began to show increased interest in mental imagery (chapter 6). Much experimental and computational research since the 1980s has concerned analogical thinking, also known as case-based reasoning (chapter 5). The most exciting development of the 1980s was the rise of connectionist theories of mental representation and processing modeled loosely on neural networks in the brain (chapter 7). Each of these approaches has contributed to the understanding of mind, and chapter 8 provides a summary and evaluation of their advantages and disadvantages.

Many challenges and extensions have been made to the central view that the mind should be understood in terms of mental representations and procedures, and these are addressed in part II of the book (chapters 9–14). The 1990s saw a rapid increase in the use of brain scanning technologies to study how specific areas of the brain contribute to thinking, and currently there is much work on neurologically realistic computational models of mind (chapter 9). These models are suggesting new ways to understand emotions and consciousness (chapters 10 and 11). Chapters 12 and 13 address challenges to the computational-representational approach based on the role that bodies, physical environments, and social environments play in human thinking. Finally, chapter 14 discusses the future of cognitive science, including suggestions for how students can pursue further interdisciplinary work.

## Methods in Cognitive Science

Cognitive science should be more than just people from different fields having lunch together to chat about the mind. But before we can begin to see the unifying ideas of cognitive science, we have to appreciate the diversity of outlooks and methods that researchers in different fields bring to the study of mind and intelligence.

Although cognitive psychologists today often engage in theorizing and computational modeling, their primary method is experimentation with human participants. People, usually undergraduates satisfying course requirements, are brought into the laboratory so that different kinds of thinking can be studied under controlled conditions. To take some examples from later chapters, psychologists have experimentally examined the kinds of mistakes people make in deductive reasoning, the ways that people form and apply concepts, the speed of people thinking with mental images, and the performance of people solving problems using analogies. Our conclusions about how the mind works must be based on more than "common sense" and introspection, since these can give a misleading picture of mental operations, many of which are not consciously accessible. Psychological experiments that carefully approach mental operations from diverse directions are therefore crucial for cognitive science to be scientific.

Although theory without experiment is empty, experiment without theory is blind. To address the crucial questions about the nature of mind, the psychological experiments need to be interpretable within a theoretical framework that postulates mental representations and procedures. One of the best ways of developing theoretical frameworks is by forming and testing computational models intended to be analogous to mental operations. To complement psychological experiments on deductive reasoning, concept formation, mental imagery, and analogical problem solving, researchers have developed computational models that simulate aspects of human performance. Designing, building, and experimenting with computational models is the central method of artificial intelligence (AI), the branch of computer science concerned with intelligent systems. Ideally in cognitive science, computational models and psychological experimentation go hand in hand, but much important work in AI has examined the power of different approaches to knowledge representation in relative isolation from experimental psychology.

Although some linguists do psychological experiments or develop computational models, most currently use different methods. For linguists in the Chomskyan tradition, the main theoretical task is to identify grammatical principles that provide the basic structure of human languages. Identification takes place by noticing subtle differences between grammatical and ungrammatical utterances. In English, for example, the sentences "She hit the ball" and "What do you like?" are grammatical, but "She the hit ball" and "What does you like?" are not. A grammar of English will explain why the former are acceptable but not the latter. Later chapters give additional examples of the theoretical and empirical work performed by linguists in both the Chomskyan tradition and others.

Like cognitive psychologists, neuroscientists often perform controlled experiments, but their observations are very different, since neuroscientists are concerned directly with the nature of the brain. With nonhuman subjects, researchers can insert electrodes and record the firing of individual neurons. With humans for whom this technique would be too invasive, it has become possible in recent years to use magnetic and positronic scanning devices to observe what is happening in different parts of the brain while people are doing various mental tasks. For example, brain scans have identified the regions of the brain involved in mental imagery and word interpretation. Additional evidence about brain functioning is gathered by observing the performance of people whose brains have been damaged in identifiable ways. A stroke, for example, in a part of the brain dedicated to language can produce deficits such as the inability to utter sentences. Like cognitive psychology, neuroscience is often theoretical as well as experimental, and theory development is frequently aided by developing computational models of the behavior of sets of neurons.

Cognitive anthropology expands the examination of human thinking to consider how thought works in different cultural settings. The study of mind should obviously not be restricted to how English speakers think but should consider possible differences in modes of thinking across cultures. Chapters 12 and 13 describe how cognitive science is becoming increasingly aware of the need to view the operations of mind in particular physical and social environments. For cultural anthropologists, the main method is ethnography, which requires living and interacting with members of a culture to a sufficient extent that their social and cognitive systems become apparent. Cognitive anthropologists have investigated, for example, the similarities and differences across cultures in words for colors.

With a few exceptions, philosophers generally do not perform systematic empirical observations or construct computational models. But philosophy remains important to cognitive science because it deals with fundamental issues that underlie the experimental and computational approaches to mind. Abstract issues such as the nature of representation and computation need not be addressed in the everyday practice of psychology or artificial intelligence, but they inevitably arise when researchers think deeply about what they are doing. Philosophy also deals with general questions such as the relation of mind and body and with methodological questions such as the nature of explanations found in cognitive science.

In addition to descriptive questions about how people think, philosophy concerns itself with normative questions about how they *should* think. Along with the theoretical goal of understanding human thinking, cognitive science can have the practical goal of improving it, which requires normative reflection on what we want thinking to be. Philosophy of mind does not have a distinct method, but should share with the best theoretical work in other fields a concern with empirical results.

In its weakest form, cognitive science is merely the sum of the fields just mentioned: psychology, artificial intelligence, linguistics, neuroscience, anthropology, and philosophy. Interdisciplinary work becomes much more interesting when there is theoretical and experimental convergence on conclusions about the nature of mind. Later chapters provide examples of such convergences that show cognitive science working at the intersection of various fields. For example, psychology and artificial intelligence can be combined through computational models of how people behave in experiments. The best way to grasp the complexity of human thinking is to use multiple methods, especially combining psychological and neurological experiments with computational models. Theoretically, the most fertile approach has been to understand the mind in terms of representation and computation.

## The Computational-Representational Understanding of Mind

Here is the central hypothesis of cognitive science: Thinking can best be understood in terms of representational structures in the mind and computational procedures that operate on those structures. Although there is much disagreement about the nature of the representations and computations that constitute thinking, the central hypothesis is general enough to encompass the current range of thinking in cognitive science, including connectionist theories. For short, I call the approach to understanding the mind based on this central hypothesis *CRUM*, for *Computational-Representational Understanding of Mind.*

CRUM might be wrong. Part II of this book presents some fundamental challenges to this approach that suggest that ideas about representation and computation might be inadequate to explain fundamental facts about the mind. But in evaluating the successes of different theories of knowledge representation, we will be able to see the considerable progress in understanding the mind that CRUM has made possible. Without a doubt, CRUM has been the most theoretically and experimentally successful approach to mind ever developed. Not everyone in the cognitive science disciplines agrees with CRUM, but inspection of the leading journals in psychology and other fields reveals that CRUM is currently the dominant approach to cognitive science.

Much of CRUM's success has been due to the fact that it employs a fertile analogy derived from the development of computers. As chapter 5 describes, analogies often contribute to new scientific ideas, and comparing the mind with computers has provided a much more powerful way of approaching the mind than previous metaphors such as the telephone switchboard. Readers with a background in computer science will be familiar with the characterization of a computer program as consisting of data structures and algorithms. Modern programming languages include a variety of data structures including strings of letters such as "abc," numbers such as 3, and more complex structures such as lists (A B C) and trees. Algorithms—mechanical procedures—can be defined to operate on various kinds of structures. For example, children in elementary school learn an algorithm for operating on numbers to perform long division. Another simple algorithm can be defined to reverse a list, turning (A B C) into (C B A). This procedure is built up out of smaller procedures for taking an element from one list and adding it to the beginning of another, enabling a computer to build a reversed list by forming (A), then (B A), then (C B A). Similarly, CRUM assumes that the mind has mental representations analogous to data structures, and computational procedures similar to algorithms. Schematically:

| *Program* | *Mind* |
|---|---|
| data structures + algorithms = running programs | mental representations + computational procedures = thinking |

This has been the dominant analogy in cognitive science, although it has taken on a novel twist from the use of another analog, the brain. Connectionists have proposed novel ideas about representation and computation that use neurons and their connections as inspirations for data structures, and neuron firing and spreading activation as inspirations for algorithms. CRUM then works with a complex three-way analogy among the mind, the brain, and computers, as depicted in figure 1.1. Mind, brain,

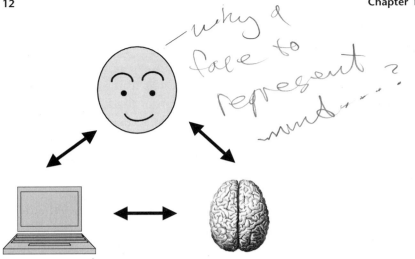

**Figure 1.1**
Three-way analogy between minds, computers, and brains.

and computation can each be used to suggest new ideas about the others. There is no single computational model of mind, since different kinds of computers and programming approaches suggest different ways in which the mind might work. The computers that most of us work with today are serial processors, performing one instruction at a time, but the brain and some recently developed computers are parallel processors, capable of doing many operations at once.

If you already know a lot about computers, thinking about the mind computationally should come fairly naturally, even if you do not agree that the mind is fundamentally like a computer. Readers who have never written a computer program but have used cookbooks can consider another analogy. A recipe usually has two parts: a list of ingredients and a set of instructions for what to do with them. A dish results from applying cooking instructions to the ingredients, just as a running program results from applying algorithms to data structures such as numbers and lists, and just as thinking (according to CRUM) results from applying computational procedures to mental representations. The recipe analogy for thinking is weak, since ingredients are not representations and cooking instructions require someone to interpret them. Chapters 2–7 provide simple examples of computational procedures that map much more directly onto the operations of mind.

## Theories, Models, and Programs

Computer models are often very useful for theoretical investigation of mental processes. Comprehension of cognitive science models requires noting the distinctions and the connections among four crucial elements: theory, model, program, and platform. A cognitive *theory* postulates a set of representational structures and a set of processes that operate on these structures. A computational *model* makes these structures and processes more precise by interpreting them by analogy with computer programs that consist of data structures and algorithms. Vague ideas about representations can be supplemented by precise computational ideas about data structures, and mental processes can be defined algorithmically. To test the model, it must be implemented in a software *program* in a programming language such as LISP or Java. This program may run on a variety of hardware *platforms* such as Macintoshes, Sun Workstations, or IBM PCs, or it may be specially designed for a specific kind of hardware that has many processors working in parallel. Many kinds of structures and processes can be investigated in this way, from the rules and search strategies of some traditional sorts of artificial intelligence, to the distributed representations and spreading activation processes of newer connectionist views.

Suppose, for example, that you want to understand how children learn to add numbers together in problems such as $13 + 28 = ?$ A cognitive theory would postulate how children represent these numbers and how they process the representations to accomplish addition. The theory would propose whether 13 is to be represented by a single structure, a combined structure such as *10 plus 3*, or by a complex of neuronlike structures. The theory would also propose processes that operate on the structures to produce a result such as 41, including the carrying operation that somehow turns 30-plus-11 into 41. A computational model would specify the nature of the representations and processes more precisely by characterizing programmable structures and algorithms that are intended to be analogous to the mental representations and processes for addition. To evaluate the theory and model, we can write a computer program in a computer language such as LISP, running the program to compare its performance with human adders and checking that the program not only gets the same right answers as the humans but also makes the same kind of mistakes. Our program might run on any number of different platforms such as PCs, or it might be specially tailored to a particular kind of computer such as one that mimics the neuronal structure of the brain.

The analogy between mind and computer is useful at all three stages of the development of cognitive theories: discovery, modification, and evaluation. Computational ideas about different kinds of programs often suggest new kinds of mental structures and processes. Theory development, model development, and program development often go hand in hand, since writing the program may lead to the invention of new kinds of data structures and algorithms that become part of the model and have analogs in the theory. For example, in writing a computer program to simulate human addition, a programmer might think of a kind of data structure that suggests new ideas about how children represent numbers. Similarly, evaluation of theory, model, and program often involves all three, since our confidence in the theory depends on the model's validity as shown by the program's performance. If the computer program for doing addition cannot add, or if it adds more perfectly than humans, we have reason to believe that the corresponding cognitive theory of addition is inadequate.

The running program can contribute to evaluation of the model and theory in three ways. First, it helps to show that the postulated representations and processes are computationally realizable. This is important, since many algorithms that seem reasonable at first glance do not scale up to large problems on real computers. Second, in order to show not only the computational realizability of a theory but also its psychological plausibility, the program can be applied qualitatively to various examples of thinking. Our addition program, for example, should be able to get the same kinds of right and wrong answers as children. Third, to show a much more detailed fit between the theory and human thinking, the program can be used quantitatively to generate detailed predictions about human thinking that can be compared with the results of psychological experiments. If there are psychological experiments that show that children get a certain percentage of a class of addition problems right, then the computer program should get roughly the same percentage right. Cognitive theories by themselves are normally not precise enough to generate such quantitative predictions, but a model and program may fill the gap between theory and observation.

**Box 1.1**
Criteria for evaluating theories of mental representation.

(1) Representational power
(2) Computational power
  (a) Problem solving
    (i)   Planning
    (ii)  Decision
    (iii) Explanation
  (b) Learning
  (c) Language
(3) Psychological plausibility
(4) Neurological plausibility
(5) Practical applicability
  (a) Education
  (b) Design
  (c) Intelligent systems
  (d) Mental illness

*aren't there an infinite # of even yet unknown practical applications?*

**Evaluating Approaches to Mental Representations**

We can now be more specific about what to expect of a theory of mental
representation. Box 1.1 lists five complex criteria for evaluating a particular account of the representations and computations that can be claimed
to explain thought. Chapters 2–7 use these criteria to evaluate six different approaches to mental representation: logic, rules, concepts, images,
cases, and connections (artificial neural networks).

Each of the approaches described in chapters 2–7 proposes a particular
kind of representation and a corresponding set of computational procedures. The first criterion, representational power, concerns how much
information a particular kind of representation can express. For example,
a university calendar urges: "Once admitted to the University, students are
advised to preregister for their courses well in advance of the beginning of
lectures." Students who take such advice seriously will need to represent
it internally in a form that leads to further inferences, such as the conclusion that they should get over to the registrar's office to sign up for next

term's courses. We will see that different proposed kinds of mental representation vary greatly in representational power.

Mental representations are important not only for what they express, but especially for what you can do with them. We can evaluate the computational power of an approach to mental representation in terms of how it accounts for three important kinds of high-level thinking. The first is problem solving: a theory of mental representation should be able to explain how people can reason to accomplish their goals. There are at least three kinds of problem solving to be explained: planning, decision making, and explanation. Planning requires a reasoner to figure out how to get from an initial state to a goal state by traversing various intermediate states. Planning problems include mundane issues such as how to get to the airport before your flight leaves, to the sort of exercise students are commonly posed in their textbooks and their exams. In these questions, students are given some information and need to figure out how to calculate the answer. The starting state involves what the student knows and the information in the problem description, and the goal state includes having an answer. The student has to find a solution by constructing a successful sequence of calculations.

In decision making, people are faced with a number of different means for accomplishing their goals and need to select the best one. For example, a student about to graduate may need to choose among looking for a job, going to graduate school, or attending a professional school such as law or business. Such decisions are very difficult, since they require students to identify their goals and figure out which course of action will best accomplish those goals. In planning problems, the task is to find a successful sequence of actions, whereas in decision problems the task is to choose the best plan from among a number of possible actions.

Explanation problems are ones that require people to figure out *why* something happened. They range from mundane questions such as why a friend is late for dinner, to deep scientific questions such as why human language has evolved. Every minimally intelligent human being is capable of planning, decision making, and generating explanations. A cognitive theory must have sufficient computational power to offer possible explanations for how people solve these kinds of problems.

The computational power of a system of representations and procedures is not just a matter of how much the system can compute, but must also take into account how efficient the computation is. Imagine a procedure that takes only a second to be applied once, but twice as long the second time, and twice as long as that the third time, and so on. Then twenty applications would take $2^{20}$ seconds, which are more seconds than there have been in the approximately 15 billion years since the universe was formed. Both naturally and artificially intelligent systems need to have sufficient speed to work effectively in their environments.

When people solve a problem, they are usually able to learn from the experience and thereby solve it much more easily the next time. For example, the first time that students register for classes is usually very confusing since they do not know what procedures to follow or how to go about choosing good classes. Subsequently, however, registering typically gets a lot easier. Part of being intelligent involves being able to learn from experience, so a theory of mental representation must have sufficient computational power to explain how people learn. In discussing different approaches to mental representation, we will encounter diverse kinds of human learning, ranging from the acquisition of new concepts such as *registration* and rules such as *Never sign up for an 8:30 class* to more subtle kinds of adjustment in performance.

In addition to problem solving and learning, a general cognitive theory must account for human language use. Ours is the only species on Earth capable of complex use of language. General principles of problem solving and learning might account for language use, but it is also possible that language is a unique cognitive capacity that must be dealt with specially. At least three aspects of language use need to be explained: people's ability to comprehend language, their ability to produce utterances, and children's universal ability to learn language. Different approaches to knowledge representation provide very different answers to how these work.

If artificial intelligence is viewed as a branch of engineering, it can develop computational models of problem solving, learning, and language that ignore how people accomplish these tasks; the question is just how to get computers to do them. But cognitive science has the goal of understanding *human* cognition, so it is crucial that a theory of mental representation not only have a lot of representational and computational power, but also be concerned with how people think. Accordingly, the third criterion for evaluating a theory of mental representation is psychological plausibility, which requires accounting not just for the qualitative capacities of humans but also for the quantitative results of psychological experiments concerning these capacities. Relevant experiments include ones dealing with the same high-level tasks that were discussed under the heading of computational power: problem solving, learning, and language. The difference between this criterion and the last is that a cognitive theory of mental representation must not only show how a task is possible computationally, but also try to explain the particular ways that humans do it.

Similarly, since human thought is accomplished by the human brain, a theory of mental representation must at least be consistent with the results of neuroscientific experiments. Until recently, neurological techniques such as recording EEGs of brain waves seemed too crude to tell us much about high-level cognition, but the past two decades have brought new scanning techniques that can identify where and when in the brain certain cognitive tasks are performed. Cognitive neuroscience has thereby become an important part of reflection on the operations of mind, so we should try to assess each approach to knowledge representation in terms of neurological plausibility, even though information about how the brain produces cognition is still limited (see chapter 9).

The fifth and final criterion for evaluating theories of mental representation is practical applicability. Although the main goal of cognitive science is to understand the mind, there are many desirable practical results to which such understanding can lead. This book considers what each of the approaches to knowledge representation has to tell us about four important kinds of application: education, design, intelligent systems, and mental illness. For educational purposes, cognitive science should be able to increase understanding of how students learn, and also to suggest how to teach them better. Design problems, such as how to make computer interfaces that people like to use, should benefit from an understanding of how people are thinking when they perform such tasks. Developing intelligent systems to act either as stand-alone experts or as tools to support human decisions can directly benefit from computational ideas about how humans think. Different theories of mental representation have given rise to very different sorts of expert computer systems, including rule-based, case-based, and connectionist tools. Other potential practical applications of cognitive science include understanding and treatment of mental illness.

As we will see, no single approach to mental representation fully satisfies all these criteria. Moreover, there are aspects of human thinking such as perception (sight, hearing, touch, smell, taste), emotion, and motor control that are not included in these criteria (see chapters 10–12). Nevertheless, the criteria provide a framework for comparing and evaluating current theories of mental representation with respect to their accomplishments as well as their shortcomings.

## Summary

Researchers in psychology, artificial intelligence, neuroscience, linguistics, anthropology, and philosophy have adopted very different methods for studying the mind, but ideally these methods can converge on a common interpretation of how the mind works. A unified view of cognitive science comes from seeing various theoretical approaches as all concerned with mental representations and procedures that are analogous to the representations and procedures familiar in computer programs. The Computational-Representational Understanding of Mind operates with the following kind of explanation schema:

Explanation target

Why do people have a particular kind of **intelligent behavior**?

Explanatory pattern

People have mental **representations**.

People have algorithmic **processes** that operate on those **representations**.

The **processes**, applied to the **representations**, produce the **behavior**.

The words in boldface are placeholders, indicating that to explain various kinds of intelligent behavior, various kinds of representations and processes can be considered. Currently, there are six main approaches to modeling the mind, involving logic, rules, concepts, analogies, images, and neural connections. These can be evaluated according to five criteria: representational power, computational power, psychological plausibility, neurological plausibility, and practical applicability.

The fundamental presuppositions that have guided the writing of this book are:

1. The study of mind is exciting and important. It is exciting for theoretical reasons, since the attempt to investigate the nature of mind is as challenging as anything attempted by science. It is also exciting for practical reasons, since knowing how the mind works is important for such diverse endeavors as improving education, improving design of computers and other artifacts, and developing intelligent computational systems that can aid or replace human experts.

2. The study of mind is interdisciplinary. It requires the insights that have been gained by philosophers, psychologists, computer scientists, linguists, neuroscientists, anthropologists, and other thinkers. Moreover, it requires the diversity of methodologies that these fields have developed.

3. The interdisciplinary study of mind (cognitive science) has a core: the Computational-Representational Understanding of Mind (CRUM). Thinking is the result of mental representations and computational processes that operate on those representations.

4. CRUM is multifarious. Many kinds of representations and computations are important to understanding human thought, and no single computational-representational account now available does justice to the full range of human thinking. This book reviews (in chapters 2–8) the six major current approaches to understanding the mind in terms of representations and computation.

5. CRUM is successful. The computational-representational approach has exceeded all previous theories of mind in its theoretical ability to account for psychological performance and its practical ability to improve that performance.

6. CRUM is incomplete. Not all aspects of human thought and intelligence can be accounted for in purely computational-representational terms. Substantial challenges have been made to CRUM that show the necessity of integrating it with biological research (neuroscience) and with research on social aspects of thought and knowledge.

## Discussion Questions

1. What are additional examples of things that students learn when they go to college or university?

2. Why have researchers in different fields adopted different methods for studying the mind?

3. Can you think of any alternatives to the computational-representational understanding of mind?

4. What aspects of human thinking are most difficult for computers to perform or model? What would it take to convince you that a computer is intelligent?

5. Are theories and models in cognitive science like theories and models in physics and other fields?

6. Are there additional criteria that you would want a theory of mental representation to meet?

## Further Reading

Three recent reference works contain valuable articles on many aspects of cognitive science: *The MIT Encyclopedia of the Cognitive Sciences* (Wilson and Keil 1999), *A Companion to Cognitive Science* (Bechtel and Graham 1998), and *Encyclopedia of Cognitive Science* (Nadel 2003).

On the history of cognitive science, see Gardner 1985 and Thagard 1992, chap. 9. Other introductions to cognitive science include Johnson-Laird 1988, Stillings et al. 1995, Dawson 1998, and Sobel 2001. General collections of articles include Polk and Seifert 2002 and Thagard 1998.

Textbooks on cognitive psychology include Anderson 2000, Medin, Ross, and Markman 2001, and Sternberg 2003. For introductions to artificial intelligence, see Russell and Norvig 2003 and Winston 1993. Graham 1998 and Clark 2001 provide introductions to the philosophy of mind and cognitive science. An introductory linguistics text is Akmajian et al. 2001. For accessible introductions to cognitive neuroscience, see LeDoux 2002 and Kosslyn and Koenig 1992; Churchland and Sejnowski 1992 present a more computational approach. D'Andrade 1995 provides an introduction to cognitive anthropology.

## Web Sites

Note: Live links to all the sites mentioned in this book can be found at my own Web site, http://cogsci.uwaterloo.ca/courses/resources.html.

Artificial Intelligence in the news (American Association for Artificial Intelligence): http://www.aaai.org/AITopics/html/current.html

Artificial intelligence on the Web: http://aima.cs.berkeley.edu/ai.html

Biographies of major contributors to cognitive science: http://mechanism. ucsd.edu/~bill/research/ANAUT.html

Cognitive Science dictionary, University of Alberta: http://web.psych. ualberta.ca/~mike/Pearl_Street/Dictionary/dictionary.html

Cognitive Science Society: http://www.cognitivesciencesociety.org/

Cogprints (archive of papers on cognitive science): http://cogprints.ecs. soton.ac.uk/

Dictionary of Philosophy of Mind: http://www.artsci.wustl.edu/~philos/ MindDict/

Science Daily (mind and brain news): http://www.sciencedaily.com/news/ mind_brain.htm

Yahoo! Cognitive Science page: http://dir.yahoo.com/Science/cognitive_ science/

## Notes

Discussions of thinking as computation often begin with an abstract model of computation such as the Turing machine, a simple device that consists of a tape and a mechanical head that can write symbols on spaces on the tape. Although it can be proven mathematically that such a machine can in principle do anything that any other computer can, the Turing machine is an excessively abstract analog of thinking, which is much better discussed in terms of higher-level computational ideas such as data structures and algorithms.

For more on explanation schemas and patterns, see Kitcher 1993, Leake 1992, Schank 1986, and Thagard 1999.

# 2 Logic

Although formal logic has not been the most influential psychological approach to mental representation, there are several reasons for beginning our survey with it. First, many basic ideas about representation and computation have grown out of the logical tradition. Second, many philosophers and artificial intelligence researchers today take logic as central to work on reasoning. Third, logic has substantial representational power that must be matched by other approaches to mental representation that may have more computational efficiency and psychological plausibility.

Formal logic began with the Greek philosopher Aristotle more than two thousand years ago. He systematically studied such inferences as

All students are overworked.

Mary is a student.

So, Mary is overworked.

Such patterns of inference, with two premises and a conclusion, are called *syllogisms*. In addition to cataloging many different kinds of syllogism, Aristotle showed how they can be analyzed purely in terms of their form. For the conclusion in the example to follow from the two premises, it does not matter that the syllogism is about overworked students. We can substitute "sausage" for "student," "orange" for "overworked," and "Marvin" for "Mary," and the conclusion that Marvin is orange follows from the revised premises even if it makes little sense. Aristotle initiated the use of symbols to show the form of the inference:

All $S$ are $O$.

$M$ is $S$.

So, $M$ is $O$.

Aristotle's discovery of how to analyze syllogisms purely in terms of their form, ignoring their content, has had a major influence on logic. The discovery's usefulness, however, has been challenged from a psychological perspective, as we will see below in the section on psychological validity.

The syllogism is a form of *deductive* inference, in which the conclusion follows necessarily from the premises: if the premises are true, the conclusion is true also. *Inductive* inference is more dangerous since it introduces uncertainty. If all the students you know are overworked, you might inductively infer that all students are overworked. But your conclusion might well be erroneous—for example, if there are basket-weaving majors you do not know who take it easy.

Although the syllogism dominated discussions of formal logic for two thousand years, it is not sufficient to represent all inferences. Syllogisms are fine for simple predicates like "is a student" but they can not handle relations such as *take* in sentences like "Students who take courses get credit for them." Here *take* is a relation between a student and a course. Modern logic began in 1879 with the work of the German mathematician Gottlob Frege (1960), who devised a formal system of logic much more general than Aristotle's. Subsequently, Bertrand Russell and many other logicians have found ways of increasing the representational and deductive power of formal logic.

The early theory of computation was developed by logicians such as Alonzo Church and Alan Turing. In the 1930s, Church, Turing, and others developed mathematical schemes for specifying what could be effectively computed. These schemes turned out to be mathematically equivalent to each other, providing support for the thesis that the intuitive concept of effective computability can be identified with well-defined mathematical concepts such as Turing-machine computability. When digital computers became available in the late 1940s and 1950s, the mathematical theory of computability provided a powerful tool for understanding their operations. It is not surprising that, when artificial intelligence began in the mid-1950s, mathematically trained researchers such as John McCarthy took logic to be the most appropriate tool. We shall see, however, that other pioneers such as Allen Newell, Herbert Simon, and Marvin Minsky preferred different approaches.

## Representational Power

Modern formal logic has the resources to represent many kinds of deductive inferences. The simplest system of formal logic is propositional logic, in which formulas like "$p$" and "$q$" are used to stand for sentences such as "Paula is in the library" and "Quincy is in the library." Simple formulas can be combined into more complex ones using symbols such as "&" for "and," "v" for "or," and "→" for "if-then." For example, the sentence

If Paula is in the library, then Quincy is in the library.

becomes

$p \rightarrow q$.

Such if-then sentences are called conditionals, consisting of antecedents (the "if" part) and consequents (the "then" part). To express negation, "*not-p*" can be written $\sim p$. From these building blocks we can construct formalizations for complex statements such as "If Paula or Quincy is in the library, then Debra is not," which can be formalized as

$(p \: v \: q) \rightarrow \sim d$.

Here, "$p$" stands for "Paula is in the library," "$q$" stands for "Quincy is in the library," and "$d$" stands for "Debra is in the library."

More complicated logics have been developed that allow different kinds of propositional operators. Modal logic adds operators for necessity and possibility, so that we can represent statements such as "It is possible that Paula is in the library." Epistemic logic adds operators for knowledge and belief, so that $Kp$ represents "It is known that $p$." Deontic logic represents moral ideas such as that $p$ is permissible or forbidden.

Propositional logic requires treating statements such as "Paula is a student" as an indivisible whole, but predicate logic allows us to break them down. Predicate calculus distinguishes between predicates such as "is a student" and constants referring to such individuals as Paula or Quincy. In the version of predicate calculus usually taught in philosophy courses, "Paula is a student" is formalized as "$S(p)$," where "$p$" now stands for Paula rather than a whole proposition. Computer scientists tend to express this more mnemonically as "is-student (paula)." In addition to simple properties, predicates can be used to express relations between two or more things. For example, "Paula takes Philosophy 256" becomes: "takes (Paula, Phil256)."

Predicate calculus can formalize sentences with quantifiers such as "all" and "some" by using variables such as "*x*" and "*y*." For example, "All students are overworked" becomes

(for-all $x$) (student($x$) → overworked ($x$)).

Literally, this says "For any $x$, if $x$ is a student, then $x$ is overworked," which is equivalent to saying that all students are overworked. The sentence "Students who take courses get credit for them" could be formalized as

(for-all $x$) (for-all $y$) [(student ($x$) & course ($y$) & take ($x$, $y$)) → get-credit-for ($x$, $y$)]

This looks complicated, but what it is saying in English is "For any $x$ and $y$, if $x$ is a student, $y$ is a course, and $x$ takes $y$, then $x$ gets credit for $y$."

Readers whose interest lies predominantly in human psychology might now be asking, why are you throwing these mathematical symbols at me? The answer is that some rudiments of formal logic are required for understanding much current work in cognitive science, including some proposals about how humans do deduction. At a minimum, we have to notice that people can comprehend such statements as "Students who pass courses get credit for them" and use them to make inferences. Predicate logic, unlike some other approaches to representation we will discuss, has sufficient representational power to handle this example.

Although predicate logic is useful for many purposes, it has limitations that become obvious as soon as we try to translate a natural language text. For example, try to put the last paragraph into logical form. Its first sentence includes the word "now," and extending predicate logic to deal with time is not an easy matter. It also contains the word "you," which the reader can figure out refers to Paul Thagard, the author of this book, but it is not obvious how to express this in logic. Moreover, the structure of this sentence includes the relation "asks," which involves both an asker and the proposition that is asked, so that we need to be able to embed a proposition within a proposition, which is not naturally done in the usual formalism for predicate logic. If translation from language to logical formalism were easier, we could have greater confidence that formal logic captures everything that is necessary for mental representation.

Propositional and predicate logic work well for making assertions that take statements to be true or false, but they provide no means to deal with uncertainty, as in "Paula is probably in the library." For such assertions, formal logic can be supplemented with probability theory, which assigns numbers between 0 and 1 to propositions. We can then write *"P(p) = 0.7"* to symbolize that the probability that Paula is in the library is 0.7.

## Computational Power

Representations by themselves do nothing. To support thinking, there must be operations on the representations. To derive a conclusion in logic, we apply *rules of inference* to a set of premises. Two of the most common rules of inference make it possible to draw conclusions using conditionals (if-then sentences):

*Modus ponens*

$p \rightarrow q$

$p$

Therefore, *q*.

*Modus tollens*

$p \rightarrow q$

*not-q*

Therefore, *not-p*.

From the conditional "If Paula is in the library, then Quincy is in the library" and the information that Paula is in the library, modus ponens enables us to infer that Quincy is in the library. From the information that Quincy is not in the library, it follows by modus tollens that Paula is not in the library.

In predicate logic, there are rules of inference for dealing with the quantifiers "all" and "some." For example, the rule of universal instantiation allows the derivation of an instance from a general statement, licensing the inference from (for-all *x*)(cool (*x*)) to cool(Paula), that is, from "Everything is cool" to "Paula is cool." A more complicated application applies the generalization that all students are overworked: (for-all *x*) (student(*x*) $\rightarrow$ overworked (*x*)). Applying this to Mary, we get the conclusion that if Mary is a student, she is overworked: student (Mary) $\rightarrow$ overworked (Mary).

Abstract rules of inference such as modus ponens are not in themselves processing operations. To produce computations, they need to be part of a human or machine system that can apply them to sentences with the appropriate logical form. From a logical perspective, deductive reasoning consists of applying formal inference rules that consider only the logical form of the premises.

### Problem Solving

**Planning**  Many planning problems are open to solutions that employ logical deduction. Suppose Tiffany is a student who wants to get a degree in psychology. Her college or university catalog tells her that she needs to take ten psychology courses, including two statistics courses, Statistics 1 and Statistics 2. The first of these is a prerequisite for the other, and the second is a prerequisite for Research Methods, which is also required for the degree. From the general description in the catalog, Tiffany can infer by the inference rule universal instantiation the conditionals that apply to her, including

take (Tiffany, Stat1) → can-take (Tiffany, Stat2)

can-take (Tiffany, Stat2) & open (Stat2) → take (Tiffany, Stat2)

take (Tiffany, Stat2) → can-take (Tiffany, RM)

can-take (Tiffany, RM) & open (RM) → take (Tiffany, RM)

take (Tiffany, RM) & take (Tiffany, Stat1) & take (Tiffany, Stat2) & take (Tiffany, seven-other-courses) → graduate-with (Tiffany, psychology-degree).

The last conditional is a somewhat awkward formalization of the statement that if Tiffany takes Research Methods, the two statistics courses, and seven other courses, then she can graduate with a psychology degree. Tiffany can use these conditionals and the inference rule modus ponens to derive a plan, which in logical terms is a deduction from her initial state, where she has taken no psychology courses, to the goal state, where she graduates. Tiffany can construct the deductive plan that she can take Statistics 1, and then Statistics 2, and then Research Methods, and then seven other courses, and finally graduate with a psychology degree.

For planning to be computationally realizable, deduction must be more constrained than the general set of inference rules found in formal logic. For example, propositional logic contains the following conjunction rule:

*Conjunction*

*p*

*q*

Therefore, *p* & *q*.

This rule is fine logically, but computationally it is potentially disastrous. If Tiffany has taken both statistics courses, she could usefully infer

take (Tiffany, Stat1) & take (Tiffany, Stat2).

But it would gain her nothing to make the additional valid inference to

take (Tiffany, Stat1) & take (Tiffany, Stat2) & take (Tiffany, Stat1) & take (Tiffany, Stat2).

Uncontrolled inference of this sort would quickly exhaust the memory of any human or machine system.

The deductive method of planning is intuitively appealing, but it encounters a number of computational problems. First, it tends to be slow, with an enormous amount of inference required to accomplish even simple plans, although various computational strategies have been developed to make deduction more effective. Second, purely deductive planning is *monotonic*: it can only draw new conclusions and not reject previous ones. (A monotonic mathematical function is one whose values continuously increase or continuously decrease without oscillation; reasoning is not monotonic because we do not continuously add new beliefs, since sometimes old beliefs must be abandoned.) AI researchers have developed several techniques to make logic nonmonotonic, but they are computationally expensive. Third, a purely deductive planner is not capable of learning from experience. Having solved a problem once, it will go through the same laborious deductive process when faced with it again, unless some method of learning from its experience has been added.

I have barely scratched the surface in describing artificial intelligence work on deductive planning (see, for example, Dean and Wellman 1991; Russell and Norvig 2003). The reader should see that logical deduction can be a useful way to describe how planning problems are solved, but that this view of planning has some difficulties. Later chapters will describe numerous other approaches to planning.

**Decision**  Deductive planning finds a logical path from an initial state to a goal state. But what happens if there is more than one reasonable path?

In the example in the last section, Tiffany's deduced plan was to take Statistics 1, then Statistics 2, then Research Methods. But often she will face decisions that require her to choose between actions. For example, she may be required to take a humanities course, and therefore will have to choose among philosophy, English, and Spanish. Deductive planning will not tell her which choice to make, since each path will take her to the desired goal state of satisfying the humanities requirement. Tiffany needs to decide which of the courses will satisfy her other goals, such as learning something interesting, not working too hard, and taking a course that fits reasonably with the rest of her schedule. Deduction may be relevant to working out the consequences of some possible choices. If Spanish is only offered at 8:30 in the morning, Tiffany might deduce that she would have to get up early in the morning if she took it. But other consequences might not be so clear, since students are often not sure about what a course will be like.

Hence, decision making often requires considering of probabilities. Tiffany might believe that philosophy will probably be more interesting than English, or vice versa, or that Spanish will probably be more useful than English. Hence, she needs to base her decision both on what her goals are and on her estimated probabilities that the actions will accomplish those goals. There is thus room for judgments that apply the formal theory of probability. We can write $P(p/q)$ to represent the probability of $p$ given $q$, so that "$P$(interesting course/English course)" could express the probability that Tiffany gets an interesting course given that she takes an English course. To estimate this probability, she could use her background knowledge of what proportion of English courses on her campus are interesting. In deciding whether to take philosophy, English, or Spanish, Tiffany will have to calculate the *expected value* of each choice, taking into account both the probability of various outcomes and the extent to which her goals are satisfied by the outcomes.

Computational systems for decision making based on probabilities have been developed. Holtzman (1989) used probability theory and other formal ideas to develop an intelligent decision system for helping infertile couples decide what kind of treatment to use. Developing probabilistic computer systems is tricky, because using probability can be computationally explosive: the number of probabilities needed can increase exponentially as the number of propositions or variables in the model increase. Clever techniques have been developed for keeping probabilistic reasoning computationally tractable (Neapolitan 1990; Pearl 1988, 2000). A different issue treated below is whether people's normal decision making uses probabilities.

**Explanation**   Whereas in a planning problem you are trying to figure out how to accomplish a goal, in an explanation you are trying to understand why something happened. Suppose that Sarah was expecting to meet Frank at the student bar, but he did not show up. She would naturally try to generate an explanation for his absence. Like plans, explanations can sometimes be viewed as logical deductions: you can try to deduce what you want to explain for what you know. Someone might tell Sarah that Frank is studying for an exam, and that whenever he studies he forgets about social engagements. From this information Sarah can deductively explain why Frank did not show up.

The view that explanations are logical deductions was developed and defended by the philosopher of science Carl Hempel (1965). Especially in mathematical areas of science such as physics, explanations can be described as logical deductions. We shall see in later chapters, however, that not all explanations are deductive. Moreover, not all deductions are explanations. For example, we can deduce the height of a flagpole from information about its shadow along with trigonometry and laws of optics, but it seems odd to say that the length of a flagpole's shadow explains the flagpole's height.

In rare cases, the reason Frank did not show up could be deduced—for example if he is a rigid person who misses appointments if and only if he is sick. Sarah could then apply modus ponens: if Frank misses an appointment, he is sick; Frank missed an appointment; therefore Frank is sick. But normally there will more than one explanation available. Just like a planner constructing multiple paths to a goal, Sarah might be able to construct several deductive explanations based on conditionals such as

If Frank is sick, then he will not arrive.

If Frank has had a car accident, then he will not arrive.

If Frank has fallen in love with someone else, then he will not arrive.

If Sarah did not actually know that Frank is sick, or that he has had a car accident, or that he has fallen in love, then she would not immediately be able to deduce that he will not arrive. But the three conditionals just given can be used to form hypotheses about what happened: maybe he's sick, or maybe he had a car accident, or maybe he has fallen in love. This kind of inference, where you form a hypothesis in order to generate an explanation, was called *abduction* by the nineteenth-century American philosopher Charles Peirce (1992). Sarah may abduce that Frank is sick because this hypothesis, in conjunction with the rule that if Frank is sick he will not arrive, allows her to deductively explain why Frank did not arrive. Abductive inference is a risky but powerful kind of learning.

## Learning

Intelligent systems should be able not only to solve various kinds of problems but also to use experience to improve their performance. How can we improve planning, decision making, and explanation? Little work has been done within the logical approach on direct improvements to problem solving, but logical representations are useful for describing some kinds of learning programs.

Consider the learning problem faced by students first arriving on campus. They usually start with little knowledge about the kinds of course offerings available or the kinds of people they will meet. But they quickly accumulate information about particular examples of courses or types of people and naturally proceed to make inductive *generalizations* about them. Crude generalizations might include such statements as that philosophy classes are fun (or boring, as the case may be) and that statistics classes are demanding. These generalizations are inductive in that they involve uncertainty, a leap from what is definitely known to what is at best probable. Students who have taken two philosophy classes might be prepared to generalize from information that could be expressed in logical form as follows:

fun (Phil100)

fun (Phil200)

Therefore, (for-all *x*) (philosophy-course (*x*) → fun (*x*)).

The conclusion is that all philosophy courses are fun. But it is obviously possible that these two courses might be fun whereas other philosophy courses (e.g., Philosophy of Basket Weaving) are boring.

Computer programs for inductive generalization do not always use logical representations for input. One of the most widely used learning programs is Quinlan's (1983) ID3 program. It can be classified as within the logical approach because it uses probabilities to form generalizations from sets of instances. For example, it could be given a sample of students from different sections of a university along with a description of their traits. It could then start to form generalizations concerning how students from such areas as arts, sciences, and engineering differ with respect to personal, social, and intellectual characteristics.

Like inductive generalization, but unlike deduction, abduction is obviously a very risky sort of inference. There may be all sorts of reasons unknown to Sarah that explain why Frank did not show up for an appointment with her. But abduction is indispensable in science and everyday life, whether paleontologists are trying to generate explanations of why the dinosaurs became extinct or students are trying to understand their friends' behavior. Since abduction's purpose is to generate explanations, and explanations can sometimes be understood in terms of logical deduction, it is natural to treat abduction within a logical framework (e.g., Konolige 1992). Later chapters describe alternative ways of thinking about abduction.

Sarah does not want to find just *some* explanation of why Frank did not arrive, she wants to find the *best* explanation. From a logical perspective, assessing the best explanation involves probabilities. Sarah will want to be able to assess the conditional probability of Frank being sick, given that he did not arrive, as well as the conditional probabilities of all the other hypotheses. A theorem of the probability calculus, Bayes's theorem, is potentially very useful. In words, it says that the probability of a hypothesis given the evidence is equal to the result of multiplying the prior probability of the hypothesis, $P(h)$, by the probability of the evidence given the hypothesis, all divided by the probability of the evidence. For Sarah, the prior probability that Frank is sick is her estimate of how likely he is to be sick in general, without considering his failure to arrive. To apply Bayes's theorem, she also needs to consider the probability of his failure to arrive, assuming he is sick. Probabilistic approaches to the problem of how to choose explanatory hypotheses have been popular in both artificial intelligence (Pearl 1988, 2000) and philosophy (Howson and Urbach 1989; Glymour 2001). But alternative approaches are available, as we will see in chapter 7.

The term "induction" can be very confusing, since it has both a broad and a narrow sense. The broad sense covers any inference that, unlike deduction, introduces uncertainty. The narrow sense covers only inductive generalization, in which general conclusions are reached from particular examples. Abduction (forming explanatory hypotheses) is induction in the broad sense but not in the narrow one. My practice in this book is to use "learning" for the broad sense of induction and "inductive generalization" for the narrow sense. Additional computational accounts of learning will be encountered in later chapters.

## Language

Linguists have sometimes taken formal logic to be a natural tool for understanding the structure of language. There are even two editions of a book called *Everything That Linguists Have Always Wanted to Know about Logic—But Were Ashamed to Ask* (McCawley 1993). The philosopher Richard Montague (1974) contended that there are no important theoretical differences between natural languages and the artificial languages of logicians. Most linguists and psychologists would disagree with this claim, however, and formal logic has played a minor role in the understanding of human language. Stabler (1992) has used logic to formalize some of Chomsky's recent ideas about language, which include the postulation of a level of "logical form" at which meaning is most explicitly represented (Chomsky 1980). Later chapters discuss how other kinds of representation, particularly rules and concepts, have been used to describe and explain human use of language.

## Psychological Plausibility

Historically, logicians have disagreed about the mutual relevance of logic and psychology. Some early writers on logic, such as John Stuart Mill, saw an intimate connection between human psychology and logic, which was construed as the art and science of reasoning. In contrast, the founders of modern formal logic, Gottlob Frege and Charles Peirce, emphatically distanced their work from psychology. Today, we can distinguish at least three positions concerning the relations and relative merits of formal logic and psychology:

1. Formal logic is an important part of human reasoning.

2. Formal logic is only distantly related to human reasoning, but the distance does not matter, since the role of logic in philosophy and artificial

intelligence is to provide a mathematical analysis of what constitutes optimal reasoning.

3. Formal logic is only distantly related to human reasoning, so cognitive science should pursue other approaches.

The first position is advocated by a few psychologists who have provided experimental evidence that people use rules like modus ponens. The second position is popular among philosophers and artificial intelligence researchers who prefer formal approaches. The third position is probably now the dominant view in psychology, but is less popular in philosophy and artificial intelligence.

The psychologists who have most aggressively defended the first position are Martin Braine (1978; Braine and O'Brien 1998) and Lance Rips (1983, 1986, 1994). Rips (1986, 279) lists several kinds of psychological evidence for mental logic. Theories of mental logic successfully predict the validity judgments that subjects give for a fairly wide range of propositional arguments. For example, people recognize as valid arguments that have the same form as modus ponens, but reject arguments of the form "If A, then C; C, therefore, A." Theories of mental logic also account for reaction times and help make sense of what subjects say when they think aloud about validity decisions.

Nevertheless, other kinds of experiments have made many psychologists skeptical about mental logic. The best-known experimental technique uses Wason's (1966) selection task, in which subjects are informed that they will be shown cards that have numbers on one side and letters on the other. They are then given a rule such as *If a card has an A on one side, then it has a 4 on the other.* The subjects are then shown four cards and asked to indicate exactly which cards must be turned over to determine whether the rule holds. They can be given, for example, the four cards shown in figure 2.1. Then they must decide which of these cards should be turned over. Most people realize that it is necessary to turn the A over to check whether it has a 4 on the other side. This can be interpreted as an application of modus ponens, since the rule *If A then 4* combined with the premise A suggests checking to see if there is a 4. On the other hand, a great many people neglect to check the 7, failing to realize that if this card has an A on the other side, it refutes the rule in question. Recognition that the card with a 7 needs to be turned over requires an appreciation of modus tollens:" If A then 4; 7 means not-4; so not-A is required for the rule to hold." Some

**Figure 2.1**
Cards in Wason's selection task.

people are confused enough about the task to turn over the cards with B and 4 on them, even though these are irrelevant to determining the truth of the rule.

The point of this kind of experiment is not to show that people are stupid in violating the rules of formal logic. Rather, the experiment becomes interesting if it suggests that people approach this kind of reasoning task with representations and computations quite different from those used in formal logic. Subsequent experiments have shown that people have little difficulty with tasks like Wason's card problem if they are given familiar concrete examples. Suppose that people are told that the cards have on one side information about whether individuals are in a bar and on the other side numbers representing their ages. They can then be given a rule such as *If a person is in the bar, then he or she is over 21*. They can then be asked what cards need to be turned over to determine whether this rule holds, choosing, for example, from IN-BAR, NOT-IN-BAR, 23, 18. In contrast to the way they perform on abstract problems with letters and numbers, most people can recognize that it is necessary not only to turn over the IN-BAR card to check the age of the person, but also to turn over the 18 card to make sure that the person is not in the bar.

Cheng and Holyoak (1985) have argued that people approach these tasks, not with mental logic, but with *pragmatic reasoning schemas*. For example, a permission schema has the form *If one is to do X, then one must satisfy precondition Y*. Then the reason that people do so much better with the concrete bar-and-age example than with the abstract letter-and-number example is that the permission schema is naturally applied to the former. The psychological application of rules and schemas is discussed further in chapters 3 and 4.

The most persistent critic of the mental logic view has been the psychologist Philip Johnson-Laird (1983). Johnson-Laird and Byrne (1991) argue that deductive reasoning is carried out neither by formal logical rules nor by content-specific rules or schemas, but by *mental models*, which are mental representations that correspond in structure to the situations that they represent. Johnson-Laird and Byrne claim that when people interpret a conditional such as "If a card has an A on one side, then it has a 4 on the other," they construct a mental representation something like this:

[A] 4

Here "[A]" indicates a model in which a card has an A on it, and "4" adds that in this model it also has a 4 on the other side. Johnson-Laird and Byrne explain many people's performance in the selection task by supposing that they consider only those cards that are explicitly represented in their models of the rule. Hence, people turn over the A card because it is represented in the model they have constructed, but fail to turn over the 7 card because it is not represented.

The theory of mental models has also been applied to many kinds of reasoning with the quantifiers "all" and "some." From a formal logic perspective, reasoning with quantifiers proceeds by first using inference rules such as universal instantiation (presented above) to remove quantifiers, then using propositional rules of inference such as modus ponens to make inferences, and finally reapplying quantifiers using additional rules of inference. Consider the simple reasoning:

All football players are strong.

Anyone strong can lift heavy objects.

Therefore, all football players can lift heavy objects.

In logic, it can be confirmed that this is a valid form of inference by instantiating it into nonquantified statements such as "If $x$ is a football player, then $x$ is strong" and "If $x$ is strong then $x$ can lift heavy objects." Propositional logic then yields "If $x$ is a football player, then $x$ can lift heavy objects," which can be generalized by a deductive inference rule to hold for any x. In contrast, Johnson-Laird maintains that people work with models rather than abstract forms, constructing the following sort of model:

football-player strong lifts-heavy-objects

In the model constructed, there are no football players who cannot lift heavy objects, so the conclusion that all football players can lift heavy objects goes through. More complicated kinds of inference with mixtures of "all" and "some" and "not" require more complex kinds of models.

Johnson-Laird argues that the comparative difficulties that people have with different kinds of inferences of this sort correspond exactly to the complexity of different kinds of models that have to be constructed. Rips (1994) and O'Brien, Braine, and Yang (1994) have responded with arguments that mental logic accounts for the psychological evidence about deductive inference better than mental models do. But mental model theory has been applied to many kinds of human thinking, including causal reasoning (Goldvarg and Johnson-Laird 2001).

Just as Johnson-Laird has challenged the relevance of formal logic to human deductive reasoning, psychologists have done experiments that suggest that human inductive reasoning may not have much to do with probability theory. Tversky and Kahneman (1983), for example, have shown that people sometimes violate the rule that the probability of a conjunction will also be less than or equal to the probability of one its conjuncts, $P(p \ \& \ q) \leq P(p)$. Suppose you are told that Frank likes to read a lot of serious literature, attend foreign movies, and discuss world politics. You are then asked to estimate the probability that Frank is college educated, that Frank is a carpenter, and that Frank is a college-educated carpenter. Not surprisingly, people in experiments like this one tend to judge it to be more probable that Frank is college educated than that he is a carpenter, but they often violate probability theory by judging it to be more likely that Frank is a college-educated carpenter than that he is a carpenter. When people approach such examples, they seem to employ a kind of matching process that judges the degree of fit between the description of the individual and their stereotypes such as college-educated and carpenter (see chapter 4). Numerous other instances have been found where people's inductive reasoning appears to be based on something other than formal rules of probability theory (Kahneman, Slovic, and Tversky 1982; Gilovich, Griffin, and Kahneman 2002). However, just as Rips and others have defended mental deductive logic, some psychologists have offered different interpretations of Tversky and Kahneman's results that are consistent with the view that people employ probabilistic reasoning (Gigerenzer, Hoffrage, and Kleinbölting 1991; Gigerenzer 2000).

One open possibility is that mental logic may give an appropriate account of some narrow kinds of human reasoning such as applying modus ponens, whereas more vivid representations such as mental models are needed to account for more complex kinds of human reasoning such as that involving "all" and "some." It is at least obvious that the logical approach is not the only possible way of understanding human thinking, and various alternatives are discussed in the chapters to come. Of course, philosophers and artificial intelligence researchers not interested in psychology can maintain that whether or not people use logic in their thinking is less important than developing formal logical models of how people and other intelligent systems *should* think. What they risk missing is the appreciation that human intelligence and the kind of machine intelligence we want to build may rest on representational structures and computational processes that differ markedly from those that logic affords.

**Neurological Plausibility**

Until recently, little was known about the neurological plausibility of formal logic. Metaphorically, every synaptic connection between neurons looks like a miniature inference using modus ponens: if neuron 1 fires, then neuron 2 fires. Neuron 1 fires, so neuron 2 fires. However, it is obvious that single neurons do not represent whole propositions, and how groups of neurons perform inferences is unknown. However, it is now possible to investigate at a larger scale how the brain performs deductive reasoning. Brain scanning experiments are being used to determine whether people perform deductions using just the left half of the their brains, as suggested by the mental logic view that deduction is formal and independent of content. The alternative hypothesis is that people perform deductions using the right half of their brains, as suggested by the mental models view that deduction requires regions in the right hemisphere of the brain that involve spatial reasoning (Wharton and Grafman 1998). (See chapter 8 for an introduction to how brain scanning is used to identify neural correlates of different kinds of thinking.)

Goel et al. (1998) used brain scans to identify regions involved in reasoning tasks such as syllogisms. They found no significant right-hemisphere activation, suggesting that deductive reasoning is purely linguistic as implied by the mental logic theory. However, Kroger, Cohen, and Johnson-Laird (forthcoming) compared brain regions involved in logical reasoning and mathematical calculation and found that parts of the right half of the brain were more active in reasoning than in calculation. They judged that their results are incompatible with a purely linguistic theory of logical reasoning based on formal rules of inference. Goel (2003) reviewed several neuroimaging studies of syllogistic reasoning and argued that it involves two neural pathways, including both linguistic and visual-spatial systems. The debate between mental logic and mental model accounts of deductive reasoning now involves three of the methodologies of cognitive science: psychological experiments, computational models, and neurological experiments.

## Practical Applicability

The logical approach to cognitive science has not been of great educational use from the perspective of providing deeper understanding of human learning. Piaget and Inhelder (1969) tried to base some of the principles of human cognitive development on logical categories, but claims about the role of propositional logic in developmental stages are not part of modern educational theory. Logic is, however, useful from another educational perspective, in that it can suggest ways that people should reason better. Courses on informal logic and critical thinking have proliferated because of the perceived need to improve people's reasoning. Formal deductive logic and probability theory certainly do provide useful tools for prescribing how some kinds of thinking should be done.

According to Dym and Levitt (1991), engineering design often involves satisfying requirements that may be expressed as logical statements. For example, a structural code may state "If a beam is simply supported, its depth shall be greater than one-thirtieth of its clear span." PROLOG, a programming language that uses logic representations and deductive techniques, has been applied to problems such as designing buildings that satisfy physical and legal constraints. Levesque et al. (1997) have developed a logic-based programming language intended for applications in high-level control of robots and industrial processes. Although logic has been a favored tool of artificial intelligence theorists, practical intelligent systems have tended to use techniques such as rules, cases, and neural networks discussed in later chapters. However, there is a growing use of probabilistic reasoning in intelligent systems, for example, in a tutoring computer program that deals with uncertainty about the knowledge and goals of the students it teaches (Conati, Gertner, and Vanlehn 2002).

## Summary

Formal logic provides some powerful tools for looking at the nature of representation and computation. Propositional and predicate calculus serve to express many complex kinds of knowledge, and many inferences can be understood in terms of logical deduction with inference rules such as modus ponens. The explanation schema for the logical approach is as follows:

Explanation target

Why do people make the inferences they do?

Explanatory pattern

People have mental representations similar to sentences in predicate logic.

People have deductive and inductive procedures that operate on those sentences.

The deductive and inductive procedures, applied to the sentences, produce the inferences.

It is not certain, however, that logic provides the core ideas about representation and computation needed for cognitive science, since more efficient and psychologically natural methods of computation may be needed to explain human thinking.

## Discussion Questions

1. What do you know that is hard to express in formal logic?

2. Are people logical? Should they be?

3. Is deduction a central kind of human thinking? How do people make deductions?

4. Is nondeductive reasoning done in accord with the laws of probability?

5. Is natural language based on logic?

## Further Reading

On the history of logic, see Prior 1967. There are many good introductory logic textbooks; for example, Bergmann, Moor, and Nelson 2003. Pollock 1995 approaches philosophical problems from a computational perspective based on formal logic. The logical approach to artificial intelligence is expounded in Genesereth and Nilsson 1987 and Russell and Norvig 2003. Rips 1994 develops and defends a logical approach to human deductive reasoning.

## Web Sites

Introduction to logic: http://people.hofstra.edu/faculty/Stefan_Waner/RealWorld/logic/logicintro.html

Logic programming: http://www.afm.sbu.ac.uk/logic-prog/

Mental models: http://www.tcd.ie/Psychology/Ruth_Byrne/mental_models/index.html

## Notes

Formal logic is concerned not only with syntax, the structure of sentences that I have described in this chapter, but also with semantics, the truth conditions of sentences. For example, the conjunction $p$ & $q$ is true just in case $p$ is true and $q$ is true, and false otherwise.

Most logic-based planners in artificial intelligence do not use a full set of logical inference rules, but instead use an inference procedure based on a simple rule of inference known as the *resolution principle* (Genesereth and Nilsson 1987). Resolution is too complicated to explain in detail here, but what it does is take expressions that have been translated into a simplified version of predicate calculus and apply a powerful kind of operator to them to see what can be deduced. Fikes and Nilsson (1971) used logical deduction in a planning system called STRIPS that has been applied to robotics and other applications.

In symbols, Bayes's theorem can be written

$$P(h/e) = \{P(h) * P(e/h) \}/ P(e).$$

In artificial intelligence research, logic and probability are often considered to be alternative approaches to knowledge representation, but I have combined them because they both base inference on highly general and abstract principles.

This chapter has focused on one approach to mental models, but other kinds of model-based reasoning are also important (Magnani, Nersessian, and Thagard 1999).

# 3   Rules

Rules are if-then structures such as: *IF you pass forty Arts courses, THEN you graduate with a B.A.* These structures are very similar to the conditionals discussed in chapter 2, but they have different representational and computational properties. Whereas most logic-based computational models have not been intended as models of human cognition, rule-based models have had psychological aims from the start. The first artificial intelligence program was the Logic Theorist of Allen Newell, Cliff Shaw, and Herbert Simon (1958). Written in 1956 on a primitive computer, this program did proofs in formal logic. Its proving behavior was intended not just as a mathematically sophisticated intelligent system, but also as a model of how humans do proofs in logic. In addition to logical rules of inference, the Logic Theorist included strategic rules for finding proofs efficiently. The Logic Theorist was soon generalized into the first broad framework for understanding human thinking, GPS (the General Problem Solver; Newell and Simon 1972). GPS used rules to simulate human solutions to various kinds of problems, such as cryptarithmetic problems described later in this chapter. In artificial intelligence, rules are often called productions.

Since GPS, two different rule-based cognitive systems have had a substantial impact on cognitive science because of their broad applicability to human cognition. The ACT system of John Anderson (1983, 1993) has had a wealth of psychological applications. More recently, Allan Newell, in collaboration with John Laird and Paul Rosenbloom, developed SOAR, a powerful rule-based program that has had many technological and psychological applications (Newell 1990; Rosenbloom, Laird, and Newell 1993).

The thrust of this chapter is not to describe any of these systems in detail, but rather to convey what makes rules so computationally and psychologically powerful. Later chapters, however, will provide alternative views of cognition that suggest that rules do not tell the whole story about human thinking.

### Representational Power

Although rules have a very simple structure, with just an IF part (sometimes called the *condition*) and a THEN part (called the *action*), they can be used to represent many different kinds of knowledge. First, they can represent general information about the world, such as that students are overworked: *IF x is a student, THEN x is overworked*. Second, they can represent information about how to do things in the world: *IF you register early, THEN you will get the courses you want*. Third, rules can represent linguistic regularities such as *IF an English sentence has a plural subject, THEN it has a plural verb*. Fourth, rules of inference such as modus ponens can be recast in rule form: *IF you have an if-then rule and the if part is true, THEN the then part will be true too*. As this example shows, rules can have multiple conditions (multiple clauses in the IF part). They can also have multiple actions: *IF you register early, THEN you get the classes you want, and you have a short line to stand in*.

It may seem surprising at first that rule-based systems have been so important in cognitive science, since rules are not as representationally elegant as formal logic. Logic provides a standardized way of representing relations and basic operations such as "and," "or," and "not," whereas these can be implemented in various nonstandard ways in rule-based systems. But the developers of rule-based systems have been happy to lose some of the representational rigor of logic-based systems for the sake of increased computational power. One advantage comes from the fact that rules do not have to be interpreted as universally true. The logical generalization (for all x) (student (x) → overworked (x)) must be interpreted as saying that every student is overworked. But the rule that *IF x is a student THEN x is overworked* can be interpreted as a *default*, that is, as a rough generalization that can admit exceptions. We might have another rule that says that *IF x is a student and x is taking only easy courses, THEN x is not overworked*. These two rules might coexist in the same system, but the result need not be the contradictory conclusion that a particular student is both overworked and not overworked, since the computational operations of the rule-based system can ensure that only the more appropriate rule is applied.

Unlike logic, rule-based systems can also easily represent strategic information about what to do. Rules often contain actions that represent goals, such as *IF you want to go home for the weekend, and you have bus fare, THEN you can catch a bus*. Such information about goals serves to focus the rule-based problem solver on the task at hand. Hence, although the rules in a rule-based system may not have the full representational power of formal logic, they can be expressed in ways that enhance computational power and psychological plausibility.

## Computational Power

### Problem Solving

In logic-based systems the fundamental operation of thinking is logical deduction, but from the perspective of rule-based systems the fundamental operation of thinking is *search*. When you have a problem to solve—for example, how to write an essay for a course—you have a *space* of possibilities that you must navigate. This space includes the possible topics you might write on, the range of available library resources you might consult, and the means you might employ to actually write the essay. Accomplishing your assigned task requires you to search through the space of possible actions to find a path that will get you from your current state (essay to be done) to the desired state (finished essay that will earn a good grade). Rule-based systems can efficiently perform this kind of search for a solution.

In complex problems, it is impossible to search the space exhaustively for the very best solution. Suppose, for example, you wear four different articles of clothing (shirts, socks, etc.) and you have ten pieces of each article (ten shirts, etc.). Then there are ten thousand ($10^4$) different combinations of clothes that you might wear each day, but no one has the time or interest to consider all these possibilities. Instead, people rely on *heuristics*, which are rules of thumb that contribute to satisfactory solutions without considering all possibilities. A heuristic such as "Wear brown shoes with brown pants but not with black pants" helps to provide an efficient solution to the problem of planning what to wear. Problem solving, learning, and language use can all be described in terms of rule-based heuristic search through a complex space of possibilities.

Psychologists make an important distinction between long-term memory, the mind's permanent store of information, and short-term memory, a much smaller selection of information immediately available for processing. From the rule-based perspective, you have many rules in long-term memory, but only a small selection of rules and facts are active in your short-term memory and ready for current use. You probably have your mother's birthday in long-term memory, but reading this sentence may make you conscious of it as it becomes active in short-term memory.

Computer scientists and psychologists make an important distinction between serial processing, in which thinking proceeds one step at a time, and parallel processing, in which many steps occur at once. Rule-based processing can be either serial, with one rule being applied at a time, or parallel, with many rules being applied simultaneously. Conscious thought tends to be serial, as we notice ourselves making one inference at a time, but these inferences may depend on numerous rules of which we are not conscious being applied simultaneously. Chapter 11 discusses the role of consciousness in thinking.

**Planning**   Many students go to college or university in a town or city away from their home town or city, so they frequently face the problem of how to get home for the weekend or at the end of term. The available means for getting from university to home can be expressed in collections of rules, such as

IF you drive on highway 1, THEN you can get from university city to home city.

IF you take the parkway, THEN you can get from university city to the highway.

IF you take Main Street from the university, THEN you can get from the university to the parkway.

IF you take a bus from the bus depot, THEN you can get from university city to home city.

IF you take a bus from the university to the bus depot, THEN you can get to the bus depot.

Other possibilities may also exist, such as taking the train or hitchhiking. Students who must solve the problem of how to get home for the weekend can search the space of possible actions (go to the bus depot, head for the highway) and put together a plan that gets them where they want to be.

Rules can be used to reason either *forward* or *backward*. Reasoning backward, a student might think that "To get home, I can take the highway, which requires taking the parkway, which requires taking Main Street, which requires getting a car." The goal is to get home, but the plan is constructed by considering a series of subgoals such as getting to the highway. Reasoning forward, the student might use inference akin to modus ponens to see that "Main Street gets me to the parkway, which gets me to the highway." Forward and backward reasoning both try to find a series of rules that can be used to get from the starting point to the goal, but they differ in the search strategy employed.

Another possible reasoning strategy is *bidirectional* search, which combines working forward from the starting place with working backward from the goal. Although many planning problems can be understood in terms of rule-based reasoning, planning in this way is difficult when there are many potentially relevant rules and the reasoner has to select which ones to use at the key points in problem solving. Rule-based problem solving sounds a lot like logical deduction, but it differs in that much more attention is paid to strategies for applying the right rules at the right time.

The same is true for the sort of planning problems that students encounter in courses. A mathematical word problem gives you some information and requires you to calculate an answer. For example, you may be told that it takes 75 minutes to get from the university city to the home city, a distance of 65 miles (100 kilometers), and be asked to calculate the average speed of the trip. Rules, embodied in mathematical operations, show you how to move forward from the information given to an answer that can be derived from it. Often, however, it will be more effective instead or in addition to work backward from the goal—the desired answer—toward the initial information given. In either case, you are trying to find a sequence of rules that provides a path between the start and the goal. Not all planning, however, is rule based. We will see in later chapters how schemas and analogies can help to solve planning problems.

**Decision** Although rules are very useful for finding plans, they are not always very helpful for deciding between competing plans. A student may be able to use rules to construct two different ways of getting home for the weekend, but the result does not provide guidance about which plan to adopt. Driving, taking the bus, and taking the train will all get you home, but which way you go will require a more complex balancing of goals such as wanting to minimize cost, time, and hassle. For decision making, therefore, rule-based reasoning needs to be supplemented by other processes, such as the expected-value calculation mentioned in chapter 2, or the deliberative coherence determination described in chapter 7.

**Explanation**   As we saw in chapter 2, explanation can often be viewed as a kind of deductive process, which rules can perform as well as logical deduction. Some kinds of hypothesis formation can be described as a search for explanations performed by rules. Suppose you try to register for a course and it turns out to be full. Various rules might apply:

IF a course is required for many programs, THEN it fills up quickly.

IF a course has a popular instructor, THEN it fills up quickly.

Knowing that the course's instructor is popular, in conjunction with the second rule just stated, allows you to explain why it was full when you tried to sign up for it. Even if you do not know for sure that the course has a popular instructor or is required for many programs, you can conjecture that these might be true (see the discussion of abductive learning below). Thus, solving explanation problems can be understood in terms of rule-based reasoning, if there is a sequence of rules that allows you to generate what needs to be explained from what you already know.

### Learning

Numerous important kinds of learning are naturally understood in terms of the acquisition, modification, and application of rules. Some rules may be innate, comprising part of the biological equipment with which we are born. A physical rule such as *IF something is coming toward your eyes, THEN blink* is not one that people or other organisms have to learn. More controversially, some cognitive scientists discussed in the next section believe that many rules of language are innate. But no one would claim that rules for how to register for university courses are innate, so how are they acquired?

Like the logical statements described in chapter 2, rules can be learned by *inductive generalization*, in which examples are summarized by means of a rule. Sometimes rules require many examples to support them: you should not conclude from just one engineering class that all engineering classes are hard or from just one philosophy course that all philosophy courses are interesting. But students do gradually acquire from experience such rules as *IF x is a programming class, THEN x will be time consuming* and *IF you want to get into popular courses, THEN you should register early.*

In inductive generalization, rules are formed from examples; but rules can also be formed from other rules by a process that in the SOAR model of cognition is called *chunking* and in the ACT model is called *composition*. Suppose that you have used lots of rules to plan how to get from university to home and found a good series of rules about how to get from university to the parkway to the highway home. The next time you want to go home, you need not go through the whole search. Instead, you can chunk the rules into a general rule like *IF you want to get from university to home, THEN drive.* Similarly, the first time you put together a class schedule, you may have to do lots of complex searching for a plan, but with experience you can use a higher-level rule such as *IF you want a good schedule, THEN arrange your classes at close times rather than spread over five days.* We will see in the section on psychological plausibility that the computational process of chunking rules has been used to model many kinds of human learning.

Another way that rules can be formed from rules is by *specialization*, in which an existing rule is modified to deal with a specific situation. If driving home on Friday afternoon may be slow because of heavy traffic, experience might lead you to produce the specialized rule *IF you want to get from university to home and it is Friday afternoon and you are in a hurry, THEN don't drive.*

As we saw in chapter 2, rules can also be used in abductive learning. Suppose a friend of yours is angry and depressed. Naturally, you try to construct explanations of what is bothering him or her. Suppose you have acquired by inductive generalization the rule *IF a student gets a bad grade, THEN the student is angry and depressed.* You could then generate a possible explanation of why your friend is angry and depressed by conjecturing that he or she might have received a bad grade. This is abductive reasoning, in which a rule is run backward to provide a possible explanation of what happened. Obviously, this kind of inference is highly risky, since there might be a much better explanation of your friend's state of mind—

for example, one based on the rule *IF someone is rejected by a partner THEN he or she becomes angry and depressed*. Picking the best explanation requires a more complex kind of inference discussed in chapter 7. But rules can be very useful for generating hypotheses such as that your friend got a bad grade. Hence abductive inference fits naturally with rule-based reasoning (Thagard 1988), although we will see other kinds of representation that also support it.

Rules can also be used to describe slow incremental learning, if each rule has a numerical value representing the usefulness or plausibility associated with it. The more a rule gets used successfully, the more it is judged to be plausible and useful. For example, each time a student successfully applies the rule, *IF you want to get from university to home, THEN drive*, the stronger the rule gets and the more likely it is to be used in the future. In sum, rules can be created from examples, created from other rules, applied abductively, and quantitatively evaluated based on their performance.

## Language

Before the cognitive revolution of the 1950s, language was widely thought to consist of behavior learned by association. Through repeated experience with pairs of words, people come to expect to hear them used together. The linguist Noam Chomsky developed a very different view of language beginning with his 1957 book *Syntactic Structures*. Chomsky argued that the behaviorist learning models could not account for the generativity of language, the fact that there are an indefinite number of sentences that people can produce and understand. You have probably never encountered the sentence "She rode to the university on a purple camel," but you have no trouble understanding it.

According to Chomsky, our ability to speak and understand language depends on our possessing a complex grammar that consists of rules that we do not consciously know we have. Children who learn English, for example, start forming the past tenses of verbs by adding "ed," without being aware that they are applying a rule like *IF you want to use a verb to describe the past, THEN add "ed" to the verb*. Notoriously, children under five overgeneralize the rule, saying "goed" and "bringed" rather than using the irregular forms that are exceptions to the rule. Pinker (1999) argues at length that rules such as adding "ed" to make past tenses are an essential ingredient of our ability to produce and comprehend language. Taatgen and Anderson (2002) use the ACT system to model how children acquire past tenses in English. Akmajian et al. (2001) describe rules that apply to several different aspects of language. For example, as English speakers we know how to form nouns from verbs by adding "er," as in turning "write" into "writer." We also know phonetic rules such as how to pronounce plurals: compare the predictably different pronunciations of the "s" in "cats"/"huts" and "dogs"/"hugs." Syntactic rules enable us systematically to turn statements into questions, as when we turn "I am happy" into "Am I happy?" by moving the auxiliary verb "am" to the beginning of the sentence.

Chomsky's influential views have been controversial on a number of issues. In chapter 7, we will consider connectionist views that language consists not of rules but of looser associations represented by weights between simple units. Independent of the issue of whether our knowledge of language is best represented by rules, there is the issue of whether it is learned or innate. Chomsky continues to maintain that every human is born with an innate universal grammar. In a departure from his early views, in which children acquire the ability to use language abductively by forming hypotheses about what rules apply to their own individual languages (Chomsky 1972), he currently holds that children learn a language automatically by merely recognizing which of a finite set of possibilities that language employs (Chomsky 1988). All human languages have nouns, verbs, adjectives, and prepositions or postpositions. But languages such as Japanese do not have articles like "the" and "a" in English, so a child learning Japanese has to instantiate universal grammar in a different way than child learning English. Most recently, Chomsky (2002) has raised doubts about whether grammar is a system of rules.

## Psychological Plausibility

Of all the computational-representational approaches described in this book, which has had the most psychological applications? The answer is clear: rule-based systems. I cannot attempt to give a comprehensive review of all of these applications, but I will provide a sample of some typical ways in which rule-based systems have been used to account for human thought.

Newell (1990) has shown how SOAR, a sophisticated current rule-based model, can be applied to a wide range of interesting psychological phenomena. For example, he describes how SOAR solves cryptarithmetic problems, which are puzzles in which letters are substituted for numbers (see also Newell and Simon 1972). One puzzle is *DONALD + GERALD = ROBERT*, where each letter must be replaced by a distinct number between 0 and 9 in a way that makes the equation true. Rules can be very useful for solving this problem, which for our usual addition algorithm is more perspicuously represented as

DONALD

GERALD

---

ROBERT

How does one begin to solve this puzzle? You might notice that in the second column from the left *O* added to *E* produces *O*. This might bring to mind the rule: *IF 0 (zero) is added to a number THEN the number is unchanged.* This rule suggests that *E* is 0. Then, looking at the fourth column, you could see that since $A + A = 0$, *A* should be 5. But following this line of reasoning is likely to get you into trouble, because this assumes that no carry was involved in adding *L* and *L* to get *R* or in adding *N* and *R* to get *B*. So somehow *R* needs to be twice as big as *L*, yet small enough that adding *N* to it in the third column does not produce a carry. Carrying in our familiar addition algorithm involves the rule *IF the digits added exceed 10, THEN write down the second digit of the sum and carry 1 over to the next column to the left.* This rule shows that there is another possible value for *E*: if $E = 9$, then $O + E = O$, provided that there is a carry from the column $N + R = B$. Working out the consequences of this starting point using rules about addition and carrying, along with additional knowledge such as that *IF a digit is at the beginning of a number, THEN the digit is not 0*, allows you (with considerable effort) to come up with a solution. SOAR is able to model aspects of this effort by having various operators that suggest numerical values for the digits and checking to see whether the results are consistent with each other.

SOAR has also been used to model other kinds of high-level reasoning tasks such as determining what follows from "Some archers are not bowlers" and "All canoeists are bowlers." SOAR uses neither mental logic nor mental models, the two approaches to deduction described in chapter 2, but instead does a search through a space of possible inferences, eventually forming the conclusion that "Some archers are canoeists." This is logically incorrect, but the point of a cognitive account of deduction is to model how people reason, including how they sometimes make errors.

Newell also uses SOAR to account for many aspects of human learning, particularly the power law of practice, according to which the rate of learning slows down as more is learned. This law applies to many tasks such as typing and learning to write reversed letters the way they appear in a mirror. Chunking in SOAR provides an explanation of why learning slows down as people become more experienced with a task. At the beginning of practice on a task, people can build more chunks rapidly, and as chunks build up, the speed of performance increases. For example, someone learning to type may make rapid early progress in speed and accuracy. But as higher-level chunks build up, they become less and less useful, because the situations they apply to are rare. So the learning rate of a rule-based system slows down with practice, just like that of people.

Holland et al. (1986) used rule-based systems to account for many different kinds of learning. Conditioning in rats—for example, when they learn to avoid shocks—can be explained by supposing that part of learning with rules is adjusting the strengths of different rules that are used. Every time a rat presses a lever to get food, the rule *IF lever, THEN food* gets strengthened. On the other hand, a shock can produce the conflicting rule *IF lever, THEN shock* and lead to the rat's ceasing to press the lever. Rules can also be used to describe the dynamic mental models that people have of changes in the physical world, such as *IF a car hits a pole, THEN the pole is damaged.* People's abilities and limitations in dealing with the physical and social worlds can also be understood in terms of rules. For example, once people learn a social stereotype, they tend to apply it too generally.

Crowley and Siegler (1993) have shown how variations in children's ability to play tic-tac-toe, a simple game in which the goal is to get 3 Xs or 3 Os in a row, can be understood in terms of their acquisition of rules. Children need to acquire rules about what moves to make, as well as strategic knowledge about what rules to apply when. Here are some of the rules:

*Win* IF there is a row, column, or diagonal with two of my pieces and a blank space, THEN play the blank space to win.

*Block* IF there is a row, column, or diagonal with two of my opponent's pieces and a blank space, THEN play the blank space to block the opponent.

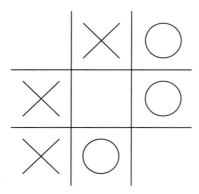

**Figure 3.1**
Rule application in tac-tac-toe. X's turn matches the IF part of four different rules: Win (a move to the top left); Block (a move to the bottom right); Play Center (a move to the middle); and Play empty corner (a move to either empty corner. Adapted with permission from Crowley and Siegler 1993, p. 537.

*Play center*   IF the center is blank, THEN play the center.

*Play empty corner*   IF there is an empty corner, THEN move to an empty corner.

Figure 3.1 shows a partially played game in which all four of these rules are applicable. Children's ability to play tic-tac-toe improves as they acquire rules such as these as well as recognition of the priority of rules. For example, many preschoolers do not have the blocking rule, and many who do have it will apply it even when they have a chance to win.

   Rule-based systems have also been used to account for the acquisition and use of language. Anderson (1983) describes human knowledge of English in terms of such rules as this one (in simplified form):

IF the goal is to communicate a meaning structure of the form (relation, agent, object), THEN set as subgoals

1. to describe agent

2. to describe relation

3. to describe object.

Additional rules show how the mentioned subgoals can be accomplished so that eventually a full sentence, such as "The girl threw the ball," is produced to describe what the agent did to the object. Anderson (1993) describes numerous applications of his ACT rule-based system to acquiring skills such as geometry problem solving and computer programming. There are many examples of a fit between the performance of rule-based systems and the behavior of human thinkers.

### Neurological Plausibility

There is a crude analogy between rules and neurons connected by synapses, in that IF one neuron fires, it can THEN cause the firing of the neuron connected to it. But this similarity is superficial and in fact little is known about how rules might be implemented in the brain. Anderson (1993) sketches a possible neural implementation of ACT, and simple rule-based systems have been implemented in artificial neural nets (see chapter 7). More recently, Anderson et al. (forthcoming) have related the newest version of the ACT system, ACT-R, to specific brain regions. Based on brain scans of people solving problems, Anderson et al. infer that production rules are implemented by the brain's basal ganglia, which are a collection of nuclei deep in the white matter of the cerebral cortex. They also estimate that the facts that the rules matched are stored in a set of buffers in the prefrontal cortex. Thus the ACT system, which originated as a purely cognitive model, is becoming a neurological model as well. For more on brains, brain scans, and neurological models, see chapter 9.

### Practical Applicability

If what we learn consists of rules, then education must be concerned with helping children and other students better acquire those rules. Anderson (1993) discusses numerous educational applications of ACT rule-based systems, including understanding how people learn computer programming, text editing, and doing proofs in geometry. Rule-based systems have been used not only to model learners' performance, but also to build computer tutors that can help them learn.

Design in engineering and other fields can also be understood in terms of rules. Newell (1990) describes a version of SOAR that designs computer algorithms by using operators that generate and test program specifications to search a space of possible algorithms. He and his collaborators have also discussed the implications of viewing human computer users as rule-based systems for designing computers that people can easily use (Card, Moran, and Newell 1983). SOAR is now being incorporated into computer games such as Quake, in order to produce opponents that behave like humans (Laird 2001). Characters in computer games usually have very limited flexibility, but SOAR can give them some of the complex decision making that make human opponents challenging.

Most expert systems used in industry and government are rule-based systems, which were the first kind of applied intelligent system to be developed (Buchanan and Shortliffe 1984; Feigenbaum, McCorduck, and Nii 1988). Expertise in many domains, from configuring computers to prospecting for oil, can be captured in terms of rules. Recent examples of rule-based expert systems (and other kinds as well) can be found in the *Proceedings of the Nineteenth* (and previous) *Innovative Applications of Artificial Intelligence Conference*, published by AAAI Press. Langley and Simon (1995) provide numerous examples of industrial application of computer programs that learn rules from examples, including systems for chemical process control, making credit decisions, and diagnosis of mechanical devices.

## Summary

Much of human knowledge is naturally described in terms of rules, and many kinds of thinking such as planning can be modeled by rule-based systems. The explanation schema used is as follows:

Explanation target

Why do people have a particular kind of intelligent behavior?

Explanatory pattern

People have mental rules.

People have procedures for using these rules to search a space of possible solutions, and procedures for generating new rules.

Procedures for using and forming rules produce the behavior.

Computational models based on rules have provided detailed simulations of a wide range of psychological experiments, from cryptarithmetic problem solving to skill acquisition to language use. Rule-based systems have also been of practical importance in suggesting how to improve learning and how to develop intelligent machine systems.

## Discussion Questions

1. What areas of knowledge do you have that are easily described in terms of rules?

2. What areas of knowledge do you have that are difficult to describe in terms of rules?

3. How does the rule-based approach differ from the logic approach described in chapter 2?

4. How might the brain implement rules?

5. Is knowledge of language innate or learned?

## Further Reading

Classic sources on the mind as a rule-based system include Newell and Simon 1972, Newell 1990, and Anderson 1983, 1993. Holland et al. 1986 discusses many kinds of learning in terms of rule-based systems. Smith, Langston, and Nisbett 1992 makes the case for rules in reasoning; see also Nisbett 1993. Pinker 1994 is an entertaining defense of the Chomskyan approach to language, including the importance of rules to language. Pinker 2002 emphasizes the role of innateness in human behavior in general, but see Elman et al. 1996 and Quartz and Sejnowski 2002 for skeptical discussions of innateness claims.

## Web Sites

ACT home page at Carnegie Mellon University: http://act-r.psy.cmu.edu/

John Anderson's home page: http://act-r.psy.cmu.edu/people/ja/

Stephen Pinker's home page: http://pinker.wjh.harvard.edu/

SOAR home page at the University of Michigan: http://sitemaker.umich.edu/soar

## Notes

Non-rule-based approaches can also be described in terms of search, but historically that description has been most closely associated with rule-based systems. The search metaphor works well with well-defined problems where the states and operators can be specified, but is much less clear for problems where the task involves learning new representations and operators.

More technically, the power law of practice can be expressed as "If the logarithm of the reaction time in a task is plotted against the logarithm of the number of practice trials, the result is a straight line that slopes downward."

# 4  Concepts

When students learn their way around their colleges or universities, they acquire new rules about them, but they also acquire new concepts. Many new administrative concepts must be acquired, such as *major, register,* and *transcript.* Students also quickly learn new concepts for describing courses, such as *bird* or *gut* or *cake* for an unusually easy course. Social knowledge increases dramatically too, as students learn concepts for describing their fellow students, such as *computer geek, jock, artsie,* (Arts student), and *keener* (eager student). Students who encounter different kinds of classes like seminars and huge lectures must modify the concept of *class* they acquired in high school.

Concern with the role of concepts in knowledge goes back more than two thousand years to the Greek philosopher Plato. He asked questions such as "What is justice?" and "What is knowledge?" and showed that concepts such as *justice* and *knowledge* are very hard to define. Plato believed that knowledge of such concepts is innate and that education can serve to remind us of the essence of these concepts. Just as Chomsky argues that linguistic rules are innate, Plato and later philosophers such as Leibniz and Descartes contended that the most important concepts are purely in the mind.

Other philosophers such as Locke and Hume contended that concepts are learned through sensory experience. The way you acquire a concept such as *dog,* for instance, is not just by thinking about what dogs are, but by encountering a variety of examples of dogs. Although Jerry Fodor (1975), a contemporary philosopher heavily influenced by Chomsky, maintains that concepts are largely innate, most cognitive scientists today are interested in processes by which concepts are learned from experience and from other concepts.

Psychological and computational interest in the nature of the concepts boomed in the mid-1970s when researchers introduced terms such as "frame," "schema," and "script" to describe new views of the nature of concepts. (Somewhat similar ideas had been advanced by Bartlett (1932) and Kant (1965).) In the most influential artificial intelligence paper of the decade, Minsky (1975) argued that thinking should be understood as frame application rather than logical deduction. In a computational-psychological collaboration, Schank and Abelson (1977) showed how a great deal of our social knowledge consists of scripts, which describe typical sequential occurrences such as going to a restaurant. Around the same time, psychologists such as David Rumelhart (1980) were describing knowledge in terms of conceptlike structures called schemas that represent, not the essence of a concept such as *dog*, but what is typical of dogs. Similarly, the philosopher Hilary Putnam (1975) argued that the meaning of concepts should be thought of in terms of stereotypes, not in terms of defining conditions. During the 1980s, discussion of concepts from a computational perspective took on a different complexion through the development of connectionist models that learn concepts; we will take up this topic in chapter 7.

## Representational Power

How often have you heard someone insist, "Define your terms!"? People frequently say things like, "We can't talk about intelligence until we can define what the word 'intelligence' means." The demand requires a definition that would provide the exact rules *IF x is intelligent, THEN x has the properties y* and *IF x has the properties y, THEN x is intelligent.* But as Plato discovered with concepts such as *justice*, such definitions are very hard to come by. As an exercise, try coming up with rules that will exactly capture what is meant by *college, university, course,* or *geek.* At best, a concept such as *intelligence* will be defined at the end of an inquiry, not at the beginning, and outside of mathematics we should not expect definitions to be available at all.

Construed as frames, schemas, or scripts, concepts are understood as representations of typical entities or situations, not as strict definitions. For example, students acquire a concept of *course* in which instruction takes place by a professor and students get a grade at the end. What is expected of a course can be summarized as a set of slots, each of which can be filled in with expected information such as the instructor's name:

Course

A kind of: process (systematic series of actions)

Kinds of courses: lecture course, seminar, etc.

Instructor:

Room:

Meeting time:

Requirements: exams, essays, etc.

Instances: Philosophy 100, Mathematics 242, etc.

One of the first things a student does in signing up for a course is to find out who the instructor is, thus filling in an important slot. The *course* concept could perhaps be represented differently by a set of rules such as *IF x is a course, THEN x has an instructor*, but we will see in the next section that there are computational reasons why it is useful to think of a concept in terms of a set of slots. Although typically courses have an instructor, this should not be taken as part of the definition of a course, since there are team-taught courses with more than one instructor and correspondence courses that have no instructor.

Some concepts involve a temporal sequence, as in taking an exam:

Exam

A kind of: course requirement

Kinds of exam: written, oral, take-home, short-answer, etc.

Room:

Sequence:

Get the exam questions

Put your name on the exam paper

Answer the questions

Check your answers

Hand in your exam

Again, this concept can be thought of in terms of rules such as *IF you take an exam, THEN first get the exam questions*. But it is cognitively useful to have acquired a package of information that can be applied as a whole.

Although the slots in concepts can usually be translated into rules, it is important to realize that slots do not express universal truths, only what is expected to hold typically. The values of slots are sometimes called *defaults*, as when the default value for number of instructors in a class is one. Rules can also be understood as expressing default expectations rather than universal truths, as in the statement *IF x is a course, THEN x typically has an instructor.* Exams typically take place in a room on campus, but take-home exams are an exception in that they do not have any special room in which everyone takes the exam.

Concepts organize knowledge in important ways that are not usually found in rule-based systems. Notice that the concept *course* includes slots that state what kind of thing a course is and what kinds of things are courses. These kind relations establish a hierarchical network of concepts, as in figure 4.1. A seminar is a kind of course which is a kind of educational process, and so on. Conceptual organization of this sort has computational consequences that give concepts properties that unorganized sets of rules might lack. Another sort of slot that is important for many physical concepts is *part*, which establishes another sort of hierarchy. For example, a toe is a part of a foot, which is part of a leg, which is part of a body. Slots involving parts can also be translated into rules, such as *IF x is a toe, THEN x is part of a foot.* But organizing concepts into slots and hierarchies has computational advantages discussed in the next section.

Concepts are clearly not intended to be a complete theory of mental representation. The information that if a course is full you can still get into it by getting a signature from the professor is not part of the concept of

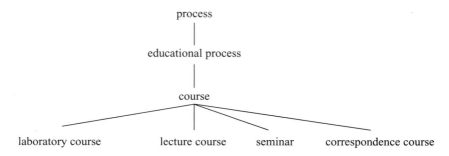

**Figure 4.1**
Hierarchical organization of the concept of a course.

*course*; rather, it is a rule you learn about courses. But concepts have computational properties that make them useful additions to rules for modeling human thinking.

## Computational Power

Packaging information into concepts that are hierarchically organized makes possible powerful kinds of computations. Large rule-based systems face the problem of selecting rules to apply. It does a system no good to have a rule that is relevant unless that rule can be retrieved from memory in order to be applied. One process that can be applied very efficiently in a concept-based system is *inheritance*, in which inferences about concepts can be quickly made using the hierarchy established by the *kind* slot. Does a seminar have an instructor? The answer to this question might not be directly represented as part of the concept of *seminar*, but it can quickly be gained by noting that a seminar is a kind of course, and courses typically have instructors. This is not a logical deduction, since not all courses have instructors. But it is reasonable to expect that a seminar has an instructor, where this expectation is inherited by virtue of a seminar's being a kind of course.

What do you think of when you hear the word "desk"? Perhaps you begin to think about chairs, studying, or lamps. Not all thinking is a matter of making inferences in the way that logic-based and rule-based systems do. One might associate desks with chairs by means of some rule such as that every desk has a chair, but this association could also come about more casually by virtue of the fact that a desk is a kind of furniture, and another kind of furniture is a chair. This kind of loose association is described computationally as a process of *spreading activation*. One concept in a system is active, and activation spreads in a network to other concepts that are linked to it by kind and other relations. Spreading activation is like a type of electronic contagion, in which one electrified object electrifies other objects connected to it. For example, if something activates your concept of *desk*, activation may spread to your concepts of *furniture* (desks are a kind of furniture) and *drawer* (a drawer is a part of a desk). Activation of these concepts may then lead to activation of related concepts such as *table* (a table is a kind of furniture) and *wood* (drawers are typically made of wood). Some rule-based systems include spreading activation as a mechanism along with rule firing for modeling how people retrieve rules from memory (Anderson 1983; Thagard 1988).

Packaging information in a concept is most useful when it can be used to deal with new situations. When a course begins, students quickly fit it into their conceptual system, categorizing it as a lecture course, a bird (easy) course, or whatever. There are two crucial steps in the process, *matching* and *inference*. Finding the most appropriate concepts to apply to a course requires matching the slots of various relevant courses against the particular information known about the course. For example, if there are only ten students enrolled in the course, this information will fit with the slot in the concept of *seminar* that suggests that class size is typically small. If instead there are a hundred students in the class, it will not fit in the size slot of the *seminar* concept, but will better match the *lecture* concept. Once a concept is matched to a situation, students can make inferences about the situation by carrying over the full set of expectations produced by the concept. Once a course is classified as a seminar, the student will probably expect it to have lots of class discussion. Thus, to understand the computational role of concepts, we need to think of these steps in a processing system:

1. The system has active concepts that represent a situation.

2. These concepts spread activation to other potentially relevant concepts.

3. Some concepts that match the current situation well are selected.

4. The system makes inferences about the situation by inheritance from the selected concepts.

### Problem Solving

**Planning**   The first time you encounter a planning situation such as registering for courses, you may need to use general rules to search for a solution. But successful registrations will make it easier for you next time around, since you can then simply follow the same sequence of operations. You have acquired a script or concept for registration. Planning then is not search or logical deduction, but concept application. Given a representation of your current situation and the goals you want to accomplish such as getting into the courses you want, you retrieve from memory a concept of registration that matches the situation and goals. This script can then be applied to tell you what to do in the appropriate order: sign up for courses, pay tuition, and so on.

Concept application, however, works only if you have an organized package of information that closely matches your current situation. After a year or more of college or university, students have a set of schemas that are useful for many educational situations, but first-year students may err by trying to apply schemas acquired in high school. Students taking the course Introduction to Cognitive Science are sometimes confused because they expect its content to be like that of courses they are already familiar with in philosophy, psychology, or computer science. They have difficulty fitting an interdisciplinary course into their previous concepts. Scripts can be very useful when they can be applied to situations that occur frequently, but they can hinder planning in novel situations where existing situations do not fit. Recall the saying: To someone whose only tool is a hammer, everything looks like a nail. The lesson is that you should not try to apply the concept of hammering to situations in which it is not relevant.

**Decision**   The same lesson applies to decision making using concepts. In some cases, making decisions based on a familiar script will not cause you problems, as when you always order the same flavor in an ice cream store. But people often apply schemas unreflectively. Hiring decisions, for example, are sometimes made not on the basis of a reasoned judgment of which candidate will best meet the needs of the organization hiring, but rather because a particular candidate fits the boss's concept of the right kind of employee. That concept might have appropriate slots that describe the intelligence and industriousness of the ideal candidate, but it also may include extraneous requirements such as race and gender. Thus, although some decisions are undoubtedly made by concept application, it is a good thing that not all are. Concept application is a quick and easy way to make a decision, but it does not always take into account the complex of concerns about actions and goals that are part of more reflective decision making.

**Explanation**   Like plans, explanations sometimes come in schematic packages. Social concepts are often used in explanations, probably more than they should be. Why did Fred stay up all night programming? Because he's a computer geek. Why does Sarah always wear black? Because she's an artsie. Why did Alice get an A in that course even though she did not study? Because it's a bird (gut, cake). In all these cases, explanation comes almost automatically by matching a concept to a situation that it seems to fit.

But concepts also have more reflective explanatory uses. Scientific explanation sometimes has the deductive flavor that logic-based and rule-based systems give to explanation. In physics, for example, there are often general laws such as *force = mass times acceleration* that can be applied mathematically to produce a deductive explanation of planetary motion. But in many fields, such as evolutionary biology and the social sciences, laws are hard to come by. Then explanation is better characterized as application of a schema that includes a target—what is to be explained—and a kind of pattern that furnishes the explanation. Here is a simplified explanatory schema for using Darwin's theory of evolution by natural selection to explain why a species has a particular trait (from Thagard 1999; see also Kitcher 1993 and Schank 1986):

Explanation target

Why does a given **species** have a particular **trait?**

Explanatory pattern

The **species** has a set of variable **traits.**

The **species** experiences environmental **pressures.**

The **pressures** favor members of the **species** that have a particular **trait.**

So members of the **species** with that **trait** will survive and reproduce better than members of the **species** that lack the **trait.**

So eventually most members of the **species** will have the **trait.**

The terms presented in boldface are variables that can be filled in by many different examples. If you want to explain, for example, why some bacteria are resistant to antibiotics, this pattern can be applied by noticing that the trait of resistance to antibiotics is variable in a species of bacteria, that antibiotics introduce environmental pressures, so that bacteria with resistance to antibiotics will survive and reproduce better until the species is resistant.

We have already seen various instances of the explanatory schema that is fundamental to cognitive science. The summary for chapter 1 provided a general explanatory schema based on representations and computational procedures, and the summaries for chapters 2–7 include explanatory schemas for particular representational approaches. Part II discusses aspects of mind and intelligence to which such schemas are harder to apply.

## Learning

We saw three kinds of answers to the question of where rules come from: they can be innate, formed from experience, or formed from other rules. The same three kinds of answer apply to concepts, which can be innate, formed from examples, or formed from other concepts. Different answers are appropriate for different concepts. Young children acquire new words and the corresponding new concepts at the rate of around ten per day.

Consider, for example, the concept of a *human face* consisting of two eyes, a nose, and a mouth. Perhaps babies learn this concept from experience as they repeatedly encounter examples of faces. But there is experimental evidence that babies do not have to learn the typical structure of faces, but rather are born expecting faces to look a certain way. Similarly, there is growing evidence that basic physical concepts such as *object* are innate, since very young infants show strong expectations about how objects should behave—for example, when they disappear behind another object and then reappear. Thus, whereas it is implausible to suppose that *all* our concepts right up to *DVD player* and *cell phone* are innate, some basic concepts as well as the mechanisms for forming new ones seem to be part of our inborn mental equipment.

Some concepts are learned from examples in much the way that some rules are formed by inductive generalization. Some concepts must be gained laboriously from many examples, as when a child learns to discriminate dogs from other animals. When you know a lot, however, you can acquire concepts quickly from a small number of examples. If you walk into a course and are surprised to discover that it has just ten students and that instead of lectures there is much discussion, you can acquire the concept of *seminar* from that example alone. Of course, the concept may be revised on the basis of subsequent examples. Just as rules are fine tuned for content and plausibility by repeated use, so concepts can be modified as additional examples are encountered. Many sophisticated computational models of concept formation from examples have been developed (Langley 1996). Connectionist methods of concept formation are discussed in chapter 7.

Not all concepts need to be formed from examples, since we can produce new concepts by combining ones we already have. Examples may play a role in filling in details of concepts such as *music television* and *electronic mail*, but much of the content is furnished by the concepts that are combined to produce the new one. Some conceptual combination is straightforward, as when we can figure out that a *pet fish* is just a fish that is kept as a pet. But other conceptual combinations are more complex; for example, a *computer geek* is not something that is both a computer and a geek, but rather a strange person obsessed with computers. Some surprising conceptual combinations can even involve an abductive component when hypotheses are required to explain how the combination might be possible. For example, the concept of *blind lawyer* is formed not simply by combining the attributes of *blind* and *lawyer*, but by adding emergent attributes such as *courageous* that are needed to explain how a blind person can become a lawyer (Kunda, Miller, and Claire 1990). There are computer models of simple kinds of conceptual combination (Thagard 1988), but not yet of the more complicated abductive kind. Costello and Keane (2000) present a computational theory that explains both the creativity and the efficiency of people's conceptual combinations.

Schemas that include causal information can be used to perform a kind of abductive inference. Here is a script for acquiring a contagious disease such as a cold:

Contagious disease

Contact: You come into contact with some germs (viruses or bacteria).

Incubation: The germs multiply.

Symptoms: The germs cause you to develop symptoms such as a runny nose.

Cure: Eventually, your body's immune system kills the germs.

If you have symptoms such as a runny nose, you can fill in the symptom slot in this schema, and then fill in the contact slot to abductively infer that you must have come in contact with some germs.

## Language

In spoken and written language, concepts are represented by words. Not all concepts need have words that describe them, but there is a close correspondence between our words and many of our concepts. In the last section, we discussed grammar in terms of linguistic rules. Knowledge of language, however, obviously cannot consist of such rules alone: we need to know words to plug into grammatical structures. A set of words in a dictionary is called a *lexicon,* so that the set of words or concepts represented in a mind is called the *mental lexicon.*

George Miller and others have argued that the mental lexicon is organized hierarchically (Fellbaum 1998). He and coworkers have produced a huge electronic lexicon called WordNet, with more than 60,000 English words. Nouns such as "dog" are organized hierarchically in terms of kinds and parts as was described in the above section on representational power (figure 4.1). Verbs that express actions such as "register" and "run" have a different kind of organization in terms of ways of doing things. For example, in one sense running is a way of traveling, and sprinting is a way of running. Adjectives such as "easy" are organized in other ways. Our use of language depends on our ability to store and use concepts for such nouns, verbs, and adjectives. Miller (1991) discusses the structure of the mental lexicon, how words are formed, and how children's vocabularies grow.

Learning a language is not just a matter of acquiring grammatical rules; it also involves developing a whole conceptual system. Linguists in the Chomskyan tradition have assumed a sharp distinction between grammar and lexicon, but the distinction is challenged by advocates of a different approach, called *cognitive grammar* (Taylor 2003). Langacker (1987) and Lakoff (1987) argue that syntactic structure is very closely tied in with the nature and meaning of concepts.

What is the meaning of a concept and how does it contribute to the meaning of a sentence? Philosophers have been particularly vexed by this question and have developed a range of possible answers to it. On the one hand, the meaning of a concept seems to derive from the meaning of other concepts, as when a child is told the meaning of *sprint* by saying it is a kind of fast running. On the other hand, the meaning of a concept is connected to observations of things in the world, as when the child actually sees someone sprinting. A concept's meaning is normally not given by definition in terms of other concepts, since successful exact definitions are rare. Nor is meaning exhausted by a set of examples, as if one identified the concept of *dog* with the set of dogs. A theory of meaning of the concepts must therefore include an account of how concepts are related both to each other and to the world (see chapter 12). Both aspects are necessary in order for us to understand how concepts underlie our ability to use language.

## Psychological Plausibility

How does one show the psychological plausibility of a particular kind of mental representation? The direct method is to perform psychological experiments producing results that follow immediately from the assumption that people have the proposed kind of mental representation. The indirect method is to use computer simulations employing the proposed kind of mental representation to explain the results of experiments concerning some general sort of performance. Much of the evidence for the psychological plausibility of rules described in chapter 3 is of the second, indirect sort—for example, the rule-based simulation of cryptarithmetic problem solving. In contrast, much of the evidence for the psychological reality of concepts comes from experiments about concepts rather than from computer simulations. Psychologists have performed a vast number of experiments designed to determine the nature of concepts and their role in categorization. Here I will mention just a small selection of important experiments.

While behaviorism dominated psychology, there was little talk of concepts or any other mental representations. When research on concept learning began in the 1950s, it presupposed the classical view of concepts as sharply defined (Bruner, Goodnow, and Austin 1956). During the 1970s, however, evidence mounted that concepts should be understood in terms of typical conditions rather than defining conditions. Defining conditions are ones that provide strict rules, as when we say that a figure is a triangle if and only if it has exactly three sides. Typical conditions allow for exceptions, as when we say that dogs typically have four legs, even though some have only three. A prototype is a set of typical conditions, so that the prototype for *dog* is something like "has four legs, is furry, barks," and so on. On the classical view, applying the concept *dog* to a particular example such as Benji is a matter of checking whether the defining conditions of *dog* apply to Benji. But on the prototype view, applying *dog* to Benji is a looser process of seeing whether the typical conditions of *dog* match Benji's characteristics.

Psychological experiments suggest that concept application fits the prototype view rather than the classical view. Posner and Keele (1970) used patterns of dots as perceptual categories. Experimental subjects were required to learn sets of four distortions of each of four prototypical patterns of dots and were then given a new set of patterns to classify. Of the new patterns, subjects found ones that matched the prototypes easiest to classify, but took longer and made more errors in classifying patterns more distant from the prototype. Similarly, people can more quickly verify the truth of the sentence "A robin is a bird" than they can verify "A goose is a bird," presumably because robins are closer to the prototype for *bird* than geese are.

Rips, Shoben, and Smith (1973) showed that people reliably rate some category members as more typical than others. For example, in North America a banana is a more typical fruit than a mango. When people are asked to list examples of a concept, they tend to produce items that are considered most typical (Rosch 1973). If you are asked to name a bird, you will be more likely to say "sparrow" than "penguin." Rosch and Mervis (1975) found that judgment of how typical a kind of bird is correlates highly with the extent to which the bird has the properties that are most commonly assigned to birds, such as flying and building nests. A robin and a penguin are both birds, and would both have to fall under the definition of *bird* if one could be produced, but cognitively they differ enormously because a robin is much closer to the prototype for *bird* than is a penguin.

Viewing concepts as prototypes helps to account for various features of how concepts are applied, including mistakes that people make. For example, when Brewer and Treyens (1981) asked subjects to recall what items were in a university office where they had been kept waiting, they often mistakenly reported that there were books in the office. Books are part of the prototype of *academic office*. Psychological experiments have also been performed that tease out some of the aspects of conceptual combination (Smith et al. 1988).

The findings about prototypes fit well with the computational view of concepts as framelike structures that list typical properties. However, there is experimental evidence that the structure of concepts is not fully captured by prototypes. Barsalou (1983) and others have argued that concepts are much more flexible and context dependent than a package of typical properties would be. Some psychologists have argued that our knowledge of a particular concept is closely tied in with the initial examples from which we learned the concept. Applying a concept is then a matter not of matching to a prototype but of comparing new examples to the old ones.

Concept application is then similar to analogical reasoning, discussed in chapter 5. Barsalou et al. (2003) argue that conceptual processing depends on specific modalities such as perception, so that a concept like *car* is tied in with memory of sensory experiences of cars.

Murphy and Medin (1985), Keil (1989), and others have argued that neither sets of typical features nor examples capture all that there is to concepts. Concept application is sometimes as much a matter of causal explanation as it is of matching features—for example, when we classify as drunk someone who jumps into a pool fully clothed. Jumping into a pool fully clothed is not a defining or typical feature of the concept *drunk*, but it fits with a theory of impaired judgment that is part of the concept: being drunk causes people to do silly things. Murphy (2002, chap. 6) reviews psychological evidence that concepts are part of our general knowledge of the world. Perhaps, therefore, we should envision concepts as involving rules such as *IF x is drunk, THEN x has impaired judgment*. Concluding that someone is drunk is not just matching a prototype, but is a kind of abductive inference based on rules. Kunda, Miller, and Claire (1990) found evidence for such inference in conceptual combination. Thus, concepts may be intimately connected with rules and examples, as well as with typical features.

## Neurological Plausibility

Spreading activation between concepts in conceptual networks is similar to the way neurons activate each other by electrochemical impulses, but little is known about how concepts are realized in the brain. Brain-scanning techniques are being used to learn more about language organization. Posner and Raichle (1994) describe studies that monitored brain responses to words such as "hammer." These studies identified distinct areas of the brain involved in word perception and speech production. Ashby and Walrdron (2000) review evidence that the prefrontal cortex and basal ganglia contribute to concept learning. Another way of learning about the neural structure of the mental lexicon is to study deficits that occur in people who have had brain damage resulting from strokes. One patient had difficulty naming inanimate objects such as musical instruments, but could comprehend the names of foods, flowers, and animals relatively well; another patient suffered a stroke and lost the ability to name fruits and vegetables (Kosslyn and Koenig 1992). Artificial neural networks (chapters 7 and 9) have provided some ideas about how concepts might be stored and used in the brain.

## Practical Applicability

One of the functions of education is to turn novices into experts in a domain such as physics or another branch of science. What is the difference between novices and experts? One answer might be that the latter have more rules, but educational research has suggested that experts have highly organized knowledge that can be described in turns of concepts or schemas (Bruer 1993). For example, students who are only beginning to learn physics have a schema for an inclined plane that includes only superficial features such as its angle and length. In contrast, the expert's schema immediately connects the concept of an inclined plane with the laws of physics that apply to it. Nersessian (1989) and Chi (1992) argue that science education is made difficult by the fact that students need to acquire abstract concepts such as *field* and *heat* that they erroneously treat as substances. Learning a complex discipline often requires active and intentional conceptual change (Sinatra and Pintrich 2003).

Any design problem involves concepts that can be represented by schemas or frames. In the context of building design, the concept of *beam* can be represented by a frame that has slots for span, load, support, and maximum stress (Allen 1992). This frame is part of a conceptual hierarchy that involves various kinds of beams, such as ones made of steel (I-beam or box-beam), concrete (reinforced or prestressed), and wood. Dym and Levitt (1991) describe an expert system called SightPlan that was developed to provide computer support for the task of locating temporary facilities on a construction site. SightPlan uses frames to represent concepts such as *construction site*, *power plant*, and various parts of power plants.

Although not so common as rule-based systems, frame-based systems have found various applications in artificial intelligence. Pure frame-based expert systems are rare, but some rule-based systems also use frames (Buchanan and Shortliffe 1984). The most ambitious current intelligent system is Cyc (originally short for "Encyclopedia"), which uses more than a million rules to encode a huge amount of commonsense knowledge that underlies intelligent performance in many domains (Lenat and Guha

1990). Cyc has a database of thousands of representations for many everyday concepts and objects, organized by means of an "ontology" of fundamental concepts such as *thing, individual,* and *animal.* The most general part of the Cyc ontology is available on the Web site listed below.

## Summary

Concepts, which partly correspond to the words in spoken and written language, are an important kind of mental representation. There are computational and psychological reasons for abandoning the classical view that concepts have strict definitions. Instead, concepts can be viewed as sets of typical features. Concept application is then a matter of getting an approximate match between concepts and the world. Schemas and scripts are more complex than concepts that correspond to words, but they are similar in that they consist of bundles of features that can be matched and applied to new situations. The explanatory schema used in concept-based systems is as follows:

Explanatory target

Why do people have a particular kind of intelligent behavior?

Explanation pattern

People have a set of concepts, organized via slots that establish *kind* and *part* hierarchies and other associations.

People have a set of procedures for concept application, including spreading activation, matching, and inheritance.

The procedures applied to the concepts produce the behavior.

Concepts can be translated into rules, but they bundle information differently than sets of rules, making possible different computational procedures.

## Discussion Questions

1. What concepts are learned? What concepts are innate?

2. What concepts can be defined? What concepts have typical features you can specify?

3. What concepts do not correspond to English words? What concepts are known only unconsciously?

4. Can concepts be reduced to rules? Can rules be reduced to concepts?

5. How does concept-based explanation differ from rule-based explanation?

6. How would you represent the concept of *mind*?

7. How are concepts related to things in the world?

## Further Reading

Murphy 2002 is a comprehensive review of psychological research on concepts. Ward, Smith, and Vaid 1997 contains many articles on conceptual combination and creative use of concepts. Aitchison 1987 and Miller 1991 provide introductions to the mental lexicon. Frame-based AI systems are reviewed in Maida 1990 and Winston 1993. Langley 1996 has several chapters on computational models of concept learning. Margolis and Laurence 1999 is a collection of important articles on concepts.

## Web Sites

Concept mapping: http://cmap.coginst.uwf.edu/info/

The Cyc ontology (organized set of thousands of concepts): http://www.cyc.com/

Visual thesaurus: http://www.visualthesaurus.com/online/index.html

WordNet, a lexical database for the English language: http://www.cogsci.princeton.edu/~wn/

## Notes

Systems of hierarchically organized concepts are sometimes called semantic networks, although in AI the term "ontology" is used. In philosophy, ontology is the study of what fundamentally exists.

Inference by inheritance is used in object-oriented programming.

Conceptual change in the major revolutions in the history of science is analyzed in Thagard 1992.

# 5 Analogies

Imagine what life would be like if you always had to figure everything out from scratch, if every class were your first class, if every date were your first date. Fortunately, people are able to remember previous experiences and learn from them. But the learning that takes place does not always establish general knowledge of the sort that is found in rules and concepts. If you are a student in your second or later year of college, you may remember how you previously registered and chose your courses. That experience may have been too limited for you to capture it in a general rule or concept, but you can still use the particular experience to guide your choices for this year. If you ended up in a particularly disastrous course, you can try to avoid courses with similar topics and instructors. On the other hand, if you had a course that was a big success for you, you can try to enroll in similar courses.

Analogical thinking consists of dealing with a new situation by adapting a similar familiar situation. Human use of analogy is documented as far back as there are written records: Homer used analogies in the *Iliad*, and parables in the Bible serve to provide analogies between stories that are told and the readers' own situations. The importance of analogies in reasoning has long been recognized by philosophers (e.g., Mill 1974; Hesse 1966), but intense psychological and computational investigation is relatively recent. Evans (1968) developed the first computational model of analogical reasoning, and numerous models have been developed since then. Today, there are several research teams working to develop sophisticated models of analogy use. Keith Holyoak and I have developed a computational theory of human analogy use (Holyoak and Thagard 1995). In ways elaborated later, our view is similar to but also different from the influential view of Dedre Gentner and her colleagues (Gentner 1983, 1989;

Forbus, Gentner, and Law 1995; Forbus 2001). In artificial intelligence today, analogical reasoning is often called *case-based* reasoning, and numerous interesting applications have been developed (Kolodner 1993; Leake 1996). Douglas Hoftstadter and his associates (Hofstadter 1995; Mitchell 1993) have developed novel models of creative analogy use.

### Representational Power

Do analogies say anything more than can be said with logic, rules, or concepts? For analogical reasoning, we need to be able to express two situations, the *target* analog representing the new situation to be reasoned about, and the *source* analog representing the old situation that can be adapted and applied to the target analog. Each analog is a representation of a situation, and the analogy is a systematic relationship between them. Representing analogs requires paying attention not only to predicates like "student" that apply to individuals but also to predicates like "teach" that describe a relation between two or more individuals. Interesting analogies hold between situations that share similar relations as well as similar features. Using the kind of logical notation introduced in chapter 2, we can represent some aspects of a course called Philosophy 999 as follows:

1. instructor (Repulso, Phil999); i.e., Professor Repulso is the instructor of Philosophy 999.

2. dull (Repulso); i.e., Repulso is dull.

3. difficult (Phil999); i.e., the course is difficult.

4. enrolled-in (you, Phil999); i.e., you're stuck in the course.

5. grade (you, Phil999, low); i.e., you're getting low grades in the course.

In addition, it may be crucial to your low grade in the course that the instructor was dull and the course was difficult:

6. cause (2 & 3, 5); i.e., the dull instructor and difficult course are causing your low grade.

Statement 6 exemplifies a kind of representational power involving causal relations between statements that is significant for many important analogies. If you are considering taking Psychology 888, which also has a dull instructor and a reputation for being difficult, you may infer by analogy to Philosophy 999 that you are likely to get a low grade in the course and therefore avoid it. Here, Philosophy 999 is the familiar source analog and

Psychology 888 is the target analog that you reason about based on the source.

More positive analogies can be used in course selection rather than course avoidance. If there has been a course that you have liked and if you can identify the features of the course that caused you to like it, then you can look for similar courses that you are also likely to enjoy. A sophisticated analogy user will ignore superficial similarities, such as that two courses both have names with the same number of letters. But how are superficial similarities to be distinguished from important ones? For one student, it may not matter what time of day a course meets; for another student, who is most alert in the morning, the time of day will be a relevant factor in choosing courses similar to ones that have already proved to be enjoyable. The key to noticing relevant differences is to appreciate the causal relations that produced outcomes relevant to your goals in taking the class. Hence, representation of analogies needs to include representation of causal relations like the one in statement 6.

Usually, analogs can be represented as collections of the kinds of representations we have already seen. Analogs are like concepts and unlike statements in logic and rules in the way that they bundle together packages of information, but they are like simple statements and unlike concepts and rules in that the information they contain describes only a particular situation. For example, the representation of Philosophy 999 in statements 1–6 provides a package of information about a course, but the pieces of information in the package apply only to that course, not to courses in general. In contrast, analogical schemas, discussed below in the learning section, include general information, like rules and concepts and unlike representations of source and target analogs.

Analogs are sometimes represented using visual images of the sort discussed in chapter 6. Figure 5.1 presents a visual analogy. People use visual analogies when, for example, they use a mental picture of a familiar building to guess how to get around in a similar unfamiliar one. Emotions can also be involved in the representation of analogs, as chapter 10 describes.

## Computational Power

If you are solving problems in a very familiar domain where you have lots of expertise, you can put to work general knowledge captured in rules and

**Figure 5.1**
A humorous visual analogy. Reprinted by permission from Holyoak and Thagard 1995, p. 14.

concepts. Analogical reasoning, in contrast, becomes useful when you have some previous experience with a domain but little general knowledge of it. Hence analogies can be computationally powerful in situations when conceptual and rule-based knowledge is not available.

Typically, analogical reasoning proceeds in four stages:

1. You face a target problem to be solved.

2. You remember a similar source problem for which a solution is known.

3. You compare the source and target problems, putting their relevant components in correspondence with each other.

4. You adapt the source problem to produce a solution to the target problem.

Understanding analogical reasoning computationally requires specifying procedures for the stages of remembering (retrieving from memory), comparison (mapping the source and target analogs to each other), and adaptation.

Retrieving potentially relevant source analogs from memory is computationally very difficult. How many experiences have you had in your life? If you have accomplished just 10 tasks per day for the past 15 years, you have potentially stored in memory 54,750 task solutions. Faced with a current task for which you hope to find a new solution, you would have somehow to compare the new problem against the very large number of stored solutions. How does the mind select usable experiences from its vast store? Suppose your current task is to register for the upcoming term or semester. Will you recall every time you had to register for something? Every time you had to stand in line? Every time you were frustrated? Every time you did something in the rain?

Current computational models of analog retrieval disagree about the factors that make for effective retrieval and that account for both the successes and failures of human use of analogies. Combining the ideas of many researchers, Keith Holyoak and I argue that retrieval is governed by three constraints: similarity, structure, and purpose (Holyoak and Thagard 1995). Two analogs are similar to each other at a superficial level if they involve similar concepts. Thinking about registering now will make you think about previous cases of registering and other bureaucratic operations that are conceptually related to registering. The similarity of visual analogs is not just conceptual, but also involves their visual appearance. One car may remind you of another car because they have similar shapes or colors.

However, powerful analogies involve not just superficial similarities, but also deeper structural relations. If registering this year is causing you to miss your favorite afternoon TV show, you may remember a previous time when paying your tuition caused you to miss a show. The correspondence between the two situations is then not just that they both involve bureaucratic tasks and missing a TV show, but the higher relation that the bureaucracy caused you to miss the show. To fully satisfy the structure constraint, two analogs must align exactly:

| Target | Source |
|---|---|
| cause: register (you) | cause: pay-tuition (you) |
| miss (you, TV show) | miss (you, TV show) |

The target analog on the left says that your registering caused you to miss your TV show. The source analog on the right says that your paying tuition caused you to miss your TV show. Even though the two situations are different in that one involved registration and the other paying tuition, they have exactly the same structure, since the relations "miss" and "cause" align perfectly.

The third constraint on retrieval is purpose: you want to remember cases that will help you to solve your current problem. In human memory (and in computer databases) there are vast amounts of information, so that retrieving all and only potentially useful information is a difficult psychological and computational problem. The problem of finding and applying source analogs to target problems can be eased by making the purpose of the analogy one of the constraints on its development. For example, if your purpose in using the analogy between registering and paying tuition is to show bureaucratic inefficiencies at your college or university, then the purpose should encourage remembering other inefficiencies.

Holyoak and I contend that it is these three constraints operating in parallel that make possible retrieval of relevant analogs from the vast number of potentially relevant ones. Other researchers on analogy disagree with us. Forbus, Gentner, and Law (1995) emphasize the role of similarity in retrieval, giving structure and purpose less of an impact. On the other hand, many researchers on case-based reasoning have stressed the constraint of purpose, urging that computer memories be indexed in ways that encourage retrieval of analogs relevant to current goals (Schank 1982; Kolodner 1993). For building expert systems, they propose developing a "generally applicable indexing vocabulary" that will apply to all domains. Whether human memory is indexed in this way can be determined only by psychological experiments (see below).

Once a potential source analog has been retrieved from memory, it must be mapped with the target problem to find the correspondences that can suggest a solution. If the two analogs are very similar, mapping is quite trivial, as when you map the current registration to the previous one. But creative analogies often involve a leap, as in the following example (Dennett 1991, 177):

The juvenile sea squirt wanders through the sea searching for a suitable rock or hunk of coral to cling to and make its home for life. For this task, it has a rudimentary nervous system. When it finds its spot and takes root, it doesn't need its brain anymore, so it eats it! (It's rather like getting tenure.)

How is a professor getting tenure like a sea squirt eating its brain? Grasping the comparison requires noticing a set of mappings: between sea squirt and professor, between finding a rock and getting tenure, and so on. Cognitive science researchers differ on which constraints play a role in such mappings. Gentner (1983, 1989) maintains that mapping is a matter of noticing structural correspondences, but Holyoak and I argue that superficial similarities and purpose also contribute to analogical mapping. Both sides of this dispute have developed computer models that aid in testing the competing theoretical claims.

If a source analog maps neatly onto a target problem, copying over the relevant part of the source to the target can generate a solution. If you solved your registration problem last time by taking an evening psychology course, you might solve it this time by taking another evening psychology course. If the exact same solution is not possible, you might adapt the previous solution somewhat—for example, by taking an evening philosophy course. The most sophisticated accounts of adaptation have been offered by researchers in case-based reasoning. Kolodner (1993) lists ten methods for adapting previous solutions, from simple substitutions like replacing a philosophy course by a psychology course, to more complex derivations like writing a computer program in one programming language by systematically adapting a program written in another computer language.

## Problem Solving

**Planning**   It should be obvious from the above discussion how analogies can contribute to solving planning problems such as registering for good courses. Under the same heading we can also put solving the kinds of problems that students are assigned in science and mathematics courses. A textbook chapter in a technical field often includes examples that show how to go about solving problems where the student is given some information and has to find an answer. For example, given some information about a chemical substance, you might have to calculate additional features of it such as density. Analogy is not the only way to go about solving such problems, but it is often useful to try to solve the exercises at the end of the chapter by flipping back and relating them to solved problems provided in the main text.

Analogies can be very useful in problem solving, but they do not always provide the best way to approach a new problem. There is always the danger that a selected analog will not have the deep relevant similarity that is needed to provide a solution to a target problem. If the target problem is genuinely novel, then no previous solution will apply and analogies will only mislead. In military planning, generals often fight the last war, using outmoded analogs. Similarly, although students can greatly simplify new assignments by perceiving them as analogous to previous ones, this strategy can backfire if the new problems require novel approaches. Techniques learned in mathematics courses are of limited use in courses that require writing essays.

**Decision**    Decisions about what actions to choose are also often made analogically. Legal reasoning frequently makes reference to previous cases that serve as precedents: these are source analogs that get mapped to the current target case. Historians have documented numerous cases of political decisions heavily guided by analogies. For example, when the United States debated in 1991 whether to attack Iraq in retaliation for Iraq's invasion of Kuwait, arguments pro and con often concerned historical analogs. President George Bush compared the Iraqi leader, Saddam Hussein, to Adolf Hitler, suggesting that the invasion of Iraq was as legitimate as the World War II invasion of Germany. Critics of the plan to invade Iraq preferred a different comparison, to the United State's disastrous involvement in Vietnam. These analogies resurfaced in 2003 when the United States again invaded Iraq. Analogies can improve decision making by both suggesting previously successful solutions and reminding leaders of previous disasters. All too often, however, decision makers become fixated on a single previous analog and do not consider how a variety of source analogs might suggest different actions to choose from.

**Explanation**    Analogies are also an important source of solutions to explanation problems, including both educational situations where teachers must convey what they understand to students and research situations where brand-new explanations are being generated. Listen for your instructors' analogies in your next few lectures. Teachers often try to help students understand unfamiliar things by comparison with what the students already know. For example, I might explain the British sport of cricket to an American by comparing it to baseball, since both involve bats, balls, and running between positions. Analogical explanations are often limited by the fact that the things being compared have many differences as well as similarities, but they can be a crucial part of getting someone new to a domain up and running. Later in this chapter, the section on educational applications discusses how to use analogies effectively in teaching.

Analogical explanation abounds in cognitive science. As we have already seen, the fundamental analogy in cognitive science is between the mind and the computer: we attempt to explain how the mind works by modeling it as a computer. The analogy is complex, however, since sometimes we get new ideas about what computing can be like by studying the mind and brain. Early ideas about computing drew heavily on psychological views, and recent connectionist computational models discussed in chapter 7 have been influenced by new views about the brain.

## Learning

Analogical thinking involves three kinds of learning. The most mundane is simply the storage of cases based on previous experience. When you figure out how to solve a problem, you can store your solution in memory. This storage does not involve analogy as such, nor does it require the kinds of generalization that underlie forming concepts and rules. But it is a necessary prelude to analogical thinking and constitutes learning at a low level. The second kind of learning is directly the result of analogizing, when you adapt a previous case to solve a new problem. This is again a more particular kind of learning than we saw with rules and concepts, since all you have learned is how to solve the particular new problem. This kind of inference can be abductive if you adapt a previous explanation problem to suggest a new explanatory hypothesis. For example, if a friend is late for a party, you may remember a previous case where somebody was late for a party because of a flat tire, and conjecture analogically that your friend in the current case might have had car trouble.

The third kind of learning introduces a general element. If you use a source analog to solve a target problem, you can abstract from the source and target and form an analogical *schema* that captures what is common to both of them. For example, figuring out how to register for courses this year based on how you registered last year can lead to an abstracted schema for registration. Analogical schemas are very much like the schemas (concepts) discussed in chapter 4, except they should not be expected to have the same degree of generality, since they are generalizations from only two instances. Having registered for courses twice, you may be able to abstract a description of registration from the two situations, an abstraction that includes rough rules concerning how to get the courses you desire. An abstracted analogical schema may be very useful for future problem solving, since it should include those aspects of the source and target analogs that are shared and relevant to problem solution. We will see in the section on psychological plausibility that forming analogical schemas improves problem solving.

## Language

Analogy plays an important role in the production and comprehension of language, since it underlies the use of metaphor. When people say that Britney Spears is the new Madonna, they do not literally mean that Britney Spears *is* Madonna. Rather, they are pointing out some systematic similarities between the two: both are female rock stars who perform provocatively. Similarly, the statement that life is a battlefield evokes a systematic comparison between a target (life) and a source (war). Other metaphors, such as that life is a party, evoke very different comparisons. The information superhighway is not a highway, but it is analogous to one in that it provides a fast and effective way of moving electronic data.

Some language theorists see metaphor as a rather deviant use of language since it does not seem to use language literally: why not just say what you mean? In contrast, various linguists, philosophers, and psychologists have viewed metaphor as a pervasive and valuable feature of language, not as an exceptional or deviant use (Glucksberg and Keysar 1990; Lakoff and Johnson 1980). All metaphors have as their underlying cognitive mechanism the sort of systematic comparison that analogical mapping performs, although metaphor may go beyond analogy by using other figurative devices to produce a broader aura of associations. Both the generation of a metaphor by a speaker and its comprehension by the hearer require the perception of an underlying analogy. If I tell you that Professor Repulso is a sea squirt, you should be able to understand that I am not saying that he is a marine animal with a saclike body, but rather that there is some relevant similarity between his mental history and that of the sea squirt.

## Psychological Plausibility

Many psychological experiments have examined how people use analogies. I will mention only a few examples that show analogy at work in problem solving, learning, and language use.

How would you go about solving the problem in box 5.1? Most people find it hard to think how the doctor can use the rays to kill the tumor without destroying the healthy tissue: Gick and Holyoak (1980) found

**Box 5.1**

The tumor problem (from Gick and Holyoak 1980).

> Suppose you are a doctor faced with a patient who has a malignant tumor in his stomach. It is impossible to operate on the patient, but unless the tumor is destroyed the patient will die. There is a kind of ray that can be used to destroy the tumor. If the rays reach the tumor all at once at a sufficiently high intensity, the tumor will be destroyed. Unfortunately, at this intensity the healthy tissue that the rays pass through on the way to the tumor will also be destroyed. At lower intensities the rays are harmless to healthy tissue, but they will not affect the tumor either. What type of procedure might be used to destroy the tumor with the rays, and at the same time avoid destroying the healthy tissue?

that only about 10 percent of college students could produce a good solution.

In contrast, 75 percent of college students could produce a good solution to the tumor problem if they were told the fortress story in box 5.2. At first glance, the fortress story has nothing to do with the tumor problem. But many people are able to use the solution in the fortress story that involves the army dividing up and then converging on the fortress to generate a solution to the tumor problem: instead of using a single high-intensity ray, the doctor could administer several low-intensity rays from different directions.

This example illustrates the simple kind of analogical learning where a new problem is solved by adapting an old one. Using the same problem, Gick and Holyoak (1983) investigated how students learn analogical schemas from more than one example. In addition to the fortress story, some students were given a story about a firefighter who extinguished an oil-well fire by using multiple small hoses. The fire was put out by converging water, just as the fortress was conquered by converging armies. Students who had two such examples and were instructed to reflect on the similarities between them were more likely to be able to remember to apply a convergence solution to the tumor problem than students who had only received a single analog. Learning analogical schemas thus contributes to more effective problem solving.

Psychological experiments concerning language have been done to address the question of metaphor use. Glucksberg and Keysar (1990) have

**Box 5.2**
The fortress story (from Gick and Holyoak 1980).

A small country fell under the iron rule of a dictator. The dictator ruled the country from a strong fortress. The fortress was situated in the middle of the country, surrounded by farms and villages. Many roads radiated outward from the fortress like spokes on a wheel. A great general arose who raised a large army at the border and vowed to capture the fortress and free the country of the dictator. The general knew that if his entire army could attack the fortress at once it could be captured. His troops were poised at the head of one of the roads leading to the fortress, ready to attack. However, a spy brought the general a disturbing report. The ruthless dictator had planted mines on each of the roads. The mines were set so that small bodies of men could pass over them safely, since the dictator needed to be able to move troops and workers to and from the fortress. However, any large force would detonate the mines. Not only would this blow up the road and render it impassable, but the dictator would destroy many villages in retaliation. A full-scale direct attack on the fortress therefore appeared impossible.

The general, however, was undaunted. He divided his army up into small groups and dispatched each group to the head of a different road. When all was ready he gave the signal, and each group charged down a different road. All of the small groups passed safely over the mines, and the army then attacked the fortress in full strength. In this way, the general was able to capture the fortress and overthrow the dictator.

shown that people find metaphorical meanings even when instructed to find literal meanings. In one study, college students were asked to decide whether or not sentences such as "Some desks are junkyards" were literally true. The students were slower to correctly respond "no" to a sentence that was literally false when it also had a metaphorical interpretation, as in the above example, than to respond to literally false sentences such as "Some desks are roads" that lack a metaphorical interpretation. Similar findings have been obtained for sentences that can be interpreted *both* literally and metaphorically. Keysar (1990) presented students with sentences such as "My son is a baby" in contexts that manipulated whether the sentence was true or false, literally or metaphorically. The students were instructed to press a key as quickly as possible to indicate the *literal* truth value of the sentence. If the sentence was literally false in the context, the students decided more quickly if it was also metaphorically false; if the sentence was literally true, they decided more quickly if it was also metaphorically true. Such findings imply that literal and metaphorical processing interact with each other. Metaphorical interpretation appears to be an obligatory process that accompanies literal processing, rather than an optional process that occurs after literal processing.

## Neurological Plausibility

Neurological research on analogical reasoning is just beginning. Boroojerdi et al. (2001) found that the left prefrontal cortex is involved in analogical reasoning by determining that magnetic stimulation of that part of the brain speeds up solution times for solving analogical problems. This is consistent with recent findings that reasoning involving complex relations, which is crucial for analogical thinking, also involves the left prefrontal cortex (Christoff et al. 2001; Kroger et al. 2002).

Recent computational models of analogy are moving in the direction of using artificial neural networks that approximate to real neuronal behavior. Hummel and Holyoak (1997, 2003) have developed a neural network model of analogy that uses synchrony of neuronal firing to represent relational information. Eliasmith and Thagard (2001) use a different technique to produce representation of complex relations that are distributed over multiple neurons. Neural network models of cognition are described in chapters 7 and 9.

## Practical Applicability

As we saw in the section on computational power, analogies can make substantial contributions to explanation. Hence, they potentially have great value in education. Effective teachers often try to help students understand the unfamiliar by systematically comparing it to the familiar. There are, however, many potential pitfalls in educational use of analogies. Avoiding pitfalls requires careful attention to what students know and to how analogies are used and misused.

Here are some brief recommendations for how educators can more successfully use analogies (see Holyoak and Thagard 1995, for more discussion and justification):

1. Use familiar sources. There is no point in explaining science or some other complex, unfamiliar target in terms of something that is equally unfamiliar. You cannot explain the structure of atoms to young children by analogy to the solar system if they do not know the structure of the solar system.

2. Make the mapping clear. With a good analogy, students should be able to figure out for themselves the basic correspondence between the source and target, but some guidance may facilitate finding a mapping. For example, in cognitive science it is important to indicate which aspects of mind correspond to which aspects of computers.

3. Use deep, systematic analogies. Instead of superficial feature comparisons, the most powerful analogies use systematic causal relations that provide clear relevance to the students' goals.

4. Describe the mismatches. Any analogy or metaphor is incomplete or misleading in some respects. Some educators have concluded that analogies are therefore too misleading to be effective in teaching, but the solution to the problem is not to abandon use of analogies but rather to indicate where they break down. No one should expect the information superhighway to have a white stripe painted down the middle.

5. Use multiple analogies. When one analogy breaks down, another can be added to provide understanding of what has been incompletely presented.

6. Perform analogy therapy. Find out what analogies students are already using and correct them as necessary.

These maxims are good advice not only for educational use of analogies but also for all the other uses of analogy, including problem solving and decision making.

Analogies are often a fertile source of creative designs. Georges de Mestral invented Velcro after he observed how burrs stuck to his dog. Alexander Graham Bell modeled the telephone partly on the human ear. New adhesives have been invented based on how the feet of gecko lizards enable them to walk up walls. Industrial designers often use the technique of reverse engineering, where they take a competitor's product apart and figure out how to produce an analogous product.

Analogies and metaphors have also contributed to computer design and discussion of computer-human interaction. The Macintosh interface, which was copied (analogically) by the Windows program on PCs, uses a desktop analogy: the screen is like a desk on which the user lays out various documents and folders. Spreadsheets make numerical calculations using a format that is analogous to a paper ledger. Word processors are in some respects like the typewriters they have replaced.

Effectiveness of design can be hampered by unsuspected analogies that users employ. One computer company reported that a woman phoned to complain that she had her foot on the mouse on the floor but the computer would not start; she seems to have thought it was like a sewing machine. A man complained that his computer would not fax a piece of paper he was holding up to its screen, which he apparently thought was like a copying machine. Designers need to consider positive analogies for consumers to use, but they also need to watch out for misleading analogies that users may come up with themselves. Customers may need analogy therapy.

Kolodner (1993) describes dozens of case-based reasoning systems. Although they differ in particular retrieval and mapping mechanisms, all fundamentally employ analogical reasoning to solve new problems on the basis of old. Lockheed, for example, uses a case-based reasoning system called Clavier to recommend how to arrange airplane parts in a large pressurized convection oven called an autoclave (Hinkle and Toomey 1994). The cases (source analogs) are records of previous loads placed in the autoclave. Although experts on autoclave use were not able to express their technique in rules, a system that stores, retrieves, and adapts cases has proven very effective. Hastings, Branting, and Lockwood (2002) developed a system that uses case-based reasoning along with rules to provide advice about how to deal with grasshopper infestations in Wyoming.

## Summary

Analogies play an important role in human thinking, in areas as diverse as problem solving, decision making, explanation, and linguistic communication. Computational models simulate how people retrieve and map source analogs in order to apply them to target situations. The explanation schema for analogies is as follows:

Explanation target

Why do people have a particular kind of intelligent behavior?

Explanatory pattern

People have verbal and visual representations of situations that can be used as cases or analogs.

People have processes of retrieval, mapping, and adaptation that operate on those analogs.

The analogical processes, applied to the representations of analogs, produce the behavior.

The constraints of similarity, structure, and purpose overcome the difficult problem of how previous experiences can be found and used to help with new problems. Not all thinking is analogical, and using inappropriate analogies can hinder thinking, but analogies can be very effective in applications such as education and design.

## Discussion Questions

1. How do analogs (cases) differ from rules and concepts?

2. When is analogical problem solving likely to be useful?

3. What are the main stages in analogical thinking? What constraints figure most prominently at each of those stages?

4. What are the main potential drawbacks of thinking by analogy?

5. How do analogies contribute to creativity? What other sources of creativity are there?

## Further Reading

Gentner, Holyoak, and Kokinov 2001 contains articles describing many current approaches to analogy. Hall 1989 reviews artificial intelligence work on analogy to that date. French 2002 surveys more recent computational models. Holyoak and Thagard 1995 gives a psychologically oriented survey. For a review of Gentner's work on analogy, see Gentner 1989. Kolodner 1993 is an excellent survey of case-based reasoning work in artificial intelligence; see also Leake 1996. For an entertaining review of the work of Hofstadter's group on creative analogies, see Hofstadter 1995.

## Web Sites

Artificial intelligence and case-based reasoning: http://www.ai-cbr.org/theindex.html

Case-based reasoning: http://www.cbr-web.org/

Conceptual metaphor: http://cogsci.berkeley.edu/lakoff

Dedre Gentner's home page: http://www.psych.northwestern.edu/psych/people/faculty/gentner/

Keith Holyoak's home page: http://www.psych.ucla.edu/Faculty/Holyoak/

# 6 Images

How many windows are there on the front of your house or apartment building? How did you answer that question? If you have never counted the windows before, you must have found a way to count them now. Perhaps you compiled a list of all the rooms that are on the front of your building and did a verbal count of their windows, but many people answer this kind of question by making a mental picture and doing a visual count. Similarly, try to remember how you get from your home to your college or university. Although you may have a purely verbal memory of how to do this ("Go to the traffic light at Main St. and turn right"), many people remember such routes by constructing a series of mental images of the roads, buildings, and other landmarks along the way.

Many philosophers, from Aristotle through Descartes and Locke, assumed that picturelike images are an essential part of human thought. In the early days of modern psychology in the late nineteenth century, researchers such as Wilhelm Wundt studied how people think with imagery and some even claimed that there was no thought without imagery. The rise of behaviorism in the twentieth century made talk of mental images and other internal representations scientifically unrespectable. But the return of cognitive psychology in the 1960s made imagery once again a suitable object of investigation, and researchers such as Paivio (1971) and Shepard and Metzler (1971) began doing experiments with visual images. Many experiments ensued, and computational models of visual imagery began to appear (Kosslyn and Shwartz 1977; Funt 1980). Some cognitive scientists remain skeptical that human thinking involves pictorial representations that are different from verbal ones (Pylyshyn 1984, 2002). But numerous computational, psychological, and neurological considerations suggest that the mind thinks with pictures as well as words.

Although cognitive scientists interested in imagery have concentrated on visual representations, we should not ignore images connected to non-visual perception. What does a pepperoni pizza taste like? If you have ever had one, you may be able to form a mental image of the taste and smell, and use it to decide whether something else—say, a submarine sandwich—tastes like a pepperoni pizza. Does a growth of beard feel like sandpaper? To answer this, you may form a tactile image of each touch and compare them. How do you hit a baseball to the opposite field, slam-dunk a basketball, or clean a mirror? If you have regularly experienced these physical activities, you may be able to construct a motor image of the bodily sensations associated with them. Finally, people can have emotional images. How did you feel when you heard that you had been admitted to your college or university? Did your friends feel the same? Chapter 10 discusses emotions and consciousness. The rest of this chapter will concentrate on visual images, the kind most investigated to date.

## Vision

For people with normal vision, seeing things seems automatic and easy. You look at a room and immediately pick out the furniture and people in it. The complexity of vision becomes apparent, however, when you try to get a computer to do the same thing. It is easy to point a video camera at a room and store the image as a set of pixels, the dots that make up an image on a TV screen. But extracting information from thousands or millions of pixels is very difficult, since the image captured by the video camera may be highly ambiguous. If a person is sitting in a chair, the pixels will reveal only part of the chair, so the computer must somehow infer that there is a chair even though it cannot see anything that matches a standard chair. Some parts of the room may be in brighter light than other parts. A rectangular object on the wall might be a picture, or it might be a mirror reflecting other parts of the room. In the past few decades, computer vision has made substantial progress, enabling robots to identify and manipulate objects under simplified circumstances. But robotic vision remains crude compared to the power of human vision.

Consider the drawing in figure 6.1. If you shift your concentration between the top and the bottom of the cube, you should be able to make it flip back and forth, seeing first one face as the front and then another

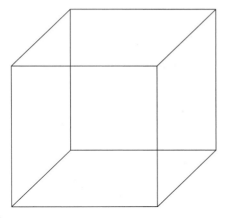

**Figure 6.1**
The Necker cube. The top edge can be seen either as being at the front or at the
back of the cube. Try to make it flip back and forth by concentrating on different
edges.

face as the front. How does this happen? Light reflects off the picture
into your eyes and onto your retina, which consists of millions of light-
detecting cells. But an enormous amount of processing is required before
your brain can interpret the picture as a cube. Your brain must detect edges,
distinguishing the lines from the background. In figure 6.1, edge detection
is trivial, but this task becomes much more difficult if there are subtle variations in brightness, grays as well as black and white. Moreover, your brain
does not receive a single image like what a video camera would produce,
but rather gets information from two eyes with slightly different perspectives on objects. The perspective differences make possible your ability to
appreciate distances and see objects in three dimensions.

The brain manages to combine inferences about edges, perspective,
colors, and other information into a coherent interpretation of objects far
more complicated than the cube in figure 6.1. See Marr 1982 and Kosslyn
1994b for much more about visual information processing. The result of
all this inference is a visual image. Such images do not depend on an
object's being present to the eyes, for we can store the images in memory,
retrieve them, and manipulate them in ways that contribute to a variety
of mental tasks.

*"Looking good!"*

**Figure 6.2**
Drawing by Gahan Wilson. © 1994, The New Yorker Magazine, Inc. Reprinted by permission.

**Representational Power**

Why do people often say that a picture is worth a thousand words? Pictures can usually be described in words. For example, we can say that figure 6.2 depicts one man sitting behind another and looking into the top of his head. Given enough sentences, we could provide a much fuller description. But the pictorial representation has various advantages. The verbal description might contain the information that the man in the chair is close to the man with his head open, who is on a couch. We could then verbally infer that the chair is close to the couch. Using the pictorial representation, however, no inference is necessary: we can just *see* that the chair is close to the couch. Figure 6.2 is an external representation that we see with our eyes. But if you cover up the picture for a moment, you may still be able to form a mental image of the picture and answer some questions about it. Roughly how old are the men? Is either of them bald? Is either wearing a tie?

Pictures and visual mental images provide powerful ways of representing how things look and how they are spatially arranged, but not all information is naturally represented in pictures. Abstract sentences like "Justice is fairness" are not visually representable, and general sentences like "All dinosaurs are extinct" are very awkward to represent pictorially. Similarly, causal statements such as "Smoking causes cancer" and "If you get a cold, then you will cough" are not straightforwardly represented by pictures. Hence, visual images complement but do not replace verbal representations of the sort we have seen in the previous chapters.

Earlier chapters assumed that representations are fundamentally verbal: the rules, concepts, and analogs discussed were all presented in words. But these structures may have visual forms as well. A rule might have the structure IF <picture 1>, THEN <picture 2>, providing a kind of movie in which picture 1 is followed by picture 2. A concept might be pictorial—for example, if my prototype for a dog is represented not by a set of features but by a picture of a dog that has those features. Similarly, source and target analogs can have visual representations such as the rabbit and shadow in figure 5.1. Hence, in addition to verbal rules, concepts, and analogs, there may be visual rules, concepts, and analogs.

What is the structure of mental images? Kosslyn (1980) and Glasgow and Papadias (1992) proposed that the mind uses arraylike structures to perform visual tasks. For example, we might represent Europe using the array shown in figure 6.3. More recently, Kosslyn (1994b) has argued that the human brain uses various kinds of neural networks to represent spatial information (see the section below on neurological plausibility).

## Computational Power

Much thinking that can be done with images can also be done with words, but verbal thinking may be much more awkward for some tasks. Visual thinking is likely to be useful for any problem whose solution depends on visual appearance or spatial relationships. Visual representations, both

| | | | | | |
|---|---|---|---|---|---|
| | | | | Sweden | |
| Wales Scotland England | | | Denmark | | |
| | | Holland | Germany | Germany | |
| | | Belgium | | | |
| | France | France | | Croatia | Serbia |
| Portugal | Spain | | | | Greece |

**Figure 6.3**
Map of Europe represented as an array. Adapted with permission from Glasgow and Papadias 1992, p. 373.

mental and external, are accessible to different kinds of computational procedures than verbal representations:

1. *Inspect*   Imagine a plate that has a knife to the left of it and a fork to the right of it. Is the knife to the left or the right of the fork? The answer could be inferred verbally using the logical properties of the relations "left" and "right," but more immediately the answer could come just by looking at the image formed and seeing that the knife is to the left of the fork. This procedure can also be used to compare two representations by inspecting them both.

2. *Find*   Where do you keep your shoes at home? To remember, you might do a mental scan of your room or rooms to find the spot they are likely to be.

3. *Zoom*   Does a frog have a tail? Some people answer this question by forming a mental image of a frog and then zooming in to look in more detail at its behind, just as you can look more closely at part of a picture.

4. *Rotate*   What does a capital letter "E" look like when it is flat on its back? One way to answer this question is to rotate the letter mentally until it is on its back.

5. *Transform*  Follow these instructions from Finke, Pinker, and Farah 1989: Imagine the letter "B." Rotate it 90 degrees to the left. Put a triangle the same width as the rotated "B" directly below it and pointing down. Remove the horizontal line. Many people see the resulting figure as a heart or double ice-cream cone. We seem to be able to alter and combine visual representations in powerful ways, including flipping and juxtaposing them as well as rotating them.

Operations such as these five make possible kinds of problem solving different from the verbal kinds considered in earlier chapters. To answer the question of whether all your shoes have the same number of holes for laces, you might retrieve an image of your closet, scan it to find your shoes, zoom in to inspect your shoes, and transform the shoe images to juxtapose laces to compare the number of holes. On the other hand, if you have only one pair of shoes, and you know the rule that two shoes from the same pair have the same number of holes, it might be easier to deduce the answer without recourse to mental imagery.

### Problem Solving

**Planning**  Suppose you have many errands to do: picking up groceries, mailing a parcel, and dropping off dry cleaning. Previous chapters suggested verbal ways in which you might plan how to accomplish these tasks in a reasonably efficient way. A set of IF-THEN rules might have guided you to the grocery store, post office, and dry cleaner's, or perhaps previous experience with these tasks might have guided you with a verbal analog or schema. Alternatively, you might construct a plan visually, imagining yourself driving into the grocery store parking lot, then driving out to the post office, and finally parking at the dry cleaner's. Such visual planning may employ a mental map that you have constructed that encodes the spatial relations of the places you have to go. Not everyone employs such mental maps: some people function better with verbally encoded landmarks. But for many others, getting around in the world is very much helped by being able to use visual images to figure out where they are and how they can get to where they want to be.

Planning with visual representations involves steps similar to those in rule-based problem solving described in chapter 2, except that the steps are executed visually. You must first construct visual representations of the starting and goal states, then construct a visual path from the start to the goal. Visual transformations can be useful in solving construction problems, such as how to build a bridge connecting two banks of a river, and even for more mundane problems in the sciences. Problem solvers often use diagrams as an external aid to supplement the more temporary benefits of mental images. In geometry, for example, it can be very helpful to draw diagrams of figures and angles as an aid to working out how to draw figures. Students solving science problems often make use of diagrams that make complex objects such as springs, molecules, and chromosomes more comprehensible.

**Decision**   Little research has been done on the contribution of imagery to decision making. But suppose you are trying to decide whether to wear your blue or your brown jacket. You might imagine how each would look with the other clothes you are planning to wear, so that the decision about what to wear would be the result of a comparison of visual images. Similarly, if you are trying to decide what to order in a restaurant, your decision might be based in part on imagining what different dishes might taste like. Emotional images can also be important for decision making, as we will see in chapter 10.

**Explanation**   Visual reasoning may be very useful in generating explanations. The great inventor Nikola Tesla could reportedly diagnose the faults in complex machinery just by forming a mental image of the machinery and running it in his head to see where breakdowns might occur. Visual explanation has not been much studied in psychology or artificial intelligence, but there is reason to believe that it is common in scientific and everyday thinking. Look at a map of the world that shows the continents of Africa and South America. Now slide these two continents together until the bulge that constitutes Brazil fits into and under West Africa. Early in this century, the fit between these two continents suggested to Alfred Wegener that they had once been joined, and he formed the hypothesis of continental drift to explain how they had come apart. This hypothesis can be stated in purely verbal terms, but the fit between Africa and South America is best represented visually and can be explained by a visual joining of the two continents. This joining mentally reverses a spatial separation conjectured to have happened long ago. As with planning, visual explanation is not a replacement for verbal reasoning, but provides a valuable complement to it.

### Learning

Athletes are often coached to improve their performances by using imagery, and there is experimental evidence that practicing by mental imaging can improve performance if mixed with actual practice (Goss et al. 1986). Someone waiting to perform a dive or to hit a baseball can imagine accomplishing the task perfectly, using both visual and motor images. Running the task through your mind can actually help you to do it better when the time comes.

Images can also be useful for generalization, as when someone uses pictures of members of a category such as *elephant* to form a fairly general mental picture of an elephant. The resulting visual representation of an elephant ignores incidental information about particular elephants (e.g., carrying a rider) in favor of general properties (e.g., being gray, wrinkled). Imagistic learning of generalizations has not received much experimental or computational attention.

Abductive learning can also be visual. If you find a long scratch on the door of your car, you can generate various verbal explanations of it. But you might also construct a kind of mental movie in which someone drives up beside you in the parking lot and opens a door that scrapes along your car just where the scratch appears. Your abductive inference that another car scraped your door is generated visually, by constructing a sequence of pictures that shows how the scratch might have come about. Other pictures are possible too, such as one showing a shopping cart rolling into the car or keys scraping along it. Shelley (1996) describes how archaeologists use visual abduction when they generate explanations of ancient objects.

### Language

Language is essentially verbal, so how could imagery be relevant to the use of language? We saw in chapter 5 that language is not just a matter of syntax and simple semantics, but is frequently metaphorical. As Lakoff and Johnson (1980) have pointed out, many metaphors are visual in origin: he's *up* today, she's *on top* of her job. Lakoff (1994) contends that much understanding involves image schemas, which are general concepts that have a visual component. For example, behind understanding of categories is visual understanding of containers: an object can be *in* or *out* of a category such as *dog*, and it can be *put into* or *removed from* such categories. Metaphors can also tie together more than one kind of sensory representation, as in "loud clothes."

Langacker (1987) defends an approach to *cognitive grammar* that takes metaphor and imagery as central to mental life, including language processing. He argues that sensory imagery plays a substantial role in conceptual structure; for example, the meaning of the word "trumpet" may be tied in part to an auditory image of the sound a trumpet makes. This approach to linguistics is controversial, but it suggests how language may depend on visual and other images as well as on words.

### Psychological Plausibility

Many psychological experiments have supported the claim that visual imagery is part of human thinking. Cooper and Shepard (1973) measured how long it took students to decide whether a rotated letter was normal or a mirror image. Figure 6.4 shows versions of the letter "R." The first "R" is normal, but the second is a mirror image. The third and fourth "R"s can be discovered to be, respectively, mirror and normal images by mentally rotating them. If letters are relatively close to the normal position, like the "R"s in cases 5 and 6, then less time is needed to determine whether they are normal or mirror images than when they are relatively far from the normal position, like the "R"s in cases 3 and 4.

In addition to rotation experiments, scanning experiments have confirmed the mental imagery hypothesis by finding that people take more time to scan longer distances across images (Kosslyn 1980). Make a mental image of your country, and identify a city on the west coast or border, one

1    2    3    4    5    6

**Figure 6.4**
Mental rotation: the amount of time it takes to determine whether a letter is normal or a mirror image is directly proportional to how much it needs to be rotated to find an answer.

in the interior of the country, and one on the east coast or border. For example, Americans should locate San Francisco, Chicago, and New York on their maps. If you are working with a visual image, then it should take longer for you to scan from the western city to the eastern city than it does to scan from the western city to the central city.

Finke, Pinker, and Farah (1989) performed experiments that show that people can assign novel interpretations to images that have been constructed out of parts or mentally transformed. In addition to the rotated "B"-into-heart example described above, they gave students instructions such as the following: Imagine the letter "Y." Put a small circle at the bottom of it. Add a horizontal line halfway up. Now rotate the figure 180 degrees. Most people see a stick person as the result of these instructions. The required transformations are shown in figure 6.5. People's frequent success in getting the right answer suggests that they are operating with visual representations. Even financial judgments may be affected by mental imagery (MacGregor et al. 2002).

Although most researchers in psychology are convinced by experiments like those just described that humans use visual imagery, some skeptics maintain that the same kind of verbal representations underlie all thought and that the experiences of imagery are illusory. Rotation, scanning, and other transformations can always be mimicked by nonimagistic computational procedures on lists of words. Within the last decade, however, neurological evidence has accumulated that provides further support for the imagery hypothesis.

## Neurological Plausibility

Kosslyn (1994b) extensively reviews two kinds of evidence that parts of the brain used in visual perception are also involved in visual mental imagery. First, patients with brain damage that produces deficits in their perceptual

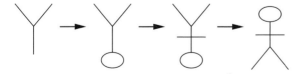

**Figure 6.5**
Sequence of transformations required to produce the stick person.

abilities sometimes have similar imagery deficits. For example, some patients unable to see one side of space during perception also are unable to see the same side of space during imagery. Damage to the occipital lobe impairs visual imagery. Second, measurements of brain activity have found that when people use visual mental imagery to perform tasks, brain areas used in visual perception become active. Imagery relies on regions of cortex that are spatially organized in ways that correspond to the structure of the retina, the networks of nerve cells that send impulses to the brain. The areas of the brain most immediately connected to the retina have a spatial organization that is structurally similar to that of the retina. Since these areas preserve some of the spatial structure of objects presented to the retina, their activation during imagery suggests that imagery involves picturelike representations, not just verbal descriptions. Kosslyn, Ganis, and Thompson (2001) review neurological studies of visual, auditory, and motor imagery.

Kosslyn describes the brain's processing of mental images in terms of computational mechanisms by which it satisfies multiple constraints in parallel. Chapter 7 describes how similar processes can be performed by artificial neural networks.

**Practical Applicability**

If mental imagery is useful in problem solving, education may profitably involve teaching people to use images more effectively. Larkin and Simon (1987) describe the conditions under which diagrams contribute to effective problem solving. Most psychological work on imagery, however, has been concerned with how people use images, not with educating them to use images better. Dehaene et al. (1999) report behavioral and brain-imaging experiments that suggest that mathematical intuition sometimes depends on visual and spatial representations; hence, mental images may be relevant to improving the teaching of mathematics.

Many strategies for improving memory rely on visual images. To remember something important, it helps to associate it with a vivid image. For example, to ensure that you will be able to recall the six kinds of mental representation discussed in this book, you might associate each of them with a mental picture of a different zoo animal that you think of as logical, rule-based, and so on.

Many kinds of design by architects, engineers, and product designers use visual representations such as sketches and blueprints. Mental imagery is presumably a part of these designers' creative mental processes, but there is little psychological evidence or computational understanding concerning the role of imagery in design. Kosslyn (1994a) presents a set of principles, based on empirical findings, for making visual displays that people can easily read and understand. Finke, Ward, and Smith (1992) discuss imagery's contribution to creative inventions.

Although artificial intelligence researchers have taken increasing interest in imagery and diagram-based systems, image-based expert systems are rare. Forbus, Nielson, and Faltings (1991) describe a system that does qualitative spatial reasoning about physical devices. Glasgow, Fortier, and Allen (1993) have used an array-based system for determining crystal and molecular structure.

## Summary

Visual and other kinds of images play an important role in human thinking. Pictorial representations capture visual and spatial information in a much more usable form than lengthy verbal descriptions. Computational procedures well suited to visual representations include inspecting, finding, zooming, rotating, and transforming. Such operations can be very useful for generating plans and explanations in domains to which pictorial representations apply. The explanatory schema for visual representation is as follows:

Explanation target

Why do people have a particular kind of intelligent behavior?

Explanatory pattern

People have visual images of situations.

People have processes such as scanning and rotation that operate on those images.

The processes for constructing and manipulating images produce the intelligent behavior.

Imagery can aid learning, and some metaphorical aspects of language may have their roots in imagery. Psychological experiments suggest that visual procedures such as scanning and rotating employ imagery, and recent neurophysiological results confirm a close physical link between reasoning with mental imagery and perception.

## Discussion Questions

1. Is introspection a reliable guide to our mental representations and procedures? Why is introspection alone not enough to show the importance of mental images?
2. Do you have sensory imagery? When do you most frequently use it?
3. What computations are potentially easier to achieve using imagistic representations?
4. In what kinds of problem solving are visual images useful? When can they become a hindrance?
5. How would a critic of mental imagery explain the psychological and neurological experiments supporting mental imagery?

## Further Reading

Kosslyn 1994b and Kosslyn, Ganis, and Thompson 2001 provide a comprehensive review of recent psychological and neurological results. Finke 1989 surveys much experimental work on imagery. Glasgow 1993 reviews the debates about imagery from a computational perspective, with discussion by AI critics. Tye 1991 provides a philosophical examination. Langacker 1987 touches on the relevance of imagery to linguistics. Marr 1982 is a classic source on human and computer vision. For the latest in the imagery debate, see Pylyshyn 2002 and Kosslyn, Ganis, and Thompson 2003.

## Web Sites

Diagrammatic reasoning: http://www.hcrc.ed.ac.uk/gal/Diagrams/

Imagination and mental imagery: http://www.calstatela.edu/faculty/nthomas/home.htm

Sports and mental imagery: http://www.vanderbilt.edu/AnS/psychology/health_psychology/mentalimagery.html

Stephen Kosslyn's home page: http://www.wjh.harvard.edu/~kwn/

Zenon Pylyshyn's home page: http://ruccs.rutgers.edu/faculty/pylyshyn.html

## Notes

One of the main reasons that computational models of imagery have been relatively rare is that the programming tools currently available are much better suited for verbal representations than for visual ones. In addition to the array representations advocated by Glasgow and Papadias (1992), graph representations can be useful for capturing some aspects of visual representations (Wong, Lu, and Rioux 1989). Croft and Thagard (2002) use scene graphs and the Java 3-D programming language to model visual analogies.

# 7 Connections

Near the end of the nineteenth century, Santiago Ramón y Cajal discovered that the brain consists of discrete cells. These neurons signal each other through contacts at specialized points called synapses. Figure 7.1 shows a simplified picture of neurons connected by synapses. The human brain has about 100 billion neurons, many of which connect to thousands of other neurons, forming neural networks.

In the early days of computational models of thinking in the 1950s and 1960s, there was much interest in modeling how neural networks might contribute to thought. But this work waned in the 1970s, as the attention of researchers in artificial intelligence and psychology shifted almost entirely to rule-based and concept-based representations. In the 1980s, however, there was a dramatic rebound of computational modeling inspired by the neuronal structure of the brain (e.g., Hinton and Anderson 1981; Rumelhart and McClelland 1986). This research is often called connectionist, because it emphasizes the importance of connections among simple neuronlike structures, but is also sometimes discussed in terms of neural networks or parallel distributed processing (PDP). A wealth of connectionist models of mind and brain have been developed, but I will concentrate on two classes of models. The first class is concerned with *local* representations in which neuronlike structures are given an identifiable interpretation in terms of specifiable concepts or propositions. The second class is concerned with *distributed* representations in networks that learn how to represent concepts or propositions in more complex ways that distribute meaning over complexes of neuronlike structures.

Both local and distributed representations can be used to perform *parallel constraint satisfaction*. Many cognitive tasks can be understood computationally in terms of processing that simultaneously satisfies numerous

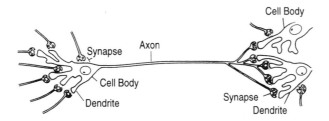

**Figure 7.1**
Neurons connected by synapses. The electrical signals flow into the dendrites and out through the axon. Adapted with permission from Rumelhart and McClelland 1986, vol. 2, p. 337.

constraints. As an initial example of a constraint satisfaction problem, consider the task faced by university administrators when they put together a new class schedule. Some of the constraints they face are inviolable: they cannot put two classes in the same room at the same time, and a student or professor cannot simultaneously be in two different classes. In contrast, many of the constraints are soft ones, involving preferences of professors and students concerning when and where their classes will take place. Coming up with a schedule that takes into account the various constraints imposed by classroom availability and the preferences of professors and students is a daunting task that is rarely accomplished in optimal fashion. Administrators typically take a previous term's schedule and adapt it as needed to handle new problems. But constraint satisfaction problems can be solved in a more general way if all the constraints are simultaneously taken into account.

Explicit models of parallel constraint satisfaction were first developed for computer vision. Marr and Poggio (1976) proposed what they called a "cooperative" algorithm for stereoscopic vision. Two eyes form slightly different images of the world: how does the brain match the two images and construct a coherent combined image? Marr and Poggio noticed that matching is governed by several constraints involving how points in one image can be put into correspondence with points in another. Creating a coherent image is then a matter of satisfying the constraints on matching points across the two images. To accomplish this task computationally, Marr and Poggio proposed using a parallel, interconnected network of processors in which the interconnections represented the constraints.

Similar networks were subsequently used by Feldman (1981) to model visual representations in memory and by McClelland and Rumelhart (1981) to model letter perception. Look back at the Necker cube presented in figure 6.1. Parallel constraint satisfaction provides a mechanism for resolving the ambiguity inherent in the Necker cube. Each of the two global interpretations can be defined in terms of a set of more elementary interpretations of the elements of the drawing. For example, under one interpretation the top-left corner in the drawing is the front-top-left corner of the cube, whereas under the other interpretation the same point is interpreted as the back-top-left corner. Furthermore, the possible local interpretations are highly interdependent, tending to either support or compete with each other in accord with the structural relations embodied in the canonical cube.

Human interpretations of the Necker cube can be modeled by a simple connectionist network that uses units to represent interpretations of the corners and links between units to represent compatibilities and incompatibilities between interpretations. In this network, parallel constraint satisfaction converges on one or the other of the two possible views, activating a subset of units that collectively represent a coherent interpretation, and deactivating the others. Research in the past decade has shown that parallel constraint satisfaction applies to many kinds of high-level cognition, not just to visual perception.

## Representational Power

Connectionist networks constitute very simple representations, since they consist only of units and links. The units are analogous to neurons and have a degree of activation that corresponds roughly to the frequency with which neurons fire in order to send signals to other neurons. In local connectionist networks, the units have a specifiable interpretation such as particular concepts or propositions. The activation of a unit can be interpreted as a judgment about the applicability of a concept or the truth of a proposition. Links can be one-way, with activation flowing from one unit to another, or symmetric, with activation flowing back and forth between two units. Links are either excitatory, with one unit raising the activation of another, or inhibitory, with one unit suppressing the activation of another. Figure 7.2 gives a simple example of a local network that might be involved

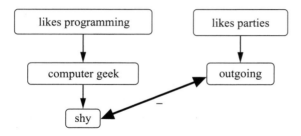

**Figure 7.2**
Simple local network with excitatory links (thin lines) and an inhibitory link (thick line with minus sign). Which of the excitatory links could plausibly be symmetric?

in making inferences about a fellow student. You meet Alice and learn that she likes programming, so you think she might be a computer geek and therefore shy. On the other hand, you learn that she likes parties, which suggests that she is outgoing. In forming a coherent impression of her, you have to decide whether she is actually shy or outgoing. The network in figure 7.2 uses a unit to represent each trait and has one-way excitatory links that make activation flow from the observed behaviors to the inferred traits. It also has a symmetric inhibitory link between shy and outgoing, reflecting the fact that it is hard to be both. The distributed networks described below include units that do not have such specific interpretations.

To understand the nature of distributed representations, we can use a visual analogy developed by Kosslyn and Koenig (1992, 20). Figure 7.3 shows an octopus network that accomplishes the task of communicating to seagulls the presence of fish near the bottom of the tidal pool. The octopi in the bottom row detect fish and signal to the octopi in the middle row by squeezing their tentacles, and the octopi in the middle row similarly signal to those in the top row, who in turn can throw up tentacles to inform the seagulls. This is a kind of *feedforward* network where information flows upward through the network. The bottom row of octopi can be thought of as an input layer, and the top row as an output layer, but what interpretation can be given to the octopi in the middle row? The information about how many fish there are is not encoded in any particular octopus, but rather is distributed over the whole network of octopi. Similarly, figure 7.4 depicts a feedforward neural network in which the hidden

**Figure 7.3**

A visual analogy for a distributed processing network. Reprinted with the permission of The Free Press, an imprint of Simon and Schuster, from *Wet Mind: The New Cognitive Neuroscience*, by Stephen M. Kosslyn and Olivier Koenig. Copyright © 1992 by Stephen M. Kosslyn and Olivier Koenig.

(neither input nor output) units in the middle layer have no initial interpretation. They acquire an interpretation through adjustments in the weights that connect them to other units, by a learning process discussed below. In *recurrent* networks, activation from the output units feeds back into the input units.

Concepts can be viewed as distributed representations in networks. A network that is trained to respond accurately to stimuli can acquire concepts that apply to the stimuli. For example, if a network has as input units

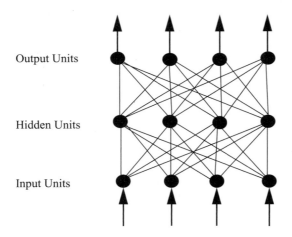

Output Units

Hidden Units

Input Units

**Figure 7.4**
A feedforward computer model, with input, hidden, and output units.

features of animals, and output units that identify kinds of animals such as dog and cat, then the network can acquire the concept of a dog or a cat. The concept does not consist of any particular node; rather, it consists of a typical pattern of activation of units that occurs when a typical set of features is given as input. The notion of a concept as a pattern of activation of nodes in a distributed network is very different from the characterization of concepts given in chapter 4, but shares with it the claim that a concept is a prototype rather than a set of necessary and sufficient conditions.

Links between units suffice for representing simple associations such as that computer geeks are shy and shy people are not outgoing. But they lack the representational power to capture more complex kinds of rules, such as that anyone who likes a computer geek is also a computer geek. In the logical symbolism presented in chapter 2, this would be something like

$(x) \{(\exists y) [\text{geek } (y) \& \text{likes } (x, y)] \rightarrow \text{geek } (x)\}$.

In words: "For any $x$, if there is a $y$ such that $y$ is a geek and $x$ likes $y$, then $x$ is a geek." Relations such as "likes" and complex logical relations are difficult to represent in connectionist networks, although ingenious attempts are underway to increase their representational power beyond that of the simple local network in figure 7.2. One promising technique is to use *synchrony* to link units that represent associated elements: a unit or package of units that represents the *x* that does the liking can be made to fire with the same temporal pattern as the *x* that likes computers (Shastri and Ajjanagadde 1993; Shastri 1999; Hummel and Holyoak 1997). Another way of representing relational information is to use vectors, which are lists of numbers that can be understood as the firing rates of groups of neurons. For example, the vector (0.3, 0.4, 0.2) can be interpreted as the relative firing activity of three neurons. Vectors can be used to distinguish between agents (e.g., what does the liking) and objects (e.g., ones that are liked). Such vectors can be combined to represent highly complex relational information needed for analogical reasoning (Smolensky 1990; Eliasmith and Thagard 2001). See chapter 9 for more discussion of neuronal representations.

Neural networks provide powerful sensory representations that make possible many more tastes and aromas than we can typically express in words (Churchland 1995). The tongue has four types of taste sensors, for sweet, sour, salty, and bitter. Consider a system that has a unit corresponding to each of these sensors, with each unit capable of ten distinct levels of activation. Then the system can discriminate $10^4 = 10,000$ different tastes, each corresponding to a different pattern of activation.

## Computational Power

### Problem Solving

Neural networks provide powerful computational tools for performing parallel constraint satisfaction. Consider the problem in figure 7.2, where the task is to decide whether Alice is outgoing or shy. This problem has both positive constraints, such as between *likes parties* and *outgoing*, and negative constraints, such as between *outgoing* and *shy*.

Once the concepts and constraints are specified, implementing this kind of model in a parallel network is easy. First, concepts such as *outgoing* are represented by units. Second, positive internal constraints are represented by excitatory connections: if two concepts are related by a positive constraint, then the units representing the elements should be linked by an excitatory link. Third, negative internal constraints are represented by inhibitory connections: if two concepts are related by a negative constraint, then the units representing the elements should be linked by an inhibitory link. Fourth, an external constraint can be captured by linking units representing elements that satisfy the external constraint to a special unit that affects the units to which it is linked either positively (by virtue of excitatory links) or negatively (by virtue of inhibitory links). In the Alice example, the external constraints are that you know that she likes programming and likes parties, so there will be links between the special unit and the units representing these two elements.

The neural network computes by spreading activation between units that are linked to each other. A unit with an excitatory link to an active unit will gain activation from it, whereas a unit with an inhibitory link to an active unit will have its own activation decreased. Some units are activated as others are deactivated, with the result depending on the interconnections among the units. A problem solution consists of when a group of units, such as those in the Alice problem, is activated by the set containing *outgoing*, while correctively deactivating the set containing *shy*. In the network in figure 7.2, *outgoing* will win out over *shy* because outgoing is more directly connected to the external information that Alice likes parties.

Constraints can be satisfied in parallel by repeatedly passing activation among all the units, until after some number of cycles of activity all units have reached stable activation levels. This process is called *relaxation*, by analogy to physical processes that involve objects gradually achieving a stable shape or temperature. Achieving stability is called *settling*. Relaxing the network means adjusting the activation of all units based on the units to which they are connected until all units have stable high or low activations.

**Planning**  Although decisions among competing plans are naturally understood in terms of parallel constraint satisfaction, constructing plans is usually a more sequential process understood in terms of rules or analogies. Your plan to graduate can be expressed in terms of a set of rules concerning what sequence of courses will give you enough courses of the required kinds. But connectionist networks can implement simple kinds of rule-based systems. Touretzky and Hinton (1988) constructed a rule-based system that uses distributed representations. It treats the process of matching the *IF* part of a rule as a kind of parallel constraint satisfaction. However, the resulting system can match only clauses with simple predicates, not relations. Nelson, Thagard, and Hardy (1994) use local representations to implement rule matching and analogy application as parallel constraint satisfaction. The resulting system models plan construction, such as how Juliet in Shakespeare's play planned to meet Romeo. Thus, connectionist systems can be indirectly relevant to modeling solutions of planning problems.

**Decision**  We can understand the process of making a decision in terms of parallel constraint satisfaction (Thagard and Millgram 1995; see also Mannes and Kintsch 1991). The elements of a decision are various actions and goals. The positive internal constraints come from facilitation relations: if an action facilitates a goal, then the action and goal tend to go together. The negative internal constraints come from incompatibility relations, when two actions or goals cannot be performed or satisfied together, as when a student cannot take two courses at the same time. The external constraint on decision making comes from goal priority: some goals are inherently desirable, providing a positive constraint. Once the elements and constraints have been specified for a particular decision problem, a constraint network can be formed such as that seen in figure 7.5.

Suppose you are facing the difficult problem of deciding what to do after graduation. Perhaps your options include going to graduate school or taking an entry-level position with a large corporation. The constraints you face are first that you cannot do both and moreover that the different options fit better with different goals that you have. Immediate employment may solve your current financial problems, but may not necessarily provide an interesting long-term career. Moreover, perhaps there are aspects of your field that you want to learn more about. On the other hand, you might be tired of taking classes. Figure 7.5 shows a simple network that captures part of what is involved in the decision. Units represent the various options and goals, and pluses and minuses indicate the excitatory and inhibitory links that embody the fundamental constraints. If a unit settles with high activation, this is interpreted as acceptance of the goal or action that it represents, whereas deactivation represents rejection. The unit representing graduate school has stronger excitatory links and therefore will get more activation than the unit representing taking a job, which will be deactivated because of the inhibitory link with the unit for graduate school.

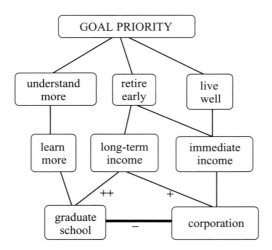

**Figure 7.5**
A constraint network for decision making. Boxes represent units, thin lines represent positive constraints based on facilitation (symmetric excitatory links), and the thin line with a minus represents a negative constraint (inhibitory link). The "goal priority" special unit pumps activation to the other nodes that have to compete for it.

Analogy can also be useful in decision making, since a past case where something like A helped to bring about something like B may help one to see that A facilitates B. But reasoning with analogies may itself depend on parallel constraint satisfaction. Chapter 5 described Holyoak's and my view that retrieving and mapping analogs involves the constraints of similarity, structure, and purpose (Holyoak and Thagard 1995). The computational models we have implemented perform parallel satisfaction of these constraints using mechanisms similar to the ones just described for decision making.

**Explanation**   Churchland (1989) has contended that explanation should be understood as activation of prototypes encoded in distributed networks. Understanding why a particular bird has a long neck can come via activation of a set of nodes representing *swan*, which include the prototypical expectation that swans have long necks. On this view, inference to the best explanation is just activation of the most appropriate prototype.

Using local networks, inference to the best explanation has been modeled via a theory of explanatory coherence (Thagard 1989, 1992, 2000). Suppose you are expecting to meet your friend Fred at the cafeteria, but Fred does not show up. Your knowledge of Fred and your general knowledge about other students may suggest various hypotheses that could explain why Fred does not show up, but you would still have to decide which hypothesis is most plausible. Perhaps Fred decided he had to study, or maybe he went dancing with someone. An extra piece of evidence that Fred was spotted in the library would clearly support one hypothesis over the other. Figure 7.6 shows a network that captures some of the relevant information as used in the program ECHO that I wrote to model explanatory coherence. Units representing pieces of evidence are linked to a special evidence unit that activates them, and activation spreads out to other units. There is an inhibitory link connecting the units representing the two competing hypotheses that Fred is in the library and that he went dancing. Choice of the best explanation can involve not only the evidence for particular hypotheses, but also explanations of why those hypotheses might be true. For example, Fred's motive for studying is that he wants high grades; alternatively, the reason he went dancing might be that he likes to party. Settling the network will provide a coherent interpretation of his behavior. In the network in figure 7.6, the network will settle with the unit for "Fred is studying" activated because it has more sources of activation than its competitor, the unit for "Fred went dancing."

**Learning**

Given the simple structure of connectionist networks, there are two basic ways in which learning can take place: add new units, or change the weights on the links between units. Work to date has concentrated on the second kind of learning. A biologically plausible kind of weight learning was proposed by Hebb (1949). He speculated that when two brain cells or systems are active at the same time, they should become associated with each other. This kind of learning has been observed in real neurons and has been modeled computationally in various ways. The idea is that if unit (neuron) A and unit B are both active at the same time, then the weight on the link between them should increase. For example, in a local network

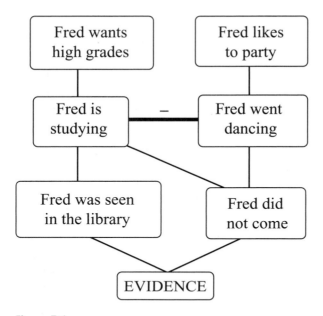

**Figure 7.6**
Network for picking the best explanation of why Fred did not show up. The thin lines are symmetric excitatory links and the thick line marked with a minus is a symmetric inhibitory link.

that has units representing both dancing and partying, if these units are frequently active at the same time, then the link between them will become stronger and stronger, implementing an association between dancing and partying. This kind of learning is unsupervised in that it does not require any teacher to tell the network when it has right or wrong answers.

The most common kind of learning in feedforward networks with distributed representations uses a technique called *backpropagation*. Figure 7.7 shows a simple network with input, hidden, and output units that is supposed to learn about social stereotypes on campus. After training, the network should be able to classify students: given a set of features activated in the input layer, it should activate an appropriate stereotype at the output layer. For example, a student who plays sports and parties (input layer) could be identified as a jock (output layer). Backpropagation can be used to train the network by adjusting the weights that connect the different

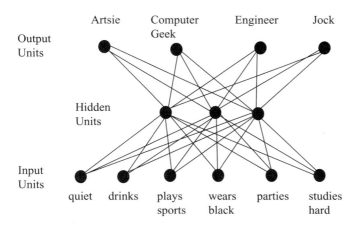

**Figure 7.7**
A network that can be trained to classify students.

units, through the following steps (see Towell and Shavlik 1994; for full details, see Rumelhart and McClelland 1986):

1. Assign weights randomly to the links between units.

2. Activate input units based on features of what you want the network to learn about.

3. Spread activation forward through the network to the hidden units and then to the output units.

4. Determine errors by calculating the difference between the computed activation of the output units and the desired activation of the output units. For example, if activation of *quiet* and *studies hard* activated *jock*, this result would be an error.

5. Propagate errors backward down the links, changing the weights in such a way that the errors will be reduced.

6. Eventually, after many examples have been presented to the network, it will correctly classify different kinds of students.

Backpropagation models have had many successful applications, in both psychology and in engineering. They do more than simply identify rules such as *IF someone plays sports THEN he or she is a jock*. Networks trained by backpropagation can identify statistical associations between input and output features that are more subtle than rules. Nevertheless, backpropagation has a number of drawbacks as a model of human learning. First, it requires a supervisor to say whether an error has been made. Much learning—for example, of language—seems to occur without much explicit supervision. Neural network models of unsupervised learning are discussed in Hinton and Sejnowski (1999). Second, backpropagation tends to be slow, requiring many hundreds or thousands of examples to train a simple network. For some kinds of human learning large numbers of trials seem appropriate, but people can also sometimes learn from very few examples. McClelland, NcNaughton, and O'Reilly (1995) advocate complementary learning systems that use both a slow-learning component for semantics as well as a fast-learning one for object names and other information.

### Language

Early connectionist models of language involved visual and auditory perception. McClelland and Rumelhart (1981) showed how word recognition can be understood as a parallel constraint satisfaction problem. Suppose you spilled coffee on this page so that some of the letters were partly covered. You would probably still be able to figure out what many of the words were, by using visible letters and the overall context. For example, in figure 7.8 it is possible to determine the ambiguous middle letter in each word, using both the presented information about the shape of the letter and the overall context given by the word that the letter appears in. Interconnected units can represent hypotheses about what letters are present and about what words are present, and relaxing the network can pick the best overall interpretation. McClelland and Elman (1986) developed a similar model of speech perception.

Just as connectionist networks can be used to disambiguate letters and sounds, they can be used also to disambiguate word meanings. Kintsch (1988, 1998) proposed a "construction-integration" model of discourse comprehension that could explain, for example, how the word "bank" is sometimes taken to mean a financial institution and at other times taken

**Figure 7.8**
Context makes possible identification of identical structures as different letters.

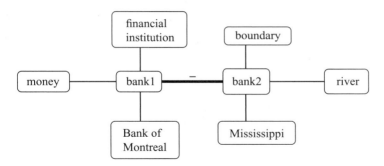

**Figure 7.9**
Meaning of "bank" is determined by activation flow in the network. Thin lines are symmetric excitatory links. Thick lines are symmetric inhibitory links.

to mean the edge of a river. Unlike what happens under the view of concepts described in chapter 4, meaning is not built into a concept but must instead be created in particular contexts by interacting elements. Figure 7.9 shows part of a network that might be useful for determining the appropriate meaning of "bank" in a particular context. Which interpretation gets activated depends on how input information will affect the various units and links.

Rumelhart and McClelland (1986) developed a parallel distributed processing model of how children learn to form the past tense of English verbs without forming explicit rules. One explanation of why young children erroneously use past tenses such as "goed" and "hitted" is that they have formed a rule that produces past tenses by simply adding "ed." Errors arise when this rule is applied too generally to include irregular verbs. But Rumelhart and McClelland showed how a connectionist network can be trained to reproduce the children's error using distributed representations rather than rules. In response, Pinker and Prince (1988) argued that the connectionist model is psychologically implausible in that it forms past tenses quite differently from how children do. MacWhinney and Leinbach (1991) replied with a new connectionist model designed to overcome these objections, and Ling and Marinov (1993) countered with a nonconnectionist model that they claimed is at least as psychologically realistic. The debate continues with Pinker and Ullman (2002) advocating a "words and rules" theory of language processing. McClelland and Patterson (2002) defend the connectionist approach.

## Psychological Plausibility

Connectionist models have furnished explanations of many psychological phenomena. McClelland and Rumelhart's (1981) model of word perception described above has explained the results of several experiments. For example, Rumelhart and McClelland (1982) described psychological experiments that confirmed their model's predictions concerning how the duration of context letters affects the perceptibility of a word. McClelland and Elman (1986) described various speech perception phenomena such as temporal effects that are explained by their model. Similarly, Kintsch's (1988) model of discourse comprehension has been confirmed by experiments in which students verified sentences of various types (Kintsch et al. 1990).

The local connectionist models of analogical mapping and retrieval not only have been used to simulate the results of previous psychological experiments, but also have suggested new ones (Holyoak and Thagard 1995; Spellman and Holyoak 1993; Wharton et al. 1994). For example, Spellman and Holyoak (1993) were able to show that the purpose of an analogy has an effect on analogical mapping in a way that Holyoak's and my computer models simulate. Similarly, to test my connectionist model of how explanatory hypotheses are evaluated, Read and Marcus-Newhall (1993) and Schank and Ranney (1991, 1992) created experiments that compared judgments of human subjects favorably with those generated by the program ECHO. Ziva Kunda and I used a simple local connectionist model to account for a dozen experimental results concerning how people form impressions of other people (Kunda and Thagard 1996).

Backpropagation techniques have simulated many psychological processes. For example, Seidenberg and McClelland (1989) used backpropagation to model visual word recognition in a way that simulates many aspects of human performance, including how words vary in processing difficulty, how novel items are pronounced, and how people make the transition from beginning to skilled reading. St. John (1992) used backpropagation to produce distributed representations that simulate many aspects of discourse comprehension. Connectionist learning mechanisms are now used to explain many aspects of human development, such as why children are quick to learn some things but slow to learn others (Bates and Elman 2002).

## Neurological Plausibility

How neurologically plausible are local connectionist networks? The artificial networks in this chapter are similar to brain structure in that they have simple elements that excite and inhibit each other. But real neural networks are much more complicated, with billions of neurons and trillions of connections. Moreover, real neurons are much more complex than the units in artificial networks, which merely pass activation to each other. Neurons have dozens of neurotransmitters that provide chemical links between them, so the brain must be considered in chemical as well as electrical terms. Real neurons undergo changes in synaptic and nonsynaptic properties that go beyond what is modeled in artificial neural networks. See chapter 9 for discussion of neurons that are much more like those found in the brain.

In local representations, each unit has a specifiable conceptual or propositional interpretation, but each neuron in the brain does not have such a local interpretation. At best, we can think of each artificial unit as representing a *neuronal group*, a complex of neurons that work together to play a processing role. Thinking of units as like neuronal groups rather than like neurons also overcomes another difference between units and neurons: many local networks use symmetric links between units, whereas synapses connecting neurons are one-way. But neuronal groups often have neural pathways that allow them to influence each other. Unlike units in artificial neural networks, a real neuron has excitatory links to other neurons or inhibitory links to other neurons, but not a mixture. The brain clearly distributes its representations over far more neurons than are found in artificial neural networks, local or distributed.

Hebbian learning that strengthens synapses between similarly active neurons has been observed in the brain, which also experiences various other kinds of learning by synapse adjustment (Churchland and Sejnowski 1992, chap. 5). However, backpropagation learning does not correspond to any process that scientists have observed in the brain. Actual neural networks do have the feedforward character of backpropagation networks, but there is no known neurological mechanism by which the same pathways that feed activation forward can also be used to propagate error correction backward. O'Reilly and Munakata (2000, 162) describe an

algorithm that is an approximation to backpropagation but is more biologically plausible.

Most connectionist models are thus only a very rough approximation to
the behavior of real neurons. Nevertheless, the analogy between the brain
and the computational mind has so far been very fruitful, and computer
models that are more authentically brainlike are under development.
Chapter 9 describes computational models that are more neurologically
realistic than the ones presented in this chapter.

### Practical Applicability

Connectionist models of learning and performance have had some interesting educational applications. Adams (1990) provides a connectionist-
style description of the various kinds of knowledge required for reading.
Figure 7.10 shows the interrelations among orthography, word meanings,
and the broader context in which a word occurs. To read a piece of text,
you need to process letters into words and simultaneously take into
account meaning and context. In the terms of this chapter, reading is a
kind of parallel constraint satisfaction where the constraints simultaneously involve spelling and meaning and context. Any narrow approach to
teaching reading that ignores some of these constraints—for example, by
neglecting phonics or by neglecting meaning and context—will make
learning to read more difficult.

Design is naturally thought of in terms of parallel constraint satisfaction.
For example, an architect's design for a building must take into account
numerous constraints such as cost, the intended use of the building, its
surroundings, and aesthetic considerations. Backpropagation techniques
have been used to assist engineers in predicting the stresses and strains of
materials needed for buildings (Allen 1992).

**Figure 7.10**
Multiple processors required for reading (Adams 1990, 138). See also Seidenberg and
McClelland 1989.

Connectionist models are widely used in intelligent systems. The back-propagation algorithm has had many engineering applications—for example, in training networks to recognize bombs, underwater objects, and handwriting. One bank trained an artificial neural network to identify which of its customers were likely to default on loans. Other networks have been trained to interpret the results of medical tests and predict the occurrence of disease. Widrow, Rumelhart, and Lehr (1994) survey applications of neural networks in industry.

## Summary

Connectionist networks consisting of simple nodes and links are very useful for understanding psychological processes that involve parallel constraint satisfaction. Such processes include aspects of vision, decision making, explanation selection, and meaning making in language comprehension. Connectionist models can simulate learning by methods that include Hebbian learning and backpropagation. The explanatory schema for the connectionist approach is as follows:

Explanation target

Why do people have a particular kind of intelligent behavior?

Explanatory pattern

People have representations that involve simple processing units linked to each other by excitatory and inhibitory connections.

People have processes that spread activation between the units via their connections, as well as processes for modifying the connections.

Applying spreading activation and learning to the units produces the behavior.

Simulations of various psychological experiments have shown the psychological relevance of the connectionist models, which are, however, only rough approximations to actual neural networks.

## Discussion Questions

1. What is the difference between a local and a distributed representation?
2. How do units in artificial neural networks differ from natural neurons?

3. How do connectionist explanations of psychological phenomena differ from rule-based explanations?

4. What psychological phenomena are most naturally explained in connectionist terms?

5. What psychological phenomena are most difficult for connectionists to explain?

## Further Reading

Introductions to neural network modeling include Bechtel and Abrahamsen 2002, Churchland and Sejnowski 1992, O'Reilly and Munakata 2000, and Rumelhart and McClelland 1986. McClelland and Rumelhart 1989 provides detailed instructions for doing your own modeling. Anderson and Rosenfeld 1988 includes some classic papers on neural networks, and Anderson and Rosenfeld 1998 contains interviews with many pioneering researchers in the field. Elman et al. 1996 applies connectionist ideas to the problem of innateness. Tesar and Smolensky 2000 discusses language acquisition from the perspective of a theory that grew out of connectionism.

## Web Sites

Jeff Elman's home page: http://crl.ucsd.edu/~elman/

Jay McClelland's home page: http://www.cnbc.cmu.edu/~jlm/

Software for neural network modeling: http://www.cnbc.cmu.edu/Resources/PDP++//PDP++.html

## Notes

The kind of spreading activation between concepts as discussed in chapter 4 is narrower than the kind discussed in this chapter, which includes inhibitory as well as excitatory mechanisms, and includes the activation of hidden units that do not represent whole concepts.

To compute activations of the units in a connectionist network, each unit is given a starting activation and repeated cycles of updating begin. There are many ways this can be done. In one technique, on each cycle the activation of a unit $j$, $a_j$, is updated according to the following equation:

$a_j(t + 1) = a_j(t)(1 - d) +$
   $net_j(max - a_j(t))$   if $net_j > 0$
   $net_j(a_j(t) - min)$   otherwise.

Here $d$ is a decay parameter (that decrements each unit at every cycle, $min$ is the minimum activation $(-1)$, $max$ is the maximum activation (1). Based on the weight $w_{ij}$ between each unit $i$ and $j$, we can calculate $net_j$, the net input to a unit, by the equation

$net_j = \Sigma_i w_{ij} a_i(t).$

# 8 Review and Evaluation

Cognitive science is about the same age as rock and roll; both emerged from diverse sources in the mid-1950s. Like rock music, cognitive science has changed in many ways through the development of new ideas and techniques. This chapter briefly summarizes the achievements of cognitive science, comparing and evaluating the representational and computational power of the six approaches described in chapters 2–7. It concludes by sketching a series of important challenges for CRUM, the Computational-Representational Understanding of Mind.

## The Achievements of Cognitive Science

Scientific understanding of problem solving, learning, and language is enormously more sophisticated now than it was fifty years ago when behaviorism reigned. We know how to design complex systems that make logical inferences. Rule- and concept-based systems have successfully modeled various aspects of problem solving and language use. In the past couple of decades, analogical thinking has been increasingly understood through a combination of psychological experiments and computational modeling. Imagery has been transformed from a topic at the fringes of scientific investigation to a subject of highly sophisticated psychological, neurological, and computational research. Connectionist models of learning and parallel constraint satisfaction have furnished explanations of numerous psychological phenomena.

One accomplishment that has eluded cognitive science is a unified theory that explains the full range of psychological phenomena, in the way that evolutionary and genetic theory unify biological phenomena, and relativity and quantum theory unify physical theory. Different

**Table 8.1**
Review of theoretical applications of computational approaches.

| | Representation | Problem solving | Learning | Language |
|---|---|---|---|---|
| Logic | Propositions Operators Predicates Quantifiers | Deduction Probability | Generalization Abduction | Logical form |
| Rules | IF-THEN | Search Forward chaining Backward chaining | Chunking Generalization Abduction | Grammar Pronunciation Spelling |
| Concepts | Frames with slots Schemas Scripts | Matching Inheritance Spreading activation | Abstraction from examples Conceptual combination | Lexicon Semantics |
| Analogies | Target and source Causal relations | Retrieval Matching Adaptation | Storage Schema formation | Metaphor |
| Images | Visual, motor, etc. | Matching, manipulating | Imaginary practice | Image schemas |
| Connections | Units and links | Parallel constraint satisfaction | Backpropagation weight adjustment | Disambiguation Pronunciation |

cognitive scientists argue that the mind is a logical system, a rule-based system, a concept-based system, an analogy-based system, an imagery-based system, and a connectionist system. The perspective of this book is that the best current answer to the final exam question "What kind of system is the mind?" is "All of the above." The mind is an extraordinarily complex system, supporting a very diverse range of kinds of thinking.

The different approaches to CRUM that were described in chapters 2–7 tend to capture different aspects of mind. Table 8.1 summarizes the different approaches and their theoretical applications. At this early stage of cognitive science research, theoretical diversity is a desirable feature rather than a flaw. Of course, we can hope that a Newton, Darwin, or Einstein of cognitive science will emerge to provide a simple, unified theory that incorporates all the insights to date. But progress can be made in understanding mind without such an overarching theory, which the complexity and

**Table 8.2**
Practical applications of cognitive science.

|             | Education                      | Design                        | Systems                           |
| ----------- | ------------------------------ | ----------------------------- | --------------------------------- |
| Logic       | Critical thinking              | Codes                         | Logic programming                 |
| Rules       | Arithmetic, skill acquisition  | Computer-human interaction    | Most expert systems               |
| Concepts    | Problem schemas                | Building specifications       | CYC, frame-based expert systems   |
| Analogies   | Problem solving                | Case-based design             | Case-based expert systems         |
| Images      | Visual problem solving         | Diagrams                      | A few expert systems              |
| Connections | Reading                        | Constraint satisfaction       | Trained expert systems            |

diversity of mind might make unattainable. One premise of cognitive science is that progress will require more than the isolated efforts of researchers in particular disciplines. Integrated, cross-disciplinary effort will continue to be essential in understanding the nature of mind.

Cognitive science has also had substantial applications to education, design, and intelligent systems. Different versions of CRUM have illuminated different aspects of applied thinking. We saw, for example, that rule-based and analogical models are useful in understanding how students solve problems, and connectionist parallel constraint satisfaction models have important implications for teaching reading. Design requires a diversity of cognitive processes, from deductive inference to imagery. Intelligent systems that mimic human abilities have drawn on a variety of kinds of representations and processes, especially rule-based, analogical (case-based), and connectionist (backpropagation) systems. Table 8.2 summarizes how the different approaches have been practically applied.

**Comparative Evaluation**

For a deeper review of the six different approaches to representation and computation, we can evaluate their comparative advantages and disadvantages, continuing to use the criteria of representational power, computational power, psychological plausibility, neurological plausibility, and practical applicability. This comparison supports the contention that no single approach currently deserves to be seen as the theoretical basis for all of cognitive science.

### Representational Power

We saw that formal logic has considerable representational power, generating complex propositions with operators such as "not" and "or" and quantifiers such as "all" and "some." Computer models that restrict themselves to rules, concepts, analogies, images, or connections have difficulty representing intricate propositions such as "No students' supervisors are responsible for some of their students' problems or worries." Even so, formal logic does not capture all the subtleties of natural language, so we have to conclude that no current computational model has the representational power to capture all of human thought.

Connectionist models have an advantage over verbal representations in that they have more flexibility in capturing a broader range of sensory experience. Patterns of activation of units can represent many tastes and smells to which verbal representations only approximate. On the other hand, connectionism has struggled with the challenge of figuring out how simple neuronlike units can represent complex relations such as those naturally included in computational models based on logic, rules, or analogies. Since the brain with its billions of neurons somehow manages to produce language, we know that a system based on interacting units can produce complex inferences, but discovering how will require connectionist models with substantially more representational power than those now available.

Computational systems that employ rules abandon the expressiveness of formal logic for a simplified format of IF-THEN rules that have computational advantages. Like propositions in formal logic, rules are concise and independent representations. In contrast, concepts, analogies, and images all bundle information together into organized structures. A concept collects a package of information about a kind of thing, and an analog collects a package of information about a situation. Images provide their own special kind of packaging since they are intimately connected with sensory functions such as vision. A visual image vividly ties together interconnected information that can be difficult to represent verbally.

In sum, a unified theory of mental representation needs to postulate structures that among them have (1) the sensory richness of images and connections, (2) the organizing capabilities of concepts, analogs, and images, and (3) the verbal expressiveness of rules and propositions in formal logic.

## Computational Power

In developing a computational model, we need to be concerned with speed and flexibility as well as abstract computational potential. There are many ways to perform computations, but for cognitive science we need computational techniques that have the speed and flexibility necessary for both psychological plausibility and practical applicability. Inference viewed as logical deduction can be elegant, but rule-based systems that emphasize heuristic search have exhibited superior performance in many domains. The effectiveness of rule-based systems has led some theorists such as Newell (1990) to advocate a unified theory of cognition based on rules. But other computational mechanisms include matching of whole structures in applying concepts, analogies, and images. Concept-based and connectionist systems implement different kinds of spreading activation. Although much human problem solving can be construed as heuristic search in a rule-based system, there are many problem solutions that are better described in terms of processes like schema application, analogical mapping, and parallel constraint satisfaction.

Similarly, human learning is not restricted to a single mechanism such as rule-based chunking. A comprehensive theory will have to account for learning of rules and concepts from examples and from combinations of other rules and concepts. It should encompass both quick, one-shot learning such as when people abductively form new hypotheses, and slow, multiple-trial learning such as when children learn to balance. Rule-based chunking and connectionist weight adjustment are both powerful learning mechanisms, but neither captures the full range of human learning capabilities.

Similarly, cognitive science still lacks a comprehensive theory of language learning and use, although different approaches have shed considerable light on different aspects of language. Some aspects of grammar and pronunciation, for example, are plausibly described in terms of rules, but rule-based approaches have helped little with understanding the nature of the lexicon or the role of metaphor in language production and comprehension. Language thus seems to depend on concepts, analogies, and images as well as on rules. Perhaps connectionism will eventually provide a neurally inspired way of saying how all these aspects are exhibited by a single system. But no comprehensive connectionist theory of language has emerged, even though connectionist models of learning and parallel constraint satisfaction have been very successful in some linguistic applications such as word sense disambiguation.

## Psychological Plausibility

Each of the six approaches to representation and computation has inspired psychological experiments as well as computational models. These experiments have addressed numerous controversial issues that continue to inspire lively debate. Are syllogistic and other kinds of logical inference done by applying logical rules, or by some more concrete method such as mental models? Is the process by which people learn to form the past tense of English verbs best described in connectionist terms or in terms of rules? Decades of experimental psychology have identified many phenomena that a general theory of mind will have to explain, but the situation so far is that different experimental results fit best with different representational theories. Rule-based models apply well to some cognitive tasks such as playing tic-tac-toe, but do not tell us much about other cases of problem solving where analogies are more prominent. Experiments support the importance of images in human thinking, but many phenomena do not seem to involve images. Although the connectionist simulations described in chapter 7 are successful in accounting for a diverse range of psychological phenomena, it would be premature to suppose that all other kinds of models are unnecessary. The connectionist models apply well to cognitive tasks that are naturally understood in terms of incremental learning and parallel constraint satisfaction. But the generation of units and constraints may require rule-based and other mechanisms that connectionist models have not yet addressed.

It would be wonderful to have a unified theory of cognition that could account for all psychological phenomena observed so far. But progress can also be made locally, applying particular theories of representation and computation to particular psychological phenomena. Cognitive science has made substantial progress in developing rich computational models of many kinds of human performance observed in psychological experiments. Discovering how the various kinds of representation and thinking fit together will undoubtedly require more experiments as well as more integrated models of the sort discussed in chapter 14.

## Neurological Plausibility

When the first edition of this book appeared in 1996, there was considerable neurological evidence linking mental imagery with the visual system in the brain, but a lack of neurological evidence for logic, rules, concepts, and analogies. Thanks to new scanning techniques for observing the operations of the brain, cognitive neuroscience has been the fastest developing part of cognitive science. Chapters 2–5 of the current edition cite some relevant neurological studies. Connectionist models gain some neurological plausibility from the analogy between artificial neural networks and the brain, although current connectionist ideas are only rough approximations to how the brain works. Chapter 9 describes computational models that are more neurologically realistic.

## Practical Applicability

Constructing a unified cognitive theory requires reconciling the conflicting claims of various cognitive scientists who hold that the mind is fundamentally a rule-based system, or a connectionist system, and so on. But accomplishing practical goals of improving education, design, and intelligent systems can proceed in a more piecemeal fashion, selectively applying insights from different approaches to cognitive science wherever they appear relevant.

Potentially, cognitive science is to education what biology is to medicine: a theoretical basis for practical remedies. Conceptions of the mind as using rules, concepts (schemas), and analogies have already contributed to understanding how people solve problems. Images are also relevant to problem solving as is evident in the usefulness of diagrams in many domains. Connectionist ideas are just starting to have an impact on educational theory and practice, and conceiving of processes such as reading in terms of parallel constraint satisfaction suggests ways of improving teaching.

To date, understanding the process of design has been most furthered by attending to the roles of rules, concepts, analogies, and images in creative design. Most expert systems that have had industrial applications have been rule-based systems, but case-based (analogical) and connectionist systems are proving increasingly useful. A manager hoping to develop an intelligent system should look carefully at the nature of the task to be accomplished and the knowledge available, critically considering what kinds of representation and computation are most appropriate.

Some advocates of particular approaches to cognitive science boldly assert that the mind is a rule-based system, or that the mind is a connectionist system, and so on. The fact that all current accounts of representation and computation have disadvantages as well as advantages suggests the need for combinations and integrations of the various approaches (see chapter 14). Some critics of CRUM have argued, however, that all of these computational approaches are inherently limited in what they can tell us about the mind.

## Challenges for Cognitive Science

Review of the major approaches taken by advocates of CRUM shows that it explains much about the nature of human problem solving, learning, and language. Although CRUM has had considerable success in illuminating the nature of mind, there remain skeptics who believe that it is fundamentally misguided and neglects crucial aspects of thinking—for example, consciousness and emotional experience. Chapters 9–13 discuss seven important challenges for CRUM:

1 *The brain challenge*   CRUM ignores crucial facts about how thinking is performed by the brain.

2 *The emotion challenge*   CRUM neglects the important role of emotions in human thinking.

3 *The consciousness challenge*   CRUM ignores the importance of consciousness in human thinking.

4 *The body challenge*   CRUM neglects the contribution of the body to human thought and action.

5 *The world challenge*   CRUM disregards the significant role of physical environments in human thinking.

6 *The dynamic systems challenge*   The mind is a dynamic system, not a computational system.

7 *The social challenge*   Human thought is inherently social in ways that CRUM ignores.

These challenges pose serious problems for CRUM and for the whole enterprise of cognitive science. There are four possible responses to them:

1. *Deny* the claims that underlie the challenge.

2. *Expand CRUM* to enable it to deal with the problems posed by the challenge, adding new computational and representational ideas.

3. *Supplement CRUM* with noncomputational, nonrepresentational considerations that together with CRUM can meet the challenge.

4. *Abandon CRUM.*

I will argue that none of the challenges provides reason to abandon CRUM. Several of them show, however, that CRUM needs to be expanded and supplemented, particularly in ways that integrate it with biological and social factors. Supplementing is different from expanding in that it requires introducing concepts and hypotheses that go beyond the computational-representational explanation pattern. Chapters 9–14 describe numerous ways in which cognitive science is currently being expanded to deal with gaps in older versions of CRUM.

## The Mind–Body Problem

Because the challenges discussed in the following chapters raise important general questions about the nature of mind and body, it will be helpful first to outline the major philosophical views about how mind and body are related. The commonsense view of persons is that they consist of two components: a body and a mind. This view is called *dualism*, since it assumes that each of us consists of two fundamentally different substances, one physical and the other mental or spiritual. Anyone whose religious views imply that a person survives after death is a dualist, since the mind can survive the body's demise only if it is something nonphysical. Although dualism is probably the most widely held view of mind, it is philosophically problematic. What evidence do we have that there is mind independent of body? If mind and body are two different substances, how do they interact? Dualism makes mind a fundamentally mysterious entity beyond scientific investigation.

In contrast to dualism, *materialism* claims that mind is not a different kind of substance from the physical matter that constitutes the body. Philosophers have defended several versions of materialism. *Reductive materialism* claims that every mental state such as being conscious of the smell of donuts is a physical state of the brain. Thus, the mental can be reduced to the physical. More radically, *eliminative materialism* claims that we should not try to identify all the aspects of our mental experience with brain events, since our commonsense views of the mind may be fundamentally wrong. Instead, as neuroscience develops, we can hope to acquire a much richer theory of mind that may replace and eliminate commonsense notions such as consciousness and belief.

Both reductive and eliminative materialism assume that understanding the mind depends fundamentally on understanding the brain. However, the computational approach to mind has frequently been associated with a different view called *functionalism*, according to which mental states are not necessarily brain states, but rather are physical states that are related to each other through causal relations that can hold among various kinds of matter. For example, an intelligent robot might be viewed as having mental states even though its thinking depends on silicon chips rather than on biological neurons. Similarly, we might encounter intelligent aliens from other planets whose mental abilities depend on very different biological structures than human brains.

These four views—dualism, reductive materialism, eliminative materialism, and functionalism—have been the favorites in recent philosophy of mind. Another view, idealism, was popular in the nineteenth century. It holds that everything in the universe is mental and nothing is material.

### Summary

The Computational-Representational Understanding of Mind has contributed to much theoretical understanding and practical application. But no single approach has emerged as the clearly most powerful explanation of human cognitive capacities. Different approaches have different representational and computational advantages and disadvantages. Psychological plausibility is shared among various approaches that have successfully modeled different kinds of thinking. But CRUM faces challenges that charge it with neglecting important aspects of mind.

### Discussion Questions

1. What are the most impressive achievements of cognitive science? In what directions does it still have the furthest to go?

2. What other challenges does CRUM need to face?

3. What are the impediments to a unified theory of the mind? Will we ever have one? Would we want one?

## Notes

My preferred version of materialism is close to what Flanagan 1992 calls "constructive naturalism" and what Foss 1995 calls "methodological materialism." Paul Churchland (1989) and Patricia Smith Churchland 1986 defend eliminative materialism. On functionalism, see Johnson-Laird 1983 and Block 1978.

Alan Turing proposed an imitation game to answer the question of whether computers can think. In this game, which has come to be known as the Turing test, an investigator communicates by typing with both a person and a computer. If the investigator cannot tell which is the human and which is the computer, then we should judge the computer to be intelligent. This test is both too loose and too restrictive. It is too loose in that a cleverly constructed program might be able to fool us for a while even though it contains little intelligence. It is too restrictive in that the computer may fall short on some fairly trivial aspect of human experience but be capable of highly intelligent functioning in other areas.

Creativity is often cited as a challenge for CRUM, but earlier chapters described several mechanisms that can model some aspects of human creativity, including abduction, conceptual combination, and analogy. Another interesting challenge is whether CRUM, neuroscience, and/or the dynamic systems view discussed in chapter 12 explain why people dream (Flanagan 2000). Bruner (1990) poses what might be called the *narrative challenge*, claiming that computational and biological approaches to thinking neglect the importance of story interpretation in how people understand each other, but researchers such as Kintsch (1998) have much to say about narrative coherence.

# II   Extensions to Cognitive Science

# 9   Brains

You probably know that your ability to think depends on your brain, but understanding of how processes in the brain contribute to thought is relatively new. Some ancient Greek philosophers believed that the brain is one of three organs of thought, along with the heart and liver. But Aristotle argued that the brain is merely a cooling device for the heart, which he took to be the center of intellectual and perceptual functions (Finger 1994). This chapter reviews the main methods for investigating the nature of brains and how they contribute to thought, ranging from looking at the effects of brain damage to using machines to scan brain activities. It then discusses how discoveries about brain processes have enriched our understanding of the representations and computations that produce thinking. The chapter then considers the relevance of molecular processes involving neurotransmitters for understanding the relation between thought and brain, and discusses the practical applicability of knowledge about the brain, especially in the treatment of mental illness.

## How Brains Are Studied

### Brain Structure and Lesions

The first important method for studying brains was dissection, in which brains were carefully cut apart to reveal their anatomical structure. In the second century A.D., the Roman physician Galen described many brain structures based on the dissection of animals such as cows and baboons. The results of dissections on human brains were not reported until the sixteenth century when Vesalius provided detailed anatomical descriptions. He thought that the ventricles, which are open spaces in the brain, are crucial for thought because they produce "animal spirit" that is distributed to the nerves. Studying the anatomy of the brain does not by itself reveal much about its physiology—how it works.

Insights into the physiology of the brain and its relation to thought came about by the method of studying *lesions*, which are injuries to specific parts of the body. Lesions of the brain can occur naturally because of tumors, blood clots, or accidents; or they can be produced by cutting or burning. In the eighteenth century, lesion experiments on dogs revealed that breathing depends on a brain area called the *medulla*: damage to the area causes severe breathing problems. Early recognition that a human cognitive function depends on a specific brain area came in the 1860s when Paul Broca attributed a patient's inability to use language to a specific part of the brain's frontal lobes now called Broca's area. Since then, the contributions of many specific parts of the brain to particular cognitive functions have been discovered, as illustrated in figure 9.1. For example, people with damage to the hippocampus have difficulty forming new memories, and damage to the amygdala can cause inability to feel fear and other emotions.

### Electrical Recording and Stimulation
In 1875, Richard Caton reported the existence of electric currents in the brain that vary with different stimuli presented. This made it possible to

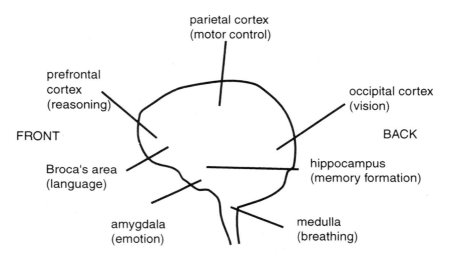

**Figure 9.1**
Some important brain areas, with their associated functions. For much more detailed maps, see the web sites listed at the end of this chapter.

determine what parts of the brain are active without having to rely on lesions. Today, electrical activity in the brain can be recorded by a machine called an *electroencephalograph*, or EEG for short. With an EEG, electrodes attached to the head detect electrical activity in different parts of the brain, and a history of this activity is transferred to a computer. EEGs can be used to monitor cognitive functions, and to diagnose brain disorders such as epilepsy, which is brought about by an abnormal electrical discharge of brain cells.

EEGs identify electrical activity in large regions of the brain, but the electrical activity of particular neurons can be identified using the technique of *single cell recording*. Electrodes are inserted into the brain to record the firing activity of specific neurons. For example, there are neurons in monkeys that respond to the texture of fat in the mouth, with especially high firing rates when the monkeys are given heavy cream (Rolls 1999, 34). Single cell recording is too invasive to be used routinely on humans, but is sometimes used during brain surgery to identify the contribution of particular neurons to specific cognitive functions.

Electrical activity in the brain can be stimulated as well as recorded—for example, during surgery by applying current to exposed parts of the brain. Less invasively, *transcranial electronic stimulation* is performed when electrodes are placed on the head to make current flow through the brain. Alternatively, *transcranial magnetic stimulation* applies powerful electromagnets to stimulate or disrupt brain activity.

### Brain Scans

Whereas EEGs can identify activity in large brain regions and single cell recording applies to individual neurons, neither method reveals much about small brain areas. In contrast, modern brain imaging technologies can identify activity in areas a few millimeters (less than 1/8 of an inch) across, comprising a few million out of the 100 billion or so neurons in the brain. The two technologies that are currently most useful are *positron emission tomography (PET)* and *magnetic resonance imaging (MRI)*.

In a PET scan, the subject is first injected with a radioactive material that spreads through the bloodstream. The most active parts of the body, including particular brain regions, require increased blood flow to nourish the cells that are producing a given activity. The PET scanner detects increases in radioactivity due to an increase in blood flow, thereby identifying groups of cells such as neurons that are most active. When you are given a particular mental task to perform, the PET scan is able to detect what parts of your brain are used to perform it. For example, if you are given a picture to look at, the PET scan will show increased blood flow to the primary visual cortex located at the back of your brain.

PET scanning has a number of limitations, including the use of radioactive material and the inability to localize activity to regions smaller than a cubic centimeter. Hence, it is now less commonly used than magnetic resonance imaging, which was originally developed to display the structure of parts of the body. With an MRI, the subject is inserted into a large magnet that generates signals from the hydrogen nuclei of water molecules in the body. The MRI machine detects these signals and uses computers to distinguish physical structures based on the different signals that they generate. For example, MRIs are often used to diagnose sports injuries by detecting changes to joints and other structures.

To investigate brain processes, specific magnetic pulses can be generated that enable the detection of changes in blood flow in a person performing a mental task; this is called *functional MRI*, or *fMRI*. Hence fMRI, like PET scans, can be used to identify brain regions with increased blood flow corresponding to increased neuronal activity. Images of the brain can be produced in a few seconds with a spatial resolution of a few millimeters. Unfortunately, fMRI does not have the temporal resolution of an electrical recording technique such as the EEG, which can detect changes in brain activity that take much less than a second. Nevertheless, fMRI studies have become crucial for helping to identify the specific brain regions involved in various kinds of thinking. For a history and review of techniques for brain mapping and imaging, see Savoy 2001 and Posner and Raichle 1994.

Now that techniques are available for identifying activity of brain regions and even of single neurons, do we still need the computational-representational understanding of mind? Why not explain thinking directly in terms of neuronal activity without talking about rules, concepts, and other representations? Why not focus on the kinds of physical processes found in the brain rather than on computational processes? To answer these questions, we need to examine how brains exhibit representational and computational properties.

## How Brains Represent

### Spiking Neurons

A representation is a structure that stands for something by virtue of relations such as similarity, causal history, and connections with other representations. For example, a photograph of you is a representation of you because it looks like you and because photography causally links it with you. The word "cat" is not similar to cats, but there is a causal link between utterances of this word and the presence of cats, as well as relations between the concept *cat* and other concepts. Let us look at how individual neurons and especially groups of neurons can serve as representations.

The artificial neurons (units) discussed in chapter 7 represent aspects of the world by means of numbers called activations that correspond roughly to the firing rates of real neurons. A typical neuron may fire hundreds of times per second, and we can think of it as representing a degree of presence or absence of what it represents. For example, if a unit represents the concept *cat*, then its firing many times per second signifies the presence of a cat. However, all natural and most artificial neural networks use distributed representations in which concepts are encoded by a population of neurons: a group of neurons represents a concept by virtue of a pattern of firing rates in all of the neurons. Thus a group of neurons, each with its own firing rate, can encode a large number of aspects of the world.

Focusing on firing rates, however, seriously underestimates the representational capacity of neurons and groups of neurons. The *spike train* of a neuron is its pattern of firing or not firing over a period of time. We can represent a spike train by a sequence of 1s (firing) and 0s (not firing). The spike train 10100 and 00011 both involve a neuron with a firing rate of 2 times out of 5, but they are different patterns. There are far more different spike trains than firing rates (see the notes at the end of this chapter). Thus, a group of neurons with varying spike trains has the capacity to encode an enormously large number of features of the world. See Maass and Bishop 1999 for analysis of the representational and computational capacities of spiking neurons, and Eliasmith and Anderson 2003 for an elegant analysis of neural representation.

We have seen that a single neuron can represent a feature of the world as the result of being tuned to fire more rapidly when that feature is presented. More powerful neural representations arise if the neuron can encode more possibilities by using the temporal properties of different spike trains, and if the neuron is part of a population of neurons that work together to represent many features. In sum, a representation in the brain is a population of neurons whose firing patterns encode information by virtue of having acquired regular responses to particular kinds of input.

## Brain Maps

The brain does not try to use all of its billions of neurons to represent everything; different brain regions represent different kinds of sensory stimuli. For example, the visual cortex at the back of the brain has neurons that respond to different visual inputs. There are neuronal groups whose firing patterns correspond spatially to the structure of the input—for example, when a column of neurons fires together to represent the fact that a line is part of the visual stimulus. Thus, different parts of the brain have groups of neurons that fire when different kinds of visual, olfactory (smell), taste, auditory, and tactile stimuli are presented. The human brain can do a lot more than just represent stimuli presented to it, because a group of neurons can respond to inputs from many groups of neurons. This can produce a combined representation of what the input neurons represent. For example, there are regions in the frontal cortex of monkeys where the sensory modalities of taste, vision, and smell converge, enabling the representation of fruits and their key properties (Rolls 1999). It is clear, therefore, that the brain is a superb representational device.

## How Brains Compute

## Transformations

But is the brain a computer? The most familiar kinds of computation involve rules for transforming symbols—for example, calculating that $2 + 2 = 4$ and inferring $q$ from $p$ and *if p then q*. Such computations are transformations of representations. The brain can also be viewed as performing transformations of representations encoded by the firing patterns of neurons. In general, a physical system is a computational system "when its physical states can be seen as representing states of some other systems, where transitions between its states can be explained as operations on the representations" (Churchland and Sejnowski 1992, 62). To put it in a slogan: *No computation without representation*. From this perspective, digital computers and brains are two different kinds of computational system.

Consider, for example, the operations of your visual system. At the back of your eye is the *retina*, millions of cells that are sensitive to light. Retinal cells respond to light reflected from objects into your eye, and send signals through a series of layers to neurons in the visual cortex. Successive layers in the cortex detect more and more complex aspects of the objects that originally sent light into the eye, as neurons in each layer abstract and transform the firing patterns of neurons in the preceding layer. Thus, the visual cortex progressively constructs representations of lines, patterns in two dimensions, and finally three-dimensional colored objects.

The brain transforms neuronal representations into new ones by means of synaptic connections. As we saw in chapter 7, the firing of one neuron can excite or inhibit the firing of another neuron. Hence, one group of neurons with its patterns of firing can alter the patterns of firing of another group of neurons to which it is connected by means of synapses between pairs of neurons. There can also be feedback connections from one group of neurons to another, enabling them to influence each other. The brain contains many such feedback influences. In general, computation in the brain consists of interactions between groups of neurons that produce transformations of firing patterns.

### Integration

The brain's operation is much more complicated than simply taking sensory input and transforming it. In order to eat a banana, a monkey needs to combine visual, tactile, and other kinds of information about it, and then use this integrated information to guide actions such as ingesting it. Hence, much of what the brain does involves operations in central brain areas that combine information from multiple other areas. At the level of individual neurons, we can describe computation in terms of the ideas about activation, excitation, and inhibition presented in chapter 7, but a full understanding of the computational accomplishments of brains requires attention to the higher level operations of transformation and integration just described. Figure 9.2 depicts some of the interconnections of the prefrontal cortex (the front of the front of the cortex) with many other brain areas. Chapter 10 describes a computational model of emotion according to which the brain makes emotional judgments by combining

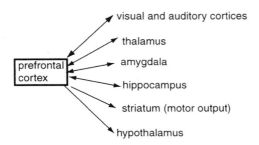

**Figure 9.2**
Inputs and outputs from prefrontal cortex. Based on Groenewegen and Uylings (2000). Note that connections usually go in both directions. Many connections between the other areas are not shown. See figure 9.1 for a better picture of the spatial organization of the brain.

information from the frontal cortex (high-level thought), the amygdala (bodily information), and the hippocampus (memory).

### Learning

One of the most impressive computational accomplishments of neural networks is learning, in which changes in the synaptic weights between neurons produce major improvements in the performance of the network. However, networks trained by the backpropagation algorithm discussed in chapter 7 exhibit a problem called *catastrophic interference* (McCloskey and Cohen 1989). This happens when a network is trained to perform one task, such as forming associations between words, and then trained to perform another similar task. When people undergo such retraining, they usually experience only some loss of the ability to perform the first task, but artificial neural networks can suffer a dramatic drop in performance on the first task when they learn the second.

McClelland, McNaughton, and O'Reilly (1995) argue that the brain's solutions to this problem is to have two complementary learning systems in two different brain regions, the hippocampus and the neocortex (the most recently evolved part of the cortex). The hippocampal system permits rapid learning of new items, whereas the neocortex learns slowly by small adjustments of synaptic strengths through something like the backpropagation algorithm. As illustrated in figure 9.3, initial storage of most information takes place in the hippocampus, and is only gradually consolidated in the neocortical system. Catastrophic interference is avoided because new

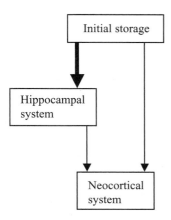

**Figure 9.3**
A two-system model of memory storage. Adapted with permission from McClelland, McNaughton, and O'Reilly 1995, p. 444.

information coming into the hippocampus has only a small and gradual effect on the neocortex, which retains most of what it already knew. Because learning depends on two different interconnected systems operating with different learning procedures, understanding of neural computation requires specification of the operations of multiple regions.

Thus, it is not metaphorical to say that the brain represents and computes, even though its computations are done differently from the kinds most familiar to us in modern digital computers. Understanding of how brains work requires attention to the roles played by particular brain regions such as the hippocampus and prefrontal cortex. Hence, we should not think of the brain as one big connectionist network of the sort described in chapter 7, but rather as a highly organized and interconnected system of specialized neural networks. This section has only begun to sketch the computational activities of brains; see Churchland and Sejnowski 1992 and Eliasmith and Anderson 2003 for much more detailed discussions.

## How Molecules Matter

If you have you ever had a cup of coffee or an alcoholic drink, then you have experienced the effects of chemicals on the brain. Coffee contains caffeine, which blocks the action of the molecule adenosine, which makes people drowsy by inhibiting the firing of some neurons. Hence, caffeine increases neuronal activity and keeps you awake. In contrast, alcohol can disrupt mental functioning by inhibiting the action of the molecule glutamate, which excites neurons. Both caffeine and alcohol also increase activity of the chemical dopamine, which produces feelings of pleasure. Adenosine, glutamate, and dopamine are all neurotransmitters, molecules that enable one neuron to influence another.

All the models of neurons and brains described earlier in this book are based on electrical activity: neurons fire and provide electrical inputs to other neurons. However, as caffeine and alcohol illustrate, the direct effects of real neurons on each other are chemical as well as electrical, in that molecules are emitted from one neuron and then passed over to another neuron, where they initiate chemical reactions that generate the electrical activity of the stimulated neuron. Figure 9.4 depicts how neurotransmitters are passed from the axon of one neuron to the dendrite of another neuron.

There are dozens of neurotransmitters operating in the human brain, some with excitatory and others with inhibitory effects. This operation is consistent with the general connectionist ideas described in chapter 7, which assumed excitatory and inhibitory links between neurons. But broader chemical effects on neural computation are produced by hormones such as estrogen and testosterone, which can affect the firing of neurons independent of direct connections. A neuron in one part of the brain such as the hypothalamus may fire and release a hormone that travels to a part of the body such as the adrenal glands, which stimulates the release of other hormones that then travel back to the brain and influence the firing of different neurons. Complex feedback loops can result, involving interactions between the neurotransmitter control of hormone

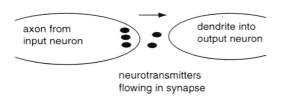

**Figure 9.4**
Neurotransmitter molecules flowing from one neuron into another.

release and the hormonal regulation of neurotransmitter release. These feedback loops can also involve the immune system, because brain cells also have receptors for cytokines, which are protein messengers produced by immune system cells such as macrophages. Thus, attention to the neurochemistry of hormones shows an important limitation to connectionist models, in that whether a neuron fires is not just a function of neurons that have synaptic inputs to it (see Thagard 2002 for further discussion).

**Practical Applicability**

Motivations for studying brains are both theoretical—how does it work?—and practical—how can we help it to work better? Many advances have been made in understanding how mental problems can arise from defects in the functioning of different brain areas and neurotransmitters. For example, children with attention deficit disorder have difficulty concentrating and often fall behind in school. They are generally treated with Ritalin, which stimulates areas of the brain involved in filtering information by increasing the activity of neurotransmitters such as dopamine.

The growth of different brain areas can help to explain variations in behavior as people age. In the past decade, brain scans of children and teenagers have revealed that the brain undergoes remarkable growth at roughly the ages of 1–2 and 11–12 years. The latter growth spurt was a big surprise to researchers, and is generating new explanations of why many teenagers display difficult and risky behavior (Strauch 2003). Areas of the prefrontal cortex are not fully developed until the early twenties, so that teenagers' decisions are often heavily driven by emotional information in the amygdala, rather than by reasoning about potential risks. They may, for example, take drugs such as ecstasy and cocaine, which provide short-term pleasure by intensely stimulating production of dopamine, but lead to addiction as the result of depletion of dopamine receptors that produces cravings for higher and higher doses.

Neurotransmitters and brain areas are also relevant to explaining many mental illnesses. Schizophrenia, in which people lose touch with reality because of bizarre beliefs and hallucinations, is associated with excess dopamine activity in the prefrontal cortex. Drugs that block dopamine reduce the symptoms of schizophrenia. On the other hand, lack of dopamine can produce the problems with motor control found in

Parkinson's disease. Depression is often treated with Prozac and other drugs that increase the availability of the excitatory neurotransmitter serotonin by decreasing its reuptake in synapses.

## Summary

The early decades of cognitive science, and even the connectionist models of the 1980s, largely ignored how brains produce thinking. But since the 1990s the brain challenge has been increasingly answered by experimental and computational investigations of how brains work. Brain scanning techniques such as PET and fMRI have provided a huge amount of information concerning how different brain regions contribute to various cognitive functions. Computational models of the brain have become biologically richer, both with respect to employing more realistic neurons such as ones that spike, and with respect to simulating the interactions between different areas of the brain such as the hippocampus and the cortex. These models are not strictly an alternative to computational accounts in terms of logic, concepts, rules, images, and connections, but should mesh with them and show how mental functioning performs at the neural level. The remarks on neurological plausibility in chapters 2–6 show that such meshing is rapidly progressing.

Moreover, there is increasing understanding of the chemical functioning of brains, in particular how different neurotransmitters and hormones affect neuronal firing. These advances do not require abandonment of the general view of thinking as representation and computation, but they do show the need to expand and supplement earlier cognitive theories.

Understanding of brain mechanisms is invaluable for explaining and treating mental illness. The explanation schema for kinds of mental illness such as schizophrenia is as follows:

Explanation target

Why do people have a particular kind of mental illness?

Explanatory pattern

People usually have normal brain function that involve identifiable brain structures and neurotransmitters.

Defects to these brain structures and chemical processes can disrupt normal functioning.

These defects produce the symptoms of the mental illness.

Many mental illnesses are treated by means of drugs that help to restore or approximate the normal functioning of chemical-electrical processes in the brain. The dramatic advances in neuroscience of recent decades do not by themselves solve the mind–body problem, since a skeptic can always maintain that there are aspects of mind such as consciousness that will never succumb to scientific explanation. But we will see in the next two chapters that even questions about the nature of emotions and con-sciousness are increasingly yielding to neurological investigation.

## Discussion Questions

1. How do different methods reveal different aspects of brain structure and function?

2. What is the relation between brain structures and the kinds of repre-sentation discussed in chapters 2–7?

3. Is brain processing really computation?

4. To understand brains, is it necessary to move down to the molecular and chemical level?

5. What aspects of thinking seem to be hardest to explain in terms of brain structures and processes?

## Further Reading

See Finger 1994 for a readable history of neuroscience. Kandel, Schwartz, and Jessell 2000 is a standard neuroscience textbook. Allman 1999 dis-cusses brain evolution. O'Reilly and Munakata 2000 describes computa-tional models for cognitive neuroscience. Churchland 2002 and Bechtel et al. 2001 provide philosophical discussions of neuroscience.

## Web Sites

Explore the brain and spinal cord: http://faculty.washington.edu/chudler/introb.html

*Science Daily* (mind and brain news): http://www.sciencedaily.com/news/mind_summaries.php

The Whole Brain Atlas: http://www.med.harvard.edu/AANLIB/home.html

## Notes

If a neuron fires up to 100 times per second, then there are 101 possible firing rates it can have, including 0. The average firing rate of the neuron might be, for example, 25 or 50 times per second. A group of 1000 neurons can then represent a huge number of possibilities, $100^{1000}$. For spiking neurons, there are $2^{100}$ different possible spike trains compared to only 101 different firing rates. The number of different possible combinations of spike trains in a group of 1000 neurons is therefore astronomical: $(2^{100})^{1000}$.

Chapter 3 mentions the debate between the view that many rules and concepts are innate and the alternative view that emphasizes learning. A related debate concerns the extent to which brain structures have been selected by biological evolution for specific functions. Evolutionary psychologists claim that the brain contains a large number of evolved computational devices that are specialized in function, such as a face recognition system, a language acquisition device, navigation specializations, and a routine for detecting cheaters in social situations (Cosmides and Tooby 1999). In contrast, Quartz and Sejnowski (2002) argue that the brain has evolved to make possible flexible learning: the main representational features of cortex are built from the dynamic interaction between neural growth mechanisms and environmentally derived neural activity.

# 10 Emotions

How do you feel about the following items? *Group A*: death, cancer, poison, traffic tickets, insults, vomit. *Group B*: lottery winnings, fine restaurants, sex, victories, babies, parties. For most people, the things in group A are associated with negative emotions such as sadness, fear, and anger, whereas the things in group B are associated with happiness and pleasure. If you think of the main events of your day so far, you will probably be able to recall the emotions that accompanied them—for example, the joy you felt when your sports team won, or the worry you felt when you realized that exams are coming soon.

Traditionally, cognitive science ignored the study of emotions, seeing it as a side issue to the more central study of cognition. Philosophers as far back as Plato have tended to view emotion as a distraction or impediment to effective thought. In the past decade, however, there has been a dramatic increase in the appreciation of the relevance of emotion to cognition, particularly with respect to decision making. On the old view, decisions can be made either rationally or emotionally, and cognitive science is mainly concerned with the rational ones. In contrast, the view now emerging is that emotions are an inherent part of even rational decision making. This chapter will describe how emotions contribute to both representation and computation. But first we need to discuss the nature of emotion.

## What Are Emotions?

Everyone is familiar with basic emotions such as happiness, sadness, fear, anger, disgust, and surprise. But there is much disagreement among cognitive scientists concerning the nature of emotions. Favored theories fall into two general camps; one viewing emotions largely as judgments about a person's general state and the other instead emphasizing bodily reactions. Suppose you were driving a car this morning and another driver suddenly cut in front of you and made you veer rapidly to the side of the road. Probably your first reaction would be fear, followed by anger at the driver who cut you off. According to the view of emotions as judgments, your fear would have consisted primarily of an inference that you were at risk of bodily harm, violating your goal of staying alive and healthy. Similarly, your anger would have consisted of a judgment that the other driver was responsible for putting you in danger. Proponents of the view that emotions are primarily judgments include Oatley (1992), Nussbaum (2001), and Scherer, Schorr, and Johnstone (2001).

Keith Oatley (1992) describes how basic human emotions are intimately connected with goal accomplishment. People are happy when their goals are being accomplished, and sad when they are not. If you do well on an exam or in a job interview, or if you get invited to a party, happiness derives from this satisfaction of your professional and social goals. Failure to satisfy such goals can produce disappointment and sadness. People become angry at whatever frustrates their goals—for example, someone stealing your parking space. You experience fear when your survival goals are threatened, as when a truck comes skidding toward your car. Disgust reflects a violation of your eating goals, as when someone offers you a chocolate-covered cockroach to eat. We can therefore see emotions as involving a very general representation of a person's overall problem-solving situation.

Why should such a general representation be used? Why not simply have verbal or visual representations that display the current status of goal accomplishment? Oatley points out that human problem solving is often very complex, in that it involves multiple conflicting goals to be accomplished, rapidly changing environments, and rich social interactions. Emotions provide a summary *appraisal* of your problem-solving situation that makes two important contributions to subsequent thinking. Appraisal that certain aspects of your situation are extremely important to your goals can lead you to *focus* on those aspects, concentrating your limited cognitive resources on what matters. Moreover, emotions provide readiness for *action*, ensuring that you will be spurred to deal with your problem-solving situation rather than being lost in thought (Frijda 1986). Thus, emotions are not just incidental, annoying features of human thought, but have important cognitive functions concerned with appraisal, focus, and action.

Because emotions play a role in human thought and action, explaining why people do what they do often requires us to refer to emotional states. "He slammed his fist into the wall because he was angry." "She was smiling all day because she was ecstatic at being admitted to medical school." Sometimes, emotion-based explanation goes beyond verbal representation when we understand other people's emotions by imagining ourselves in their situation and experiencing an emotion that approximates to what they feel. This kind of understanding is called *empathy*. It is based on analogical thinking where you develop a mapping between someone else's situation and your own that actually produces in you some image of the emotion that the other person is experiencing (Barnes and Thagard 1997).

In contrast to the view of emotions as appraisals, the opposing view emphasizes bodily reactions rather than cognitive judgments. When a driver cuts you off, you probably experience physiological changes such as increases in your heart beat, breathing rate, and blood pressure. On the physiological view, your fear and anger consist of your brain reacting to these physiological changes rather than making a judgment about your general situation. The view that emotions are largely a matter of physiological reactions originated with William James (1884). Damasio (1994) refers to the signals that the body sends to the brain concerning physiological factors as *somatic markers*.

There is no need to choose between a cognitive theory of emotions as judgments and a physiological theory of emotions as neurological reactions to bodily changes. Morris (2002) uses recent discoveries about neural functioning to argue that emotions depend on *interaction* between bodily signals and cognitive appraisals. What needs to be developed is a neuro-computational theory that shows how your emotions can involve both judgments about how the current situation is affecting your goals and neurological assessments of your body's reaction to that situation. I will describe such a theory below in the section on emotional computation, and extend it to consciousness in chapter 11.

Emotions such as fear, anger, and happiness involve reactions to particular situations: you are happy that you got a good grade on an exam, or angry that a friend failed to meet you as planned. In contrast, moods are much more long lasting and less directed toward particular situations.

You can be in a good or bad mood for hours, without there being a particular thing or event that you are in a good or bad mood about. Psychologists use the term *affect* (with the emphasis on the first syllable) to encompass emotion, mood, and sometimes also motivation.

### Representing Emotions

What do emotions add to your ability to represent the world? From the representational theories described in chapters 2–9, it might seem that there is no need for a person or robot to have any mental structures beyond propositions, concepts, rules, analogies, images, and distributed representations. But tying these kinds of mental structures to emotions provides an efficient way to guide action. If you react to the prospect of eating sheep brains with disgust, then you do not need to do a lot of inference in order to decide what to do when you are offered some. In contrast, if your emotional association with ice cream is highly positive, then you will be strongly inclined to eat it. As my group A and B examples at the beginning of this chapter show, we have positive and negative associations with many concepts.

Fazio (2001) reviews a large body of psychological experiments concerning the automatic activation of emotional attitudes attached to concepts. In these experiments, participants are given a word such as "cockroach" intended to prime a negative or positive attitude. They are then given an evaluative word such as "disgusting" and are asked to indicate as quickly as possible whether the word meant "good" or "bad." Many experiments have found that people are faster to answer when the prime concept fits emotionally with the evaluative word. For example, "cockroach" followed by "disgusting" produces a quicker response to "bad" than does "chocolate" followed by "disgusting." It therefore seems that emotional evaluations are closely tied in with the representation of concepts and objects.

People also have emotional associations with many propositions, analogs, and images. Depending on your nationality and interest in sports, the proposition that Canada won the 2002 Olympic ice hockey championship might be associated with excitement, disappointment, or boredom. Similarly, your attitude toward different rules that you have learned is probably represented not by some abstract numerical value like strength but by emotions that you associate with them. For example, the rule *IF you avoid early morning classes, THEN you can sleep more* is probably associated with happiness and relief. Analogs describe more complex situations than simple propositions and rules, but also can be associated with emotions. If you remember taking a course in which boring material and a demanding professor caused you to get a bad grade, then your memory of the course is probably associated with emotions such as disappointment and even anger. Any analogous course will prompt similar emotions that will steer you away from taking it. Images can also have positive and negative emotions: contrast your reaction to a hideous face from a horror movie with your reaction to the smiling face of your favorite movie star.

Different emotions can be distinguished with respect to two main dimensions: pleasure and arousal. Figure 10.1 charts some important emotions with respect to these two dimensions. Where would you place yourself on this wheel right now? Presumably, both the pleasant–unpleasant dimension and the aroused–unaroused dimension correlate with bodily reactions, and high arousal corresponds to more extreme physiological

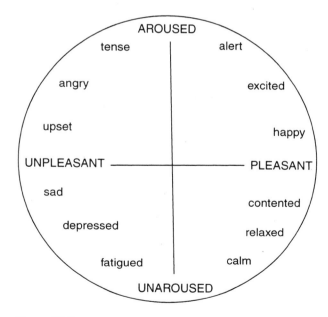

**Figure 10.1**
The structure of emotions with respect to pleasantness and intensity.

changes. But the dimensions should also correlate with cognitive appraisal of the situation that prompts the emotion, as when anger depends on realization that someone is thwarting your goals.

It is clear that emotions are represented in the brain, but it is much harder to say *how* they are represented. We have verbal concepts such as *happy*, *sad*, and *angry*, but there is a lot more to emotional thinking than just a connection between these concepts and other representations. A local neural network representation like the ones described in chapter 7 could have an excitatory link between a unit representing *ice cream* and a unit such as *happy*, but treating an emotion as just another concept conceals its links with judgment, physiology, and feeling. More plausibly, we should think of an emotion as a representation involving a pattern of activation across many neurons, as in the distributed representations discussed in chapters 7 and 9. Better yet, the neurons across which emotions are distributed should have connections to many different brain areas, including the ones involved in cognitive judgments, such as the prefrontal cortex, and the ones that receive inputs from bodily states, such as the amygdala. From this perspective, an emotion is a pattern of activation in a population of neurons with connections to both inferential and sensory brain areas. The next section will describe a computational model of how this might work.

## Computing Emotions

I once overheard the following conversation between two leading cognitive scientists. "Tell me, Maggie, could a machine have emotions?" "Well, Gordon, I'm a machine, and I have emotions." This response seems odd, because we do not usually think of people as machines or think of machines as having emotions. There are several positions to consider about the relevance of emotions to computation:

1. Emotions have nothing to do with computation.

2. Computers can be used to model emotional processing in the brain, but emotion is not really computational.

3. Emotions can be a general function of computational intelligence, so they can arise in any sufficiently complex computer or robot.

4. Emotions arise from the particular kinds of computation performed by the brain.

There is not yet conclusive evidence for any of these positions, but I think that the last one is the most plausible. Hence, the computational-representational understanding of mind should be expanded using neurological findings to encompass emotions.

The simplest way to introduce emotions into a computational model is to add emotion nodes to the kind of local connectionist network described in chapter 7. Nerb and Spada (2001) present a computational account of how media information about environmental problems influences cognition and emotion. When people hear about an environmental accident, they may respond with a variety of emotions such as sadness and anger. Following the appraisal theory of emotions, Nerb and Spada hypothesize that a negative event will lead to sadness if it is caused by situational forces outside of anyone's control. But an environmental accident will lead to anger if someone is responsible for the negative event. If people see themselves as responsible for the negative event, then they feel shame; but if people see themselves as responsible for a positive event, they feel pride. Nerb and Spada (2001) show how determinants of responsibility such as agency, controllability of the cause, motive of the agent, and knowledge about possible negative consequences can be incorporated into a coherence network called ITERA (Intuitive Thinking in Environmental Risk Appraisal).

ITERA is an extension of the impression-formation model of Kunda and Thagard (1996). The main innovation in ITERA is the addition of units corresponding to emotions such as anger and sadness, as shown in figure 10.2. ITERA is given input concerning whether or not an accident was observed to involve damage, human agency, controllability, and other factors. It then predicts a reaction of sadness or anger depending on their overall coherence with the observed features of the accident. This reaction can be thought of as a kind of emotional summary of all the available information.

Another way to introduce emotion into local neural networks is found in the HOTCO (hot coherence) model of Thagard (2000, 2003). This model differs from other neural network models in that each unit is given a valence, representing its emotional value, in addition to the normal activation, representing its applicability to the current situation. For example, the proposition that you have an exam tomorrow might get a high activation representing its truth and a negative valence representing how you

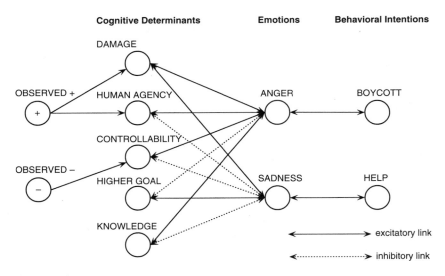

**Figure 10.2**
ITERA network for emotional reactions to environmental accidents. Solid lines are
excitatory links, and dashed lines are inhibitory links. This example represents a situation in which a media report states that there is damage caused by human agency
that could not have been controlled. Reprinted with permission from Nerb and
Spada 2001, p. 528.

feel about it. Valences spread through a network much like activations
providing an overall emotional assessment of a thing, concept, or
situation.

The ITERA and HOTCO models are unrealistic neurologically in the key
respects discussed in chapters 7 and 9: they use local units that are not like
real neurons, and they neglect the division of the brain into functional
areas. Both these limitations are overcome in the GAGE neurocomputational model of emotional decision making (Wagar and Thagard 2004).
GAGE is named in honor of Phineas Gage, a nineteenth-century railroad
worker who suffered brain damage because of a pipe that penetrated his
skull. Amazingly, he survived his injury and regained his verbal and mathematical abilities, but became incapable of making sensible decisions about
his work and personal life. Damasio (1994) describes modern patients with
similar problems, and hypothesizes that they have lost the ability to make
effective decisions because of disruptions in connections between the emotional and cognitive parts of their brain.

The particular brain area affected in Phineas Gage and similar patients is called the ventromedial (bottom-middle) prefrontal cortex, which provides links between areas of the cortex involved in judgments (the amygdala) and areas involved in emotions and memory (the hippocampus). Wagar and Thagard (2004) show how Gage's deficit and related psychological behavior can be modeled using groups of spiking neurons corresponding to each of the crucial brain areas: the ventromedial prefrontal cortex, the amygdala, and the nucleus accumbens, a region strongly associated with rewards (it is also heavily associated with addiction to drugs and alcohol). The structure of this model is shown in figure 10.3. The GAGE model uses distributed representations of input stimuli and associated emotions, and relies on the spiking properties of neurons to provide temporal coordination of the activities of different brain areas. It is thus much more neurologically realistic than either the ITERA or HOTCO models.

When GAGE operates fully as shown in figure 10.3, the nucleus accumbens serves to integrate emotional and cognitive information from different parts of the brain. But when the model is "lesioned" by disrupting the neurons corresponding to the ventromedial prefrontal cortex, the model behaves like Phineas Gage and the Damasio patients, failing to integrate cognitive and emotional information. GAGE is not a full model of cognitive/emotional processing, but it shows how a such a model can take into

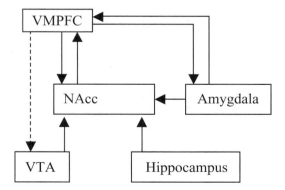

**Figure 10.3**
The GAGE model of emotional decision making, reprinted with permission from Wagar and Thagard (2004). VTA is the ventral tegmental area, VMPFC is the ventromedial prefrontal cortext, and Nacc is the nucleus accumbens.

account both the cognitive aspects of judgment and appraisal performed by the prefrontal cortex and the physiological input mediated by the amygdala. Notice that the connections in figure 10.3 among the ventromedial prefrontal cortex, nucleus accumbens, and amygdala are all bidirectional, suggesting that interaction is the right way of thinking about the relation between cognitive and physiological aspects of emotion. Thus the GAGE model shows how to integrate both cognitive appraisal and somatic marker theories of emotions.

The three models described in this section are clearly just models: no one would claim that ITERA, HOTCO, or GAGE really have emotions. The problem is not just that they lack conscious experience of emotion (see the discussion of consciousness in chapter 11), but also that they clearly do not have the bodily inputs that are a crucial part of human emotions. The GAGE model takes for granted that the amygdala collects information about bodily states, but as a computer model it does not really have any bodily input. Because robot bodies are so different from human ones, I doubt that computers and robots will ever have emotions at all like humans: see the discussions of bodies in chapter 12 and the ethical implications of artificial intelligence in chapter 14. Nevertheless, it is not implausible to describe the brain as a kind of emotional computer that integrates emotional and other sorts of information to enable people to make decisions. Psychological, neurological, and neurocomputational understanding of how emotions influence thinking is rapidly developing, so cognitive science is clearly responding well to the emotion challenge, in keeping with its response to the brain challenge.

What does the explosion of work on the neuroscience of emotions tell us about the philosophical positions in chapter 8 concerning the mind-body problem? As more and more is understood about the neurology of emotion and cognition, the dualist view that mind is sharply separate from brain becomes less and less credible. In addition, the functionalist view that mind is a purely computational construct independent of physical realization is becoming less plausible: human minds depend much more directly on human brains and bodies than functionalists would allow. Cognitive science is thus providing support for some version of brain-based materialism, while still needing to deal with the problem of consciousness discussed in chapter 11. A theory of emotions is woefully incomplete if it cannot explain why we experience *feelings* such as happiness and sadness.

Functionalists could reply that as computer power continues to increase it should become possible to develop hardware and software that duplicate the structure and function of the brain to such an extent that computers do not just model emotions, they *have* them. There are already sophisticated computer models of thousands of neurons, so why not just expand them to billions of neurons organized into the relevant brain areas? Such models will be very useful, but they will inevitably simplify the extremely complex biological functioning of the brain. Currently, it is not technically feasible to model in full chemical and biological detail the operation of a single cell, let alone the complex of neurons with electrical and chemical signaling that comprise the brain. Therefore, although emotions can be simulated computationally and can plausibly be viewed as part of the computational aspect of the brain, it is unlikely that we will ever build a machine that duplicates human emotions. The ethical implications of this limitation are discussed in chapter 14.

**Practical Applicability**

In keeping with recent dramatic advances in experimental and theoretical research on emotion, there has been a sharp rise in investigations of the significance of emotion for many practical areas, including design, management, and the study of mental illness. Donald Norman, one of the most influential thinkers on the nature of design of computers and other artifacts, has a new book emphasizing the importance of emotion for design (Norman 2003). His slogan is: *Attractive things work better.* For example, he describes an experiment performed in both Japan and Israel comparing the ease of use of two forms of automated bank teller machines. Both forms were identical in function, but only one had the button and screens arranged attractively. People found that the attractive ones were easier to use, which suggests that beauty and function are interconnected. Norman argues that emotions change the ways that people solve problems, so designers should take emotions into account when they produce objects intended for human use.

Emotion is starting to be considered as an element in the design of intelligent computers. Picard (1997) advocates *affective computing*, which is computing that relates to, arises from, or deliberately influences emotions. She notes the importance of emotion in human communication, and argues for the value of giving a computer the ability to recognize, express, and respond intelligently to human emotions. For example, learning can be a highly emotional experience: think of times when you have been bored stiff by a lecture, or when you have been excited and inspired by a dynamic teacher. We can expect a computer tutor to be much more effective if it can recognize the emotional state of the learners it is supposed to teach.

Understanding how emotions influence human thinking is also important for improving human decision making. Psychologists are increasingly appreciating that decision making is an emotional process as well as a cognitive one (Loewenstein et al. 2001). Finucane, Peters, and Slovic (2003) review evidence that judgments and decisions are influenced by positive and negative evaluations attached to mental images of different situations. For example, affect-laden imagery contributes to preferences for investing in new companies in the stock market and adolescents' decisions to choose between health-threatening or health-enhancing behaviors such as smoking or exercise. This research is consistent with the view of Damasio discussed earlier that emotion is an inherent and ineliminable part of human decision making. Hence, if you want to help people to make better decisions, it is crucial to take their emotions into account.

Understanding of emotions is also an essential component of professional success. Goleman (1995) advocates *emotional intelligence* as a complement to traditional notions of intelligence as purely cognitive. He describes how success in any social situation requires the ability to recognize and regulate one's own emotions as well as the emotions of others. Successful leaders need to be capable of empathy for others and able to inspire them by providing motivating emotions.

Finally, understanding of emotion is important for diagnosing and treating mental illnesses that involve emotional disturbances, such as schizophrenia and bipolar disorder (manic-depressive disorder). The causes of such disturbances are increasingly being identified at the molecular level, involving neurotransmitters such as dopamine and serotonin. Serotonin is a particularly important neurotransmitter that affects many kinds of behavior. Millions of people have been prescribed the drug Prozac for problems that range from depression to obsessive-compulsive disorder to excessive anger (Kramer 1993). Although side effects have been widespread, many people report substantial improvement in their emotional states as the result of Prozac therapy. Prozac increases serotonin uptake, making the neurotransmitter more readily available to particular neurons. Emotional changes such as falling in love involve neurotransmitters such as dopamine and hormones such as oxytocin. Hence, anyone interested in increasing understanding of the role of emotions in human thought and mental illness has to pay attention to evolving knowledge about the mental effects of different neurochemicals. Brain anatomy is similarly relevant: Davidson et al. (2002) review research that identifies regions of the brains involved in depression, including the prefrontal cortex, the hippocampus, and the amygdala.

## Summary

In contrast to the early decades of cognitive science, current research in psychology, neuroscience, and even artificial intelligence is seriously concerned with emotions. There is increasing recognition that mental representations are often associated with emotional evaluations that contribute to many cognitive processes, especially decision making. Brain areas that support emotional processing include the amygdala and the prefrontal cortex. Computational models are being developed that show how decision making and problem solving integrate emotions with other kinds of information. Understanding of emotions is also contributing to practical applications such as design, education, management, and mental health. Appreciation of emotions does not require abandonment of the computational-representational understanding of mind, but expands and supplements it in valuable ways that takes into account the detailed structure and functioning of the brain, right down to the molecular level of neurotransmitters. Emotion is highly relevant to the social nature of cognition, which is discussed in chapter 13.

## Discussion Questions

1. Can emotions be thought of as representations?
2. Do emotions get in the way of human thinking, or do they contribute to it? Would you want to have an emotionectomy?
3. What would it take to give a robot emotions?
4. How do emotions influence your education and work?

**Further Reading**

Research on emotion is highly diverse. For general reviews, see Davidson, Scherer, and Goldsmith 2003 and Lewis and Haviland-Jones 2000. Oatley and Jenkins 1996 surveys the psychology of emotions. On the neuroscience of emotions, see LeDoux 1996, Panksepp 1998, and Rolls 1999. Wierzbicka 1999 discusses emotion words in many languages. For philosophical discussion of emotions, see Griffiths 1997 and Nussbaum 2001.

**Web Sites**

The Emotion home page: http://emotion.salk.edu/emotion.html

Affective computing at MIT: http://affect.media.mit.edu/

University of Birmingham cognition and affect project: http://www.cs.bham.ac.uk/~axs/cogaff.html

Geneva emotion research group: http://www.unige.ch/fapse/emotion/

Kismet, a robot that models emotions: http://www.ai.mit.edu/projects/humanoid-robotics-group/kismet/kismet.html

# 11 Consciousness

What are you conscious of right now? You must be seeing this book, and maybe you are also listening to music. Perhaps you have not eaten in a while, so you are feeling hungry. I hope that you are interested rather than bored, and that your emotional state is pleasant. Consciousness includes these kinds of sensory and emotional experiences, as well as the basic awareness that you are reading a book.

No question in cognitive science is more challenging, or more fascinating, than the nature of consciousness. Until recently, the study of consciousness was usually considered a matter for philosophy rather than science, but there has been an explosion in the past decade of theories and experiments concerning how consciousness works. No consensus has emerged, but some of the neurological and computational elements of a theory of consciousness are starting to appear.

## Consciousness and the Mind–Body Problem

Understanding consciousness is crucial for a solution to the mind–body problem described in chapter 8. For each philosophical answer to this problem, there is a corresponding view of consciousness. Dualists, who see mind as separate from body, claim that consciousness is a property of spiritual minds and is not open to scientific explanation. Idealists, who think that everything is mental, can see consciousness as a property of everything in the universe. Materialists argue that consciousness is a physical process, but they differ in what kind of process they think it is. Functionalists claim that consciousness is a property of the functioning of a sufficiently complex computational system, so that consciousness may turn out to be a property of advanced robots as well as human minds. Another version of materialism that I find more plausible views consciousness as emerging from the biological complexity of the human brain, not just from its computational functions. A third version of materialism contends that consciousness is a physical process that is just too complicated to be figured out by limited human minds. This "mysterian" position may turn out to be true, but it would be defeatist to adopt it without a long and serious attempt to understand consciousness scientifically.

What would be the grounds for adopting dualism? Most people acquire dualism as part of their religious education when they are told that people have souls that survive death. This is a very appealing idea, but unfortunately there is no reliable evidence that anyone has ever managed to exist without a body. Philosophers such as Nagel (1979) and Chalmers (1996) use thought experiments to raise doubts about the prospects for a scientific explanation of consciousness. You know what it's like to be you, to have the kinds of sensory and emotional experiences that you have. Imagine what it would be like to be a bat, with a very different set of experiences. How could a computational or neurological explanation possibly account for the qualitative experiences that you have by virtue of being a human being? We can also imagine a population of zombies who function just like us biologically but who lack conscious experience. Some dualists think that this possibility shows that consciousness is not identical to any physical process.

Thought experiments can be useful in science and philosophy when they are used to suggest and elaborate new hypotheses—for example, when Einstein imagined himself riding on a beam of light when he was developing the theory of relativity. But they are never a reliable guide to the adopting of hypotheses, because our imaginations are limited by what we already believe. The *Star Trek* movies and TV shows portray "transporters" that dissolve people on a spaceship and then reassemble them on a planet. However, this process is incompatible with what we know of physics and computational complexity: taking apart the trillions of cells in a human body, transmitting them across space, and reassembling them into the original body would require unrealizable physical processes and computing power. According to the calculations of physicist Lawrence Krauss (1996, 83), "building a transporter would require us to heat matter up to a temperature a million times the temperature at the center of the Sun, expend more energy in a single machine than all of humanity presently uses, build telescopes larger than the size of the earth, improve present computers by a factor of 1000 billion billion, and avoid the laws of quantum mechanics." We can imagine transporters, but imagination is misleading because it does not reveal a real physical possibility. On the other hand, imagination is often limited by lack of knowledge: 100 years ago, no one contemplated the Internet or cell phones or the human genome project. It is likely that 100 years from now educated people will be amused that some philosophers in the twentieth century denied that consciousness could be explained scientifically.

But is there really a problem of consciousness? The philosopher Daniel Dennett (1991) argues that current puzzles about consciousness are largely the result of confusions deriving from an outmoded dualist theory of mind. The artificial intelligence researcher Drew McDermott (2001) thinks that robots will eventually have consciousness in the same way that people do, namely they will have the *illusion* that they are conscious. However, I doubt that people's experiences of sight, sound, touch, pain, and emotion are illusions. Cognitive science needs to explain these experiences, not deny them. As in the rest of science, explanation consists of identifying mechanisms that produce the observations we want to explain. This chapter will outline some of the key components and processes that currently appear to be plausible ingredients of a neurocomputational theory of consciousness.

Explanations in cognitive science, like scientific explanations in general, consist of identifying mechanisms that produce observable phenomena. To take a simple example, consider how a bicycle works. You observe the wheels turning, but explanation of why they turn requires attention to the bike's mechanisms. The bicycle consists of components such as the pedals, chain, and wheels that interact with each other: when you press down on the pedals, gears attached to it move the chain, which turns the gears on the rear wheel, propelling the bicycle forward. A mechanism consists of a group of components that have properties and relations to each other that produce regular changes in those properties and relations, as well as to the properties and relations of the whole system of which the mechanism is a part. Thus you and the bicycle move forward because its mechanism consists of components that have properties (such as the rigidity of the pedals) and relations (such as the meshing of the chain and the gears) that produce regular changes in the components (such as the wheels moving).

The bicycle's mechanism is relatively easy to understand because we can observe all the components and see them in action. Scientific explanations usually need to go beyond observation by theorizing about hidden components and processes. You cannot see, touch, or smell electrons, but your lamp and your computer work by virtue of the electrons flowing through their wires and chips. All physical objects consist of atoms, which are tiny mechanisms involving subatomic particles and their interactions. Similarly, cognitive science explains thinking by virtue of nonobservable mechanisms. Chapters 1–7 described mechanisms whose parts are representations such as rules and concepts and whose regular changes involve computed changes to systems of representations. In chapters 9 and 10, the emphasis was on neurobiological mechanisms whose components are neurons organized into brain areas and whose regular changes result from their electrical and chemical properties and interactions. What we need is a description of the components and processes of the brain that interact to produce conscious experience. We can learn a lot about a mechanism from the ways in which it breaks down, so it is useful to start with a review of ways that people sometimes cease to be conscious.

**How to Lose Consciousness**

What causes consciousness? Current scientific approaches to the study of consciousness approach this question by looking for neural correlates—that is, brain processes that occur when people are conscious (e.g., Metzinger 2000). Here I take a different approach, examining the neural correlates of loss of consciousness. Loss of consciousness can arise from many kinds of events, including death, coma, seizures, concussions, sleep, anesthesia, hypnosis, and fainting. All of these involve cases where a previously conscious person ceases to be conscious. I begin with the most obvious negative circumstance of consciousness: death. Live people are usually conscious, as we can infer from their verbal and other behaviors. But after death there is no evidence of such behaviors, so it is reasonable to infer that corpses are not conscious. In the absence of life, consciousness ceases, so it is plausible that life is at least part of the cause of consciousness.

Someone might reply that we can imagine ghosts and other souls who are conscious after death, so that life does not have to be a cause of consciousness. But science is not concerned with causality in all possible worlds, only with causality in this one. The thought experiment that we can imagine B without A is irrelevant to determining whether A in fact causes B. I can imagine a world in which thunder is caused by gods playing baseball rather than by lightning, but that is irrelevant to the inference that in our world thunder is caused by lightning. We have no evidence that there are ghosts or other postdeath souls who are conscious, so the absence of consciousness following the onset of death strongly suggests that life is among the causes of consciousness.

But what is life? Humans are alive because they consists of organs, tissues, and individual cells that are alive. Life is not a mysterious property of cells, but rather consists in them performing functions such as energy acquisition (metabolism), division (mitosis), motion, adhesion, signaling, and self-destruction (apoptosis). The molecular bases of each of these functions is well understood (Lodish et al. 2000). When people die, their cells stop functioning. For example, death by heart attack typically occurs when a clot blocks the blood supply to part of a heart muscle, which dies if it is deprived of oxygen for more than thirty minutes. If much of the heart muscle is destroyed, it loses the ability to pump blood to the rest of the body, so cells throughout the body die from lack of energy. Brain cells are particularly dependent on supplies of glucose provided by blood pumped by the heart, and neurons deprived of energy start to die within a few minutes. Brain death can also occur without damage to the heart—for example, by a gunshot wound.

Because consciousness stops when the cellular processes of energy metabolism cease, it is plausible to conclude that the causes of consciousness are biological. This is consistent with our knowledge that at least one kind of living thing is conscious, namely humans, and that nonbiological entities such as rocks exhibit none of the behaviors that display consciousness in humans. I leave open the question of whether nonhuman animals such as dogs and dolphins are conscious; for the current argument, it suffices that even if they are conscious when alive, they display no evidence of it when they are dead. The circumstance of death allows us to narrow down the causes of consciousness to biological ones, but it would be desirable to narrow them down further. Plants live and die too, but exhibit no behaviors indicative of consciousness and its loss. We can, however, get a more specific understanding of the causes of consciousness by looking at circumstances found in humans but not in plants, such as comas and concussions.

Medically, a coma is a state of unresponsiveness in which even strong stimuli fail to elicit psychological reactions (Wyngaarden, Smith, and Bennett 1992, 2049). Coma is distinguished from stupor, in which people are unconscious but can be aroused by vigorous stimulation, and syncope (fainting), in which people are unconscious only briefly. The common causes of coma include: cerebral or cerebellar hemorrhage, cerebral or cerebellar infarction, subdural or epidural hematoma, brain tumor, infections such as meningitis and encephalitis, anoxia, hypoglycemia, and drugs such as alcohol and opiates. All of these conditions affect the brain, and all can occur while the heart continues beating fairly normally. So consciousness requires proper brain functioning, indicating that the biological causes of consciousness are specifically neurological.

Comas can last for many years, but the briefer loss of consciousness associated with concussions and fainting also point to neurological causes of consciousness. A concussion is a change in mental status resulting from an external force. Typical causes of concussions are direct blows to the head or face and whiplash effects on the neck. Symptoms of mild concussions include confusion, dizziness, and memory loss, whereas more severe concussions produce total loss of consciousness. Loss of consciousness from concussion results from the rotational movements of the brain inside the cranium, with shearing forces that cause the brain to move in a swirling fashion and bump into the interior of the skull, both at the point of impact and after rebound on the opposite side of the skull. Since blows to the body other than the head are unlikely to cause loss of consciousness, the phenomena of severe concussions supports the coma-based conclusion that the causes of consciousness are neurological.

Syncope is defined medically as brief unconsciousness due to a temporary, critical reduction of cerebral blood flow. It is relatively common, and is colloquially known as fainting. Unlike coma and concussion, heart activity is directly involved in syncope, because syncope's 60 percent reduction in cerebral blood flow usually results from a large drop in cardiac output. This drop can be caused by abnormal neural reflexes, abnormal cardiovascular function, impaired right-heart filling, acute loss of blood volume, and severe hypotension. Hence, loss of consciousness in syncope does not serve to eliminate the heart as a major cause of consciousness, but its association with blood flow specifically to the brain does support the general conclusion that the causes of consciousness are at least in part neurological. Together, coma, concussions, and syncope all suggest that brain processes are causally involved in consciousness. Of course, it is desirable to have a much more specific account of what neurological processes produce consciousness, and for this we need to look at additional ways of losing consciousness.

Epilepsy is a group of disorders that involve alteration or loss of consciousness. Epilepsy is now recognized as the result of abnormal brain activity involving spontaneous and transient paroxysms. Epileptic seizures, which can involve either partial or total loss of consciousness, occur when abnormality in the cerebral cortex leads to brief, high-amplitude electrical discharges that can be recorded from the scalp by electroencephalography (EEG). Such discharges, which involve synchronized activity of many neurons, can have many causes, including brain lesions, head trauma, infections, brain tumors, physiological stress, sleep deprivation, fever, and drugs. It is clear, however, that total or partial loss of consciousness in epileptic seizures is accompanied by abnormal electrical activity in the brain. We can thus conclude that the neurological causes of consciousness are at least in part electrical.

People die only once in their lives, and most people never lose consciousness because of comas, concussions, or seizures. But we all lose consciousness every day when we fall asleep, which is marked by electrical changes in the brain. Active wakefulness is accompanied by low-amplitude, high-frequency beta waves in the EEG (Sharpley 2002). In contrast, slow-wave sleep (stages 3 and 4 following a gradual slowing of activity) is characterized by high-amplitude, low-frequency delta waves. Hence, sleep is like seizures in that loss of consciousness is marked by alterations in the electrical activities of the brain.

But recent evidence suggest that the causes of sleep are chemical as well as electrical. According to Benington and Heller (1995), the primary function of sleep is to replenish stores of glycogen, the major source of energy to neurons. As cerebral glycogen stores drop, levels of the neuromodulator adenosine increase, eventually inhibiting neuronal activity sufficiently to induce slow-wave activity that is necessary for the replenishment of glycogen. Injections of adenosine promote sleep and decrease wakefulness, whereas caffeine, which is an antagonist for adenosine receptors, promotes wakefulness (Sharpley 2002). During sleep deprivation, adenosine levels increase significantly, but the levels decrease during sleep. Other neurotransmitters whose levels are altered during sleep include dopamine, histamine, noradrenaline, acetylcholine, serotonin, and GABA (Gottesman 1999). Hence, a full explanation of the loss of consciousness involved in sleep will have to take into account chemical causes such as the accumulation of adenosine.

A similar conclusion follows from recent discoveries about how anesthesia works. General anesthetics such as ether and nitrous oxide have been used in surgery since the 1840s, but an explanation of the molecular mechanisms of anesthesia has arisen very recently (Moody and Skolnick 2001). Recent research suggests that the neural targets of general anesthetics are the ligand-gated ion channels that control synaptic transmission between neurons. For example, GABA is the main inhibitory neurotransmitter in the brain, and many general anesthetics bind to GABA receptors in presynaptic neurons, leading them to fire and transmit GABA to postsynaptic neurons. Because GABA tends to inhibit firing of postsynaptic neurons, binding of GABA receptors tends to decrease neuronal activity overall, producing anesthetic effects such as loss of consciousness, sensitivity, and mobility. However, increase in inhibitory synaptic transmission is only one of the various mechanisms used by different anesthetics, which can include stimulation of glycine-based neuronal inhibition as well as suppression of NMDA-based neuronal excitation. When patients receive injected or gaseous anesthetics, they become unconscious when the concentration of the anesthetic in the blood reaches a critical level, and regain consciousness when the concentration drops.

Hameroff (1998) argues that anesthesia shows that quantum mechanical effects are responsible for consciousness. He contends that anesthesia ablates consciousness because gas molecules act by quantum effects of van der Waals forces in hydrophobic pockets of select brain proteins. Ultimately, chemical explanations depend on quantum effects, since the bonds that conjoin atoms into molecules are currently understood in terms of quantum mechanics. But the explanation of the chemical effects of anesthetics in terms of their effects on receptors for neurotransmitters such as GABA does not draw on quantum-level phenomena. Hence, the rapidly accumulating evidence for the chemical nature of the causes of loss of consciousness does not support the hypothesis that the causes of consciousness are quantum mechanical. It may turn out, as Hameroff and his collaborator Roger Penrose contend, that an explanation of consciousness will need to descend to the quantum level, but current experimental research suggests that a descent to the chemical level may suffice.

So far, consideration of the most important ways of losing consciousness—death, coma, concussion, fainting, sleep, and anesthesia—suggests that the causes of consciousness are biological, neural, electrical, and chemical. To pin down the causes of consciousness further, we need to go into much more detail concerning the neurological processes that underlie conscious experience.

### Toward a Neurological Theory of Consciousness

Crick (1994) speculated on the neural underpinning of visual consciousness (see also Crick and Koch 1998). We saw in chapter 6 that understanding of visual imagery has been greatly aided by recent work on the brain's visual systems, and Crick tried to put the same kind of neurological discoveries to work to provide an explanation of visual awareness. From experimental psychology, he took the hint that awareness is likely to involve some form of attention. He conjectured that the mechanism by which the visual brain attends to one object rather than another involves the correlated firing of neurons. Neurons associated with the properties of a particular object tend to fire at the same moment and in the same sort of pattern. Unlike the artificial neurons described in chapter 7, but like the spiking neurons described in chapter 9, real neurons pass activation to each other in bursts, making possible a kind of coordination among neurons that fire in temporally similar bursts. Crick conjectured that neural networks may have the competitive aspect we saw in chapter 7: when some neurons fire, they tend to suppress the firing of others. A shift in visual attention from one object to another could then be the result of a group of neurons firing in coordination with each other and together suppressing another group of neurons that fire in coordination with each other.

The second hint that Crick took from experimental psychology is that consciousness involves short-term memory. In terms of CRUM, long-term memory consists of whatever representations—rules, concepts, analogs, images, and so on—are permanently stored in memory. Psychological experiments have shown that short-term memory is much more limited:

unless people chunk information into more complex structures, they can only remember about seven items at once (Miller 1956). You can remember your phone number by repeating it, but longer strings of digits require complex strategies to encode them. Short-term memory and consciousness are associated in that we tend to be conscious of the contents of short-term memory. Crick conjectured that short-term memory might work by means of neurons that have a tendency to fire for a certain time and then fade away, or by "reverbatory circuits" in which neurons in a ring tend to keep each other firing. He describes experiments in which visual neurons in monkeys fire in response to a visual target, and continue to fire for seconds after the target is removed. If they do not continue to fire, the monkeys are more likely to make mistakes in dealing with the target, suggesting that the neurons are important for the short-term memory required to perform the assigned task.

The possible neuronal correlates of attention and short-term memory discussed by Crick do not yet furnish us with a neurological explanation of visual consciousness. Much more remains to be learned about the neurological processes of attention and memory, as well as about their relevance to conscious experience. But this kind of research shows the possibility of neuroscience narrowing in on kinds of brain activity that are relevant to consciousness. Crick discussed parts of the brain, such as the thalamus, that seem to be involved in the attentional mechanisms that underlie visual awareness. Dualists will complain that no matter how much is known about the neural correlates of consciousness, they still cannot imagine how the material brain could produce consciousness. This is sometimes called the "argument from lack of imagination." It is comparable to saying that no matter how much is known about the motion of molecules, it is difficult to imagine that heat is just the energy of that motion rather than some special substance like caloric. Neuroscience is still far from having as much evidence that consciousness is caused by the firing of neurons as physics has that heat is caused by the motions of molecules, but the rapid rate of progress in cognitive neuroscience should lead us to keep a watch for further biological explanations of consciousness.

Crick and Koch's account applies only to consciousness of visual experience, and different mechanisms are needed to apply to other kinds of consciousness. Morris (2002) has formed an interesting hypothesis about the origins of emotional feelings based on neurological experiments

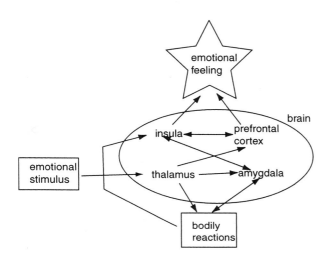

**Figure 11.1**
Origins of emotional consciousness. Adapted, with permission from Elsevier, from Morris 2002, p. 318.

concerning the neural basis of fear. Brain scanning experiments suggest that people's conscious awareness of fear depends on part of the cortex called the *insula*, which integrates information from many bodily senses. Morris conjectures that emotional feelings such as fear arise as the result of a complex interaction of the sort shown in figure 11.1. Suppose you suddenly see a scary face. This is an emotional stimulus that is processed by the visual regions of your brain and the result is transmitted to the thalamus and then on to the amygdala. Physical reactions such as increased heartbeat result, but there are also complex interactions with the insula and prefrontal cortex. Emotional feeling then emerges as the result of the overall interactions of all of these brain areas. Similarly, Edelman and Tononi (2000) propose that consciousness arises from integrated activity across numerous brain areas such as the thalamus and different regions of the cortex. See Zeman 2002 (chapter 8) for a comparative survey of current scientific theories of consciousness.

**Representation and Computation**

This chapter so far has concentrated on emerging ideas about the neurobiology of consciousness, and may seem to have left behind the representational-computational understanding of mind reviewed in earlier chapters. But a full account of consciousness will require both representation and computation.

Damasio (1999) develops a neurologically sophisticated account of two kinds of consciousness, core and extended, both of which have a representational component. Core consciousness is a simple kind that involves basic wakefulness and attention. It depends on evolutionarily older parts of the brain such as brain stem nuclei that regulate body states and map body signals, but not on newer parts such as the prefrontal cortex. According to Damasio (169): "Core consciousness occurs when the brain's representation devices generate an imaged nonverbal account of how the organism's own state is affected by the organism's processing of an object." Thus, even core consciousness is a representational process.

Extended consciousness is even more obviously representational, since it involves a sense of self based on autobiographical memory. Whereas core consciousness requires only representation of current body signals, extended consciousness requires stored representations of previous experiences as well as higher-level structures that represent these representations. Damasio thinks that these second-order structures are produced by neural activity in the cingulate cortex and other parts of the brain found only in animals that evolved relatively recently, like people and other primates. He describes how disorders of extended consciousness, such as amnesia found in Alzheimer's patients, are very different from disorders of core consciousness, such as comas caused by damage to the brain stem.

Representation has also been important in philosophical theories of consciousness developed by Lycan (1996) and Carruthers (2000). According to these theories, consciousness of your mental state such as a pain consists in a representing of that state. Lycan maintains that this representing is like perception by means of a set of internal attention mechanisms. But according to Carruthers, this representing requires only having a thought about the mental state. As in Damasio's extended consciousness, the theory that consciousness is a kind of higher order thought involves the postulation of representations of representations. If these accounts are true, then consciousness is clearly part of the representational understanding of mind.

But what about computation? Could it be that consciousness is a representational process that depends only on physical processes that are not best described as computational? Neither Damasio nor Carruthers describe representations of representations as functioning computationally. However, when more detailed models of conscious experience are presented, such as in the model in figure 11.1, it becomes natural to describe the relevant physical processes as neurocomputational. When input from a stimulus triggers activity in brain areas such as the thalamus, amygdala, insula, and prefrontal cortex, there are complex transformations of representations constituted by populations of neurons firing systematically. Not only can these transformations be modeled computationally, they are plausibly described as *being* computations, because the relevant transitions between brain states are operations on representations. Of course, some of the inputs to brain processing come from physical sources such as the sense organs and the body's sensing of its own internal states, but these get integrated computationally into composite representations found in the insula and amygdala. Hence, consciousness can plausibly be understood as a computational-representational process.

Does this mean that sufficiently complex computers will be conscious? I do not know. We do not yet understand enough about how the brain's interactive processes generate consciousness to be able to say whether causally comparable processes can be built into computers. At the very least consciousness will require robots that acquire sensory information from the world and their own physical states. Because future robots will not duplicate the full biological complexity of humans, it may be that consciousness may never emerge from their sensory and representational activities. Even if robots do acquire consciousness, there is no reason to expect that their qualitative experiences will be at all like ours, since their bodies and sense organs will be very different. Even if we use a robot to simulate in great detail human information processing, there will be many aspects of human biology that contribute to human consciousness but which will be lacking in the robot—for example, hormones and specific brain areas such as the insula. Given current limitations of knowledge, we simply do not know what it might be like to be a robot.

## Summary

Explaining consciousness is one of the most difficult problems in cognitive science, but philosophical thought experiments fail to show that no scientific explanation is possible. There is growing reason to believe that consciousness is caused by biological, neurological, electrical, and chemical mechanisms. Neurological theories of various kinds of consciousness, such as visual and emotional experience, are being developed. Core consciousness depends on the brain's ability to represent basic physical experiences, but extended consciousness requires higher level representations of the self and its history. Consciousness appears to be a representational and computational process, but it is not yet possible to say whether computers and robots can be conscious.

## Discussion Questions

1. What would it take to give a robot consciousness?
2. Can consciousness be thought of as representational?
3. Is consciousness an essential aspect of emotions?
4. How big a role does consciousness play in intelligent thought? What is its function?
5. Could consciousness be understood in terms of neurons and brain structures?

## Further Reading

For general surveys on consciousness, see Blackmore 2004 and Zeman 2002. On the neuroscience of consciousness, see Damasio 1999, Edelman and Tononi 2000, and Metzinger 2000. For philosophical discussion, see Block, Flanagan, and Güzeldere 1997, Carruthers 2000, and Churchland 2002. Merikle and Daneman 2000 is a review of the experimental psychology of conscious versus unconscious perception. On the neurochemistry of consciousness, see Perry, Ashton, and Young 2002.

## Web Sites

Association for the Scientific Study of Consciousness: http://assc. caltech.edu/

Christof Koch on the neuronal basis of consciousness: http://www.klab. caltech.edu/cns120/

David Chalmer's page, with extensive bibliographies: http://www.u. arizona.edu/~chalmers/

Representational theories of consciousness: http://plato.stanford.edu/ entries/consciousness-representational/

University of Arizona Center for Consciousness Studies: http:// consciousness.arizona.edu/

## Notes

The argument in the section on how to lose consciousness uses J. S. Mill's method of difference, which says that if you want to determine the causes of a phenomenon, it helps to look for what is missing when the phenomenon is absent.

Penrose (1994) argues that consciousness and other mental phenomena arise from the brain being a quantum computer, but there is no evidence that thought depends directly on quantum effects.

# 12   Bodies, the World, and Dynamic Systems

The three challenges (body, world, and dynamic systems) discussed in this chapter accuse CRUM of focusing too much on mental representation and neglecting the fact that thought is not a solitary, disembodied occurrence, but rather occurs in individuals who interact with a physical world. Extreme versions of these challenges totally reject the idea of mental representation, claiming that human intelligence is a matter of bodies inhabiting physical environments and operating in them in ways that are not at all like how a computer processes information. I have grouped together diverse criticisms concerning bodies and the world, and tried to give a common set of responses. This chapter also considers whether it is useful to think of the mind as a dynamic system of the sort commonly investigated in physics and biology.

## Bodies in the World

The core idea behind the body and world challenges is that thinking is not just in the head. CRUM seems to restrict thinking to computational processing occurring in the mind, ignoring the fact that most of what people do involves continuous and rich interaction between both their bodies and the world-at-large. There are diverse variants of the objection that CRUM neglects the body and the world, including psychologists who tie concepts closely to direct perception, philosophers influenced by Martin Heidegger, and researchers in robotics disaffected with standard approaches to artificial intelligence.

### Embodiment and Direct Perception

How do people interact with the world? Information needs to be conveyed from the world to the mind through the senses. CRUM treats perception as involving the inferential construction of representations that capture features of the world. Psychologists influenced by Gibson (1979) have rejected this inferential view of perception and claimed that we learn about the world more directly, by having our perceptual apparatus so attuned to the world that information is directly conveyed to the brain without requiring computations on representations. Our physical sensory apparatus is one of the contributors to our ability to interact with the world.

As we saw in the discussion of emotions, CRUM tends to treat the nature of our bodies as largely irrelevant to our cognitive processes. But Johnson (1987) and Lakoff (1987) have argued that this tradition has neglected the crucial role that our bodies play in our thinking. Many of the metaphors that permeate our language derive from body-based relations such as up and down, left and right, and in and out. If we did not have the kinds of bodies we have, operating in the kind of world we inhabit, then our systems of metaphor and our whole mental apparatus would be different from what they are. It may seem to be a virtue of CRUM that it potentially applies to computers and extraterrestrial beings independent of physical makeup, but this virtue is illusory if in fact many of the key aspects of human thinking depend on the kind of body we have and how it is attuned to the world.

Lakoff and Johnson (1999) argue that human concepts are embodied in the sense that they are crucially shaped by our bodies and brains, especially by our sensory and motor systems. For example, our concepts of color are shaped in part by two aspects of our bodies: the color cones in our retinas that absorb light of different wavelengths, and the complex neural circuitry connected to those cones. Moreover, the basic concepts that we use to categorize the world are derived in part from the way that our visual and other sensory systems detect the overall part-whole structure of the world. We can form visual images of elephant and chairs, but not of more abstract concepts such as *animal* and *furniture*. Concepts of spatial relations such as *above*, *in front of*, and *contains* are also deeply affected by the ways that our bodies perceive and react to the world. Barsalou et al. (2003) review evidence from psychological and neurological experiments that support the view that conceptual representations are grounded in specific sensory modalities. For example, your representation of a car is not an abstract, verbal symbol like the concepts in chapter 4, but rather involves neurons in the brain's visual areas that capture and reenact sensory experiences of cars.

## Being-in-the-World

How do people hammer in a nail? To answer this question from the perspective of CRUM, we would start to consider what kinds of representation we have of a hammer and a nail. For each of these, we perhaps have a concept or image that we use to represent hammers and nails, and our hammering takes place because we are able to do computational operations on these representations that somehow get translated into the physical action of hammering the nail.

The German philosopher Heidegger rejected this representational view of the practice of hammering (1962; Dreyfus 1991). He denied the division assumed in cognitive science between the representing subject and the world, and claimed that we function in the world simply because we are a part of it. He used the expression "being-in-the-world" to convey that people can perform tasks like hammering just by virtue of their physical skills, without any kinds of representation. Dreyfus (1992) mounted Heideggerian arguments against artificial intelligence, claiming that its attempt to formalize and represent knowledge is hopeless, because our intelligence is inherently nonrepresentational.

The antirepresentational view of cognition has found favor in some AI researchers who have become disaffected with the standard approach. Winograd and Flores (1986) endorse a Heideggerian perspective and conclude that the standard approach to AI is impossible, because we will never be able to represent the mass of background information underlying human performance. Smith (1991) advocates what he calls "embedded computing," which avoids the representational load of traditional computational approaches by emphasizing interaction with the world rather than internal processing. Similarly, Dourish (2001) claims that attention to embodied interaction can lead to the design of more effective interactive computers.

## Robotics

Embodiment has also been a major theme in research in robotics. Brooks (1991, 2002) has advocated an approach to building robots that is very different from that of researchers in the logic and rule-based traditions. Instead of trying to encode the knowledge that a high-level robot needs to have to plan its movements around its environment, he builds simple machines that have the capacity to learn about their environments. Rather than encoding complex rules about how to walk, Brooks gives his insect-like robots multiple processors that enable them to learn to walk by interacting with the environment, without using any of the representation techniques advocated by the six approaches to CRUM discussed in earlier chapters. The humanoid robots that Brooks and his students have built are designed to be able to recognize and respond to faces, but contain no concepts or rules for reasoning about people. Mackworth (1993) has also advised building robots that are physical systems embedded in the real world, closely coupling perception and action. He has built a system of mobile robots that rapidly play a simple version of soccer without the complex representations and plans usually used in robots based on artificial intelligence.

### Situated Action

Some anthropologists and psychologists have also argued that cognitive science has erred in overemphasizing the mental and underemphasizing the role that situations and context play in human problem solving and learning. Suchman (1987) and Lave and Wenger (1991) contend that cognitive psychologists have examined human thinking on artificial tasks, and that problem solving in realistic contexts is not so heavily dependent on mental representation, but rather depends on direct interaction with the world and other people. People who lack abstract mathematical representations can nevertheless perform more than adequately at practical tasks such as dividing a pizza up at a party. Using a complex machine like a computer is not just a matter of forming an abstract representation of it, but rather of learning how to interact with it. Suchman and Lave see people, like Brooks's simple robots, as thinking through interaction with the world rather than by means of representing it and processing those representations. Shanon (1993) argues that CRUM is incapable of appreciating the subtle, contextual ways in which people deal with the world.

### Intentionality

The relation between mind and world is also involved in what philosophers such as John Searle (1992) see as a crucial objection to CRUM. Mental states are intended to represent the world: they possess intentionality, the property of being *about* something. Your belief that your friends are at the library is not simply a representation in your head; it is about your friends and the library, which are parts of the world. Searle uses a thought experiment to contend that a computer could never have intentionality. Imagine that you are locked in a room and people pass you paper with symbols that you do not recognize. You are, however, able to use a whole set of tables to look up the symbols given to you and select other symbols that you then pass back out of the room. Unknown to you, the symbols are Chinese, and when you pass back the symbols you have looked up, you are providing sensible answers to questions that you received. Searle contends that it is obvious that you are merely manipulating symbols you do not understand, so that similarly a computer manipulating symbols is lacking in understanding. The symbols that people operate with have the semantic property of intentionality based on our interactions with the world, but representations in computers are independent of the world and therefore lacking in intentionality. Computers are purely syntactic engines lacking human semantic capabilities that provide meaning to their symbols based on their interactions with the world. Therefore, the computational view of mind is fundamentally flawed.

## Responses to the Body and World Challenges

### Denial

Can cognitive science ignore bodies and the world? Although CRUM has focused on representations and processes rather than on physical interaction, CRUM should not simply deny the world challenge. Researchers in psychology and artificial intelligence sometimes use the term "representation" to mean nothing more than "structure," but a structure is a representation only if its purpose is to stand for something.

When people solve problems and learn, they are not operating as disembodied computers unconnected with the world. Computational models developed to date have tended to ignore the details of physical environments. Most computers used in modeling have no connection with the world other than the keyboards that programmers use to type instructions. Greater appreciation of the structure of the world is important for helping designers to produce machines and tools that people can easily use (Norman 1989). Hence, CRUM needs to be expanded and supplemented to encompass the body and the world. Radical proponents of being-in-the-world, embedded computing, situated action, and intentionality will see this expansion as a waste of time, on the grounds that CRUM is utterly misguided. But CRUM's explanatory accomplishments justify asking how the body and world challenges might be met. Heideggerians may say that we do not represent the world, we just embody it, but these may not be exclusive alternatives.

### Expand CRUM

As we saw in chapters 9–11, neuroscience, emotions, and consciousness suggest the need for expanding the range of representations CRUM considers beyond the standard ones in chapters 2–7. Similarly, taking the world and the body seriously suggests the need for new sorts of representations. When I see a house on top of a hill, the linguistic encoding *on* (*house, hill*) does not capture all the knowledge that my perceptual experience has given me. Imagistic representations should include not only the visual images discussed in chapter 6, but also images derived from the other sensory modalities of smell, taste, hearing, and touch. Hammering a nail is not just a matter of representing the concepts of hammer and nail; it is also a matter of representing the kinesthetic feel of an arm doing the hammering. Abstracted from physical and neurological considerations, however, this kind of expansion of CRUM goes only a small way toward giving CRUM the capacity to explain interactions with the world.

### Supplement CRUM

Just as the structure and operations of the brain and body matter for understanding emotions, so biological matters seem relevant to any full account of interactions with the world. A possible model for such investigations is Kosslyn's (1994b) work on imagery, where visual representations are described in connection with how the brain processes them. Similarly, we can hope to learn how the brain deals with other kinds of sensory input, and at least speculate about how these tie in with our verbal representations. Not all brain processes need be thought of in computational terms: see later in this chapter for a discussion of the brain as dynamic system. But a fully integrated account of human thinking will have be able to tie together the nonrepresentational operations of the brain and body with the computational procedures that seem crucial for high-level cognition. If some proponents of CRUM have been guilty of neglecting the facts that we can walk and throw and hammer, some environmental challengers have unfortunately threatened to reduce human thought either to simplistic, insectlike responses or to mysterious, unanalyzed occurrences.

## Abandon CRUM

But if we add neuroscience into the picture, why do we need CRUM? Why not drop it out of the picture as an unnecessary middle layer of explanation between the world and the neural networks in the brain? The answer lies in the extraordinary complexity and diversity of human problem solving. Brooks's insectlike robots are very impressive in their ability to learn to scurry around their environments, but they are completely lacking in the capacity for higher-level planning such as people perform whenever they figure out how to get to another city. Similarly, being situated is a great boon for simple tasks, but people can solve complex, abstract tasks that go far beyond mere response to the environment. Images, concepts, rules and other representations enable us to carry out imaginary manipulations of the world that can take place independently of actual manipulations.

The intentionality problem is serious, but it is not beyond the range of a suitably enriched CRUM. We must grant that the desktop computers currently used to simulate thinking are syntactic engines that lack semantics: the fact that I can write "beer" in my computer program does not mean that my computer understands what a beer is. But computers are already being provided with limited capacities to learn about the world, by means of robotic interfaces that provide visual, auditory, and tactile input from the world, and by means of learning algorithms that can generate various kinds of distributed, verbal, or imagistic representations. Searle's Chinese room pumps your intuitions by making you see yourself as a disconnected symbol pusher. But if you are effective in processing Chinese symbols because you are part of a whole system that interacts with the world and thereby acquires the symbols in the lookup table, then you, together with the whole apparatus you employ, would naturally be judged to understand Chinese. Similarly, a robotic learning computer could have semantics to go with its syntax, and acquire intentionality for its internal representations. To provide a full model of human thinking, CRUM needs to take the world and our bodily interactions with it more seriously, but the required extensions are possible and natural. The theory of dynamic systems contains useful ideas for developing these extensions.

## Dynamic Systems

The summary to chapter 1 presented the explanation schema central to CRUM, and the summaries to chapters 2–7 instantiated the schema with specific kinds of representations and processes. Many scientific explanations do not use this kind of explanation pattern. Suppose we want to explain why it rained yesterday. No respectable meteorologist would talk about the beliefs or the goals of the clouds and the raindrops, which are entities that simply do not have mental representations. Instead, meteorologists make their predictions and explanations by considering a large number of variables, including temperature, humidity, and air pressure at various locations. They incorporate these variables into mathematical equations that describe how the weather system changes over time. Meteorologists treat weather as a *dynamic system*, that is, as a system whose changes over time can be characterized by a set of equations that show how current values of variables depend mathematically on previous values of those variables.

Many phenomena in physics, biology, and even economics can usefully be understood in terms of dynamic systems ideas such as state space, attractors, phase transitions, and chaos. The *state space* of a system is the set of states it can be in as determined by the variables that are used to measure it. For example, a very simple weather model that keeps track of temperature, humidity, and air pressure at five locations has a total of fifteen variables, so all the different combinations of values of these variables constitute the state space of the system. Changes in the system can be described in terms of movement from one point in the space (one combination of values of all the variables) to another. Before fast computers existed, scientists could deal only with simple systems whose changes are describable by linear equations, those of the form $y = kx + c$. In this equation, the value of the variable $y$ depends only on the value of the variable $x$ multiplied by a constant $k$ and added to a constant $c$. But complex dynamic systems need to be described by nonlinear equations such as $y = xz$, where the value of the variable $y$ depends on interaction of values of $x$ and $z$.

Nonlinear systems can have very erratic behavior, jumping from one point in the state space to another, very different point in a short period of time. The weather, for example, can change dramatically in a couple of hours with high winds and dropping temperatures when a cold front moves in. Despite these dramatic changes, dynamic systems may have relatively stable states called *attractors* that they tend to settle into. A system may have multiple attractors, so that there is more than one stable state. Change from one attractor state to another constitutes a *phase transition*, as when the weather moves from being cool and clear to being hot and humid, or when water gets cold enough that it freezes. In both these cases, what appear to be small local changes put the system into a qualitatively very different state.

A dynamic system displays *chaos* if it is very sensitive to initial conditions, that is, if very small differences in values of variables of its equations can produce dramatically different outcomes as the system develops. The weather is a chaotic system, since very small changes in variables far from some location can over time add up to dramatic changes in the weather there. This is called the butterfly effect: a butterfly flapping its wings in China may have a tiny effect on the atmospheric system there that eventually leads to a major weather change elsewhere. Chaotic systems can display abrupt changes (phase transitions) that are very hard to predict because they depend on minuscule changes in many variables. One of the reasons that the weather is very hard to predict more than a few days in advance is that meteorologists cannot measure all the slight differences in all the variables that affect the weather a few days in the future.

The dynamic systems challenge to cognitive science consists of the claim that, rather than understanding human thinking in computational-representational terms, we should think of the mind as a dynamic system. Instead of proposing a set of representations and processes, we should follow the successful example of physics and biology and try to develop equations that describe how the mind changes over time. Here is an explanation schema that employs some dynamic systems ideas:

Explanation Target

Why do people have **stable** but **unpredictable patterns of behavior**?

Explanatory Pattern

Human thought is describable by a set of **variables**.

These variables are governed by a set of nonlinear **equations**.

These **equations** establish a **state space** that has **attractors**.

The system described by the **equations** is **chaotic**.

The existence of the **attractors** explains **stable patterns** of behavior.
**Multiple attractors** explain abrupt **phase transitions**.
The **chaotic** nature of the system explains why **behavior** is **unpredictable**.

The plausibility of the dynamic systems challenge depends on the extent to which explanation schemas like this can be applied to make sense of many aspects of human thinking.

Application of dynamic systems concepts to cognition is relatively recent: most work has been published only since the 1990s. There are three different ways in which the mind has been viewed as a dynamic system. Relatively rare are cases where the explanation pattern that is so powerful in physics and biology is directly applied to cognition. It is very difficult in psychology to identify a small number of relevant variables and write equations using them that predict anything interesting. Nevertheless, dynamic systems accounts using small sets of variables and equations have been proposed for such phenomena as decision making (Busemeyer and Townsend 1993; Richards 1990) and language growth (van Geert 1991).

More commonly, researchers use dynamic systems ideas metaphorically when they cannot specify variables and equations. Even if these are unknown, it is still possible to describe changes in a complex system in terms of changes in state space, attractors, phase transitions, and chaos. Thelen and Smith (1994) interpret children's development in learning to walk in terms of transitions between attractor states. Other metaphorical applications of dynamic systems ideas have been made to clinical psychology (Barton 1994; Schmid 1991). Thagard and Nerb (2002) show how easy it is to apply dynamic systems ideas to emotions, which seem to be chaotic in the sense that small changes in your situation—for example, being insulted—can produce large changes in your emotional state and mood. On the other hand, the emotional dynamic system does have some stability, as people maintain a cheerful or terrible mood over long periods. This stability exists because the system has a tendency to evolve into a small number of general states called attractors, and the shift from one mood to another can be described as the shift from one attractor to another.

The third kind of application of dynamic systems ideas has been made by some connectionists who find describing the behavior of artificial and real neural networks in dynamic systems terms very useful. Connectionist systems are clearly dynamic systems in that they contain variables for the activations of the various units and for the strengths of the links between them, along with nonlinear equations for updating these activations and changing strengths. Connectionist dynamic systems differ from the first kind listed above in that the number of variables can be very large, since for every unit there is a separate variable representing its activation value. Concepts like attractors, phase transitions, and chaos can be shown to apply to neural networks: for example, when a network settles, it acquires a stable state in which no further activation changes occur. Connectionist models described in dynamic systems terms include those of Pollack (1991) and Skarda and Freeman (1987).

### Responses to the Dynamic Systems Challenge

### Denial

A defender of CRUM could argue that the dynamic systems approach is very limited in its application to human thinking. Although that approach has been powerful in physics and biology, the identification of small numbers of variables linked by small numbers of equations that has worked there has not so far been very useful in psychology. Instead, there has been a proliferation of metaphorical applications of dynamic systems ideas that have yielded very little in the way of precise predictions and modeling. Connectionist models have been more precise, but connectionism is part of CRUM, not an alternative to it; so dynamic systems theory is best seen as just an adjunct to connectionism rather than as an alternative to CRUM. Each of the three ways of applying dynamic systems ideas to thinking displays a limitation of this approach: human thinking is not subject to description in terms of a small number of variables, metaphorical explanation is of limited use, and connectionism does fine with only a minimal application of dynamic systems ideas.

### Expand and Supplement CRUM

The dynamic systems approach should be taken more seriously than this argument suggests, since it embodies several aspects that are relatively neglected in the CRUM approach. First, as van Gelder and Port (1995) argue, the dynamic systems approach deals with time more gracefully than CRUM typically does. It provides a new set of ideas for describing changes that may occur in intelligent systems. Second, the dynamic systems approach provides a possible way of meeting the world challenge discussed earlier in this chapter. We saw that CRUM must face the problem that minds are not disembodied processors but must interact with a changing world. From a dynamic systems perspective, the mind and the world are not distinct, but together comprise one big dynamic system. Writing the equations to describe the interactions of mind and world is obviously very difficult, but at least mind and world are treated in comparable terms. Third, the dynamic systems approach might be useful for explaining non-representational aspects of human behavior. Even if problem solving and language are best understood in terms of mental representations, there are other aspects of human behavior such as motor control, moods, and sleep that are more naturally explained using dynamic systems ideas. When a two-year-old changes in seconds from smiling to screaming prompted by some tiny event, there is more to the dramatic behavioral shift than processing involving rules, concepts, analogies, images, or distributed representations. Emotional shifts, and other changes like a child's first steps or a person falling asleep, may be best understood in terms of a dynamic system possessing attractors and phase transitions.

Thus, CRUM, particularly its connectionist version, seems open to expansion and supplementation with dynamic systems ideas. The hypothesis that mind is a dynamic system is not yet a credible alternative to CRUM, since there is so much about problem solving, learning, and language that is explainable with CRUM and that proponents of the dynamic systems approach have not even addressed. Nevertheless, a full account of the nature of mind that incorporates human biology and interactions with the world may find it useful to draw on dynamic systems explanations. Eliasmith (2003) provides a plausible account of how to integrate symbolic, connectionist, and dynamic systems explanations of how the mind works.

## Summary

According to the body and world challenges, cognitive science has not taken seriously enough the relation of minds to their physical environment. These challenges arise both in an abstract form (the problem of intentionality, which concerns how representations can be about the world) and in concrete psychological and computational forms. Some critics of CRUM have argued that our minds do not have to represent the world because they are situated in it. Although CRUM needs to be expanded and supplemented to better describe how thinking depends on interactions with the world, views of mind that emphasize the environment to the exclusion of the representational are not rich enough to account for the full range of human intelligent performance.

Instead of thinking of the mind as a computational-representational system, we might consider it as a dynamic system in which changes can be described by mathematical equations. Dynamic systems models of mind are relatively new, and fall into three classes that either use a small number of variables and equations, use dynamic systems ideas metaphorically, or use connectionist models described in dynamic systems terms. The dynamic systems approach seems promising for dealing with temporal, physical, and nonrepresentational aspects of mind, but suggests expanding and supplementing CRUM rather than abandoning it.

## Discussion Questions

1. How much of driving a car involves mental representations, and how much is just knowing how to interact with the world?
2. Could a computer acquire intentionality?
3. Do computer models of the mind have to ignore the physical context of action?
4. What are the advantages of thinking of the mind as a dynamic system?
5. Is the dynamic systems approach incompatible with CRUM?
6. Are connectionist networks dynamic systems?

## Further Reading

Clark 1997 discusses embodied and situated cognition; a briefer review is Clark 1999. On situated cognition, see Kirshner and Whitson 1997. The journal *Cognitive Science* had a special issue on situated action in January 1993, containing aggressive arguments for and against. Dietrich 1994 contains essays defending computational approaches to mind against various objections including intentionality.

Ward 2002 provides an introduction to dynamic cognitive science. See also Bechtel and Abrahamsen 2002. For a popular introduction to dynamic systems, see Gleick 1987. Abraham and Shaw 1992 gives a more rigorous introduction with applications to psychology. Works that argue for the dynamic systems approach to cognition include Thelen and Smith 1994 and Port and van Gelder 1995.

## Web Sites

Dynamic systems research groups: http://www-chaos.umd.edu/nonlinear_sites.html

Embodied cognition links: http://www.geocities.com/fastiland/embodiment.html

Robotics frequently asked questions: http://www.frc.ri.cmu.edu/robotics-faq/TOC.html

Rodney Brooks's Web site: http://www.ai.mit.edu/people/brooks/index.shtml

Situated learning course: http://inkido.indiana.edu/syllabi/R695/sitcog.html

## Notes

There has been much philosophical discussion of the problem of how representations represent. One issue concerns externalism, the extent to which content is determined by the external world. Von Eckardt 1993 contains a good discussion of recent views on content determination. I argued in chapter 4 that the meaning of concepts is a matter both of their relation to each other and of their relation to the world.

Dynamic systems are usually described using differential or difference equations. For example, consider the logistic difference equation

$$x_{t+1} = r * x_t * (1 - x_t).$$

We can interpret $x_t$ as population at time $t$, a proportion of what is possible, and interpret $r$ as rate of population growth. This simple equation displays very odd behavior: for $r$ less than 1, the population goes to 1. For $r$ between 1 and 3.57, the population is stable or oscillating between two points. For $r$ greater than 3.57, the performance is chaotic, producing apparently random results, extremely dependent on the starting value of $x$. On your computer or calculator, see the difference between starting with $x = 0.4$ and starting with $x = 0.35$.

# 13 Societies

Just as cognitive science has tended to neglect the location of thinkers in their physical environments, so it has tended to neglect the interaction of thinkers in social environments. Philosophy, cognitive psychology, and artificial intelligence have largely been concerned with the mental representations and processes that occur in individual thinkers. However, recent trends in each of these fields have pointed toward increasing appreciation of the social context of knowledge. The social challenge to CRUM concerns whether it can be expanded or supplemented to deal with social aspects of thinking.

## Social Epistemology

Epistemology is the branch of philosophy concerned with the nature and justification of knowledge. Traditionally, epistemology has been concerned with what individuals know: how do we justify our beliefs? Recently, however, there has been increasing concern with social aspects of knowledge, particularly among philosophers of science. In modern science, knowledge is obviously a social enterprise. Most published papers have more than one author, and much research is performed by teams of scientists working together. The announcement of experiments pointing to the existence of the "top quark" was made jointly by more than 400 physicists. Contributors to the social epistemology of science include Giere (1988), Kitcher (1993), Solomon (2001), and Thagard (1999).

Many other kinds of knowledge are inherently social, from business expertise shared by people working together in corporations to artistic expertise shared by people collaborating in symphonies and the theater. Goldman (1999) explores the ways that human knowledge can be increased via social transactions. He evaluates many social practices that increase knowledge, including testimony, argumentation, and communication technologies. Much of what you know depends on the testimony of your friends and acquaintances: if your professor says that there is going to be an exam next week, then you have good reason to believe it. On the other hand, you probably know some people who are unreliable on particular topics, so you do not use their testimony as the basis for your own beliefs. Because we do not have the time and resources to investigate everything we are told about, we often must rely on others to provide us with information. Discourse is not confined to only factual reports. People sometimes present reasons or evidence for what they say, and this is known as argumentation. Learning how to evaluate the arguments of others can increase the reliability of the information that we acquire from them. Similarly, we can improve the quality of our beliefs by ensuring that they arise from communication media that are reliable. Contrast the newspapers, magazines, and television shows that you trust most with others that you have learned to doubt.

### Social and Distributed Cognition

Psychologists and anthropologists have also been paying increasing attention to social aspects of knowledge. The field of social cognition studies how people make sense of their social world by reasoning about the thoughts, goals, and feelings of other people (Kunda 1999). What we believe about other people can be represented by concepts such as social stereotypes based on race and gender, or by rules about what to expect in social interactions. For example, if you meet someone for the first time, you will probably attempt to understand them by applying concepts such as *nice* or *obnoxious*. Understanding how people think and feel about each other is crucial for understanding social institutions such as marriage. Gottman et al. (2003) provide a dynamic systems model of how marriages succeed or fail as the result of how husbands and wives react to their perceptions of each other. One of their conclusions is that most marriages fail through a process of escalating negative emotions.

A more radical notion is that of *distributed cognition*, the idea that thinking occurs not just in individual minds but through the cooperation of many individuals. For example, a team of software engineers working collectively on a new computer program must ensure that they are progressing toward a common goal. They must develop a common representation of the task that the program is intended to perform, and they need continuous communication to make sure that the different parts of the project will work together. Similar communication and cooperation is necessary whenever accomplishing a task requires more than one person. The evaluation of various approaches to CRUM in chapters 2–8 discussed problem solving as an accomplishment of individual thinkers, but in today's world problems are often solved by teams of thinkers. Students sometimes work on class projects in teams, and anyone who has been involved in extracurricular activities such as a newspaper or club knows how important it is to be able to work toward common goals with other people. Contributors to the work on distributed cognition include Galegher, Kraut, and Egido (1990), Hutchins (1995), Resnick, Levine, and Behrend (1991), and Salomon (1993).

Hollan, Hutchins, and Kirsch (2000) discuss the relevance of distributed cognition for improving our use of computers. They describe three important kinds of distribution of cognitive processes. First, cognitive processes may be distributed across the members of a social group, such as a team of navigators on a ship. Second, cognitive processes may involve coordination with external structures such as computers. Third, cognitive processes may be distributed through time as people continue to interact with each other and with external objects. Because people's use of computers in fields such as science and business now involves networks of both people and computers, the theory of distributed cognition is highly relevant to understanding and improving human-computer interaction.

Researchers are also investigating the role of emotion in organizations (Fineman 2000). Group success depends not only on exchanging cognitive representations such as concepts and rules, but also on exchanging values that are based on emotional attitudes. For example, a soccer team not only needs the knowledge that winning depends on players passing to each other, but also needs each player to attach a positive emotional value to passing as opposed to individual play. Emotional communication requires special mechanisms that transmit values by verbal and nonverbal means. One direct mechanism is emotional contagion, in which people acquire the emotions of others just by witnessing and mimicking their physical expressions (Hatfield, Cacioppo, and Ratson 1994). For example, if your friends are bubbling with excitement about seeing a new movie, you may acquire their excitement. Similarly, people often acquire attitudes about what is and what is not worth doing by interacting with and observing the emotions of role models such as parents and teachers.

A more cognitively complicated mechanism for emotional communication is analogy, when people try to convince people that they will like or dislike something by comparing it to something familiar (Thagard and Shelley 2001). For example, you may try to get someone to go to the newest *Matrix* movie by having them recall how they felt about the last one or similar movies. Empathy is a particular kind of emotional analogy in which you try to understand the emotional state of someone by comparison to your own previous mental states. There is experimental evidence that the development of ethical behavior in children is heavily shaped by emotional contagion and empathy (Hoffman 2000). Hence, distributed cognition is influenced by emotional as well as other kinds of communication.

### Distributed Artificial Intelligence

Intelligent computation can also be understood as distributed. In its first few decades, AI concentrated on how individual computers might perform intelligently. Recently, however, there has been increased attention to how to get networks of computers to work together. A university campus today has thousands of computers electronically linked to each other, and the Internet links many millions of computers worldwide. Instead of trying to build a full kind of intelligence into a single computer, it might be possible to have varieties of specialized intelligence in many computers. By communicating with each other, the computers would solve problems beyond the capabilities of each working alone. Distributed artificial intelligence (DAI) is a branch of AI that investigates problems concerning how computers with different kinds of knowledge bases can be linked and put to work cooperatively. Imagine four distinct computers, each one running an expert system based respectively on logic, rules, analogies, and distributed representations. Could they be made to work together to overcome communication problems and produce an expert problem solver that exceeds in power any one of the systems? A more recent term for the field of distributed artificial intelligence is *multiagent systems*, reflecting the current concern in artificial intelligence with agents that perceive environments and act on them. For surveys, see O'Hare and Jennings 1996 and Wooldridge 2002.

One amusing application of DAI is the annual competition to build teams of soccer-playing robots (Asada et al. 2003). Just as successful human sports teams require cooperation among all their members, the success of robotic soccer teams depends on the ability of individual robots to work with each other. Robot soccer has become a useful forum for testing theories about what makes robots effective and what makes multiagent cooperation useful. Figure 13.1 shows some soccer robots in action.

DAI is similar to connectionism (chapter 7) in that both concern parallel activity of multiple processors, but differs in that each processor in a DAI system is on its own an advanced system possessing some intelligence. In contrast, the units in a connectionist system are very simple and merely pass activation to other units, not the complex messages that can be passed between computational agents in a DAI system.

**Figure 13.1**
Soccer robots in action. Reprinted with permission from Asada et al. 2003, p. 28.

## Culture

Unlike philosophers, psychologists, and AI researchers, anthropologists have always been attuned to social aspects of cognition. The central concept of anthropology is *culture*, "the systems of agreed-upon meanings that serve as recipes, or guidelines, for behavior in any particular society" (Barrett 1991, 55). The concept of culture is obviously social, for it concerns shared beliefs and values that make social interactions possible. As part of the trend to consider cognition in social contexts, some psychologists have recently been shifting their attention to culture. Hirschfeld and Gelman (1994, 4) contend that the mind is "less an all-purpose problem solver than a collection of enduring and independent subsystems designed to perform circumscribed tasks." These tasks may be specific to particular cultures, so that problem solving would show cultural variability. Similarly, emotions may not be fully wired into human thinking, but may vary in different cultures (Kitayama and Markus 1994). According to Ekman (2003), there are biologically universal human emotions such as happiness, sadness, and anger. But there also seems to be considerable variation across cultures in the linguistic description and behavioral display of emotions (Wierzbicka 1999). For example, most languages have words for sadness, but Russian contains words for subtle kinds of sadness with no English language counterparts.

Nisbett (2003) describes many differences in the styles of thought between Westerners (Europeans and North Americans) and East Asians (Chinese, Japanese, and Koreans). Psychological experiments have shown that East Asians are more likely than Westerners to notice environments and relations, whereas Westerners attend more to objects. Westerners are more likely to see stability where East Asians see change. Westerners have a tendency to explain other people's behavior in terms of their personality traits, whereas East Asians are more aware of how situations and relationships determine people's behaviors. These contrasts are not the result of any biological differences between Westerners and East Asians, but rather reflect cultural influences: Western culture emphasizes the independence of individuals, whereas East Asian culture emphasizes interdependence.

Whorf (1956) claimed that different languages carry with them such different views of the nature of space and time that people of different cultures live in different worlds. Subsequent research has indeed found that people with different languages vary with respect to their ways of thinking about space, time, objects, color, shapes, events, and other minds (Boroditsky 2003). For example, English speakers use front-back spatial terms to talk about time: childhood is behind you, and a career is ahead of you. Mandarin speakers differ in that they also use up-down spatial terms to talk about time. Thinking is a complex collaboration between linguistic and nonlinguistic representations.

Some sociologists have taken the idea of cultural variability to such an extent that they throw out any idea of objective knowledge. The world is "socially constructed," and people's belief systems arise not from their cognitive processes but from their social situations. Skepticism about cognitive explanations of knowledge has been common in sociology of science—for example, in Latour and Woolgar 1986. But recognizing the importance of social factors in the development of scientific knowledge is consistent with both the existence of cognitive factors and the objectivity of science (see Thagard 1999). All humans share the same basic perceptual and neurological apparatus, which provides a biological commonality to cultural variability.

## Responses to the Social Challenge

### Denial

How should CRUM respond to these diverse arguments that thinking should not be understood in a social vacuum but as an inherently interactive process? Denial could take the form of a doctrine philosophers of social science call *methodological individualism*. This is the view that since groups are just collections of individuals, there are is no need for explanations of group behavior to concern anything but individuals. Methodological individualism is popular among some economists who claim that explanations in terms of macroeconomic groups such as nations, corporations, and social classes are all in principle dispensable in favor of explanations of the behavior of individuals. Similarly, one could argue for an individualistic CRUM by claiming that the talk of groups, networks, and culture in the social challenge should eventually be eliminable in favor of talk of individual thinkers.

One can admit the physical fact that groups, networks, and societies consist of individuals while maintaining that explanation cannot ignore social structures. Societies are very complex systems, and their operations are so dynamic and interactive that reductive explanation of what happens in them in terms of what happens to individuals is extremely hard to achieve. We saw the same problem of complexity in chapters 9 and 12: the operations of the brain may just be the operations of neurons, but there are billions of neurons that interact with each other in highly complex ways that make it unlikely that we will every be able to specify fully the behavior of individuals on the basis of the behavior of their neurons. A more promising strategy is to take seriously all of the various levels of explanation (neurons, persons, societies) and to investigate how these levels are related to each other (see chapter 14).

## Expand CRUM

Taking the social challenge seriously requires CRUM to acquire a somewhat different perspective on representations and processes. The function of mental representations is not just for them to be representations by and for an individual, but also for them to be shared and used collectively. Propositions, rules, concepts, images, analogies, and even distributed representations need to be transmitted from one individual to another. Analogy, for example, is not just a process by which one person solves a problem alone, but can also be an important way in which someone helps someone else to solve a problem, leading to a shared representation of a situation. When you solve the problem of how to register for courses for the term or how to get a computer account, you are likely to rely heavily on information that is provided by others. Understanding consciousness may also rely on looking at cognition from a social perspective. You may not need much awareness to solve problems yourself, but consciousness is valuable for noticing what you are doing in order to teach other people. It is also crucial for empathic understanding in which you appreciate the emotions of others by analogy to your own experiences.

For representations to have a social application, there must be interpersonal processes that permit the spread of representations from one person to another. Such transmission in computer networks seems at first glance to be very simple, since electronic links make such transmissions as electronic mail and file transfers seem effortless. In fact, even simple transmissions depend on establishing protocols so that computers with very different hardware and software can communicate with each other. Distributed AI is far from trivial. Similarly, communication among humans is often very difficult. Teaching is not just a matter of dumping information into students' heads, but of striving to convey the desired representational systems. Hence, we need to expand CRUM to include descriptions of processes by which representations are transmitted among individuals.

## Supplement CRUM

Investigation of the social processes of cognition, including their psychological, computational, epistemological, and cultural aspects, is barely beginning. Although CRUM can be expanded in a social direction to include enhanced ideas about representation and computation, we should still expect that explanation of thinking will have to rely additionally on inherently social concepts such as group, network, society, culture, and communication. The brain, emotion, consciousness, body, and world challenges showed the need to supplement CRUM with biological considerations, and similarly CRUM needs to be supplemented with social considerations. We might call the desirable approach to the study of mind CRUMBS, for *Computational-Representational Understanding of Mind, Biological-Social*. This acronym invites dismissal of the whole enterprise as offering only tiny morsels of understanding about the mind. But progress is being made on numerous aspects of CRUMBS, and no other approach to mind currently offers to tell us more about the full range of mental phenomena.

One emerging area of research is computational modeling of institutions and groups (Prietula, Carley, and Gasser 1998). Just as we can understand the mechanisms of individual cognition by developing computer simulations, so we can learn about social processes by developing computer models of them. For example, I have described elsewhere a computational model of how consensus is achieved in scientific controversies such as the debate about the causes of stomach ulcers. In this model, the individual scientists are simulated using the ECHO program for explanatory coherence (described in chapter 7 of the present volume), and group consensus is reached by repeated communication between scientists (see Thagard 2000).

## Abandon CRUM

Like extreme proponents of the Heideggerian and situated-action perspectives, some social constructivists propose avoiding CRUM in favor of a purely social perspective on knowledge. Although admitting the importance of the social dimensions of human thinking, we should not forget that problem solving, learning, and language are also to be explained in terms of the representations and processes of individual minds. Mind and society are complementary explanatory notions, not competitors. Hence, the social challenge to cognitive science should be viewed as a spur to expand and supplement CRUM, not to abandon it.

## Summary

According to the social challenge, cognitive science has largely neglected the relation of minds to their social environments. But research on social epistemology, distributed cognition, multiagent systems, and culture is increasingly describing and explaining how human thought operates in societies. The social challenge does not mount an alternative to CRUM, but rather points to issues about groups, networks, societies, and cultures that cognitive science can take seriously by expanding and supplementing CRUM.

## Discussion Questions

1. What are the social contexts in which you acquire and apply knowledge?

2. How do emotions contribute to distributed cognition?

3. Would you expect a network of computers to be any more intelligent than a computer working alone?

4. Is CRUMBS coherent? Can there be a theory of mind that is biological and social as well as computational?

## Further Reading

On social epistemology, see Goldman 1999, 2002. On distributed cognition, see Hutchins 1995. On multiagent systems (distributed AI), see Wooldridge 2002. For a concise survey of cultural differences in social cognition, see Kunda 1999, chap. 11.

## Web Sites

Culture and cognition at the University of Michigan: http://www.lsa. umich.edu/psych/cultcog/index.html

RoboCup (robotic soccer): http://www.robocup.org/

Social epistemology resources: http://ucsu.colorado.edu/~brindell/soc-epistemology/

UCSD distributed cognition and human-computer interaction laboratory: http://hci.ucsd.edu/lab/

University of Massachusetts Multi-Agent Systems Lab: http://dis.cs. umass.edu/

# 14   The Future of Cognitive Science

## Integrations

Although the various challenges to the Computational-Representational Understanding of Mind show that it needs to be expanded and supplemented, we should not forget CRUM's numerous accomplishments reviewed in chapter 8. Any competing approach to mind will have to surpass CRUM in its ability to explain human problem solving, learning, and language. In the past half century, cognitive scientists have shed light on many aspects of human thought. Still, there are aspects that seem particularly elusive, such as the concerns about consciousness discussed in chapter 11. We cannot expect much progress on these difficult problems from narrowly focused research in a single discipline, but we should hope for further progress on the integration of psychological, computational, neurological, philosophical, linguistic, and anthropological research that has characterized the best investigations in cognitive science. How the mind works is the biggest puzzle that humans have ever tried to put together, and the pieces require contributions from many fields.

Extrapolating from current research, I see three kinds of integrations that we can hope will continue. First, at the most general, conceptual level, we should encounter new cross-disciplinary integrations as researchers in psychology, philosophy, artificial intelligence, anthropology, linguistics, and neuroscience continue to recognize the need to talk to each other and follow each other's work. Students and researchers interested in mind who restrict their learning to theories and methods in a single discipline are missing out, not only on a broader understanding of mind, but also on the possibility of creative advances in their own discipline that might be sparked by cross-fertilization from another. If my remarks in chapters 9–11 about neurochemicals are on the mark, then we should expect molecular biology to become an increasingly important contributor to cognitive science theory.

Second, cognitive science should continue to witness experimental integrations, through different kinds of data collected by methods used in different disciplines. Research on language, for example, will need to combine qualitative linguistic data with experimental psychological and neurological data. Ideally, diverse kinds of data should be unified conceptually so that they point toward robust conclusions about the nature of language use. Research on imagery has provided a good example of how behavioral and neurological experiments can mesh to support theoretical ideas about mental processes, and other aspects of thinking are similarly benefiting from a combination of behavioral and neurological experiments. Solving the very difficult problem of consciousness will require taking seriously not only behavioral and neurological data, but also the experiential data that each of us has by virtue of our conscious experience. Experimental data from molecular biology will also be increasingly relevant.

The third kind of integration that cognitive science should continue to see is theoretical integration made possible by computational ideas and simulations. We have seen that the analogy between thinking and computation has made two great contributions to the understanding of mind. First, it has provided a host of ideas about mental structures and processes, generating a complex account of mind that suffers neither from the explanatory poverty of behaviorism nor from the mystery making of dualism. Thinking about the mind as a kind of computer and conjecturing how it might be programmed has enabled researchers to produce far more precise and detailed accounts of mental operations than has been possible with any other theoretical approach. Second, because computational hypotheses can be made precise enough to be programmed, they can be tested by running simulations whose performance can be compared to that of human thinkers. One result of the computational view of mind has been an appreciation of how complex and diverse thinking is: simulations enable researchers to see both the limitations and the accomplishments of their theoretical ideas. Simulations have been valuable tools for understanding mechanisms at many different levels, such as the cognitive, neural, molecular, and social. I expect that computational models will increasingly aid our understanding of the relations between different levels of mechanisms—for example, helping to relate the social to the cognitive, the cognitive to the neural, and the neural to the molecular. Models may need to incorporate multiple levels, as when neural mechanisms are applied to help understand social phenomena in the emerging field of social neuroscience (Cacioppo 2002). It is possible that molecular mechanisms such as those contributing to consciousness may be relevant to understanding cognition.

Increasingly, computational theories have been integrated in that they cross the boundaries of the different approaches that I have described in isolation. We saw that theories of mental models, concepts, rules, analogies, and imagery are increasingly being tied, both experimentally and theoretically, to neural activity. Computational models that use multiple representations—for example, both concepts and rules—have been developed. Such cross-fertilization and hybridization, perhaps further enriched by dynamic systems ideas, will continue to be part of cognitive science. We can also expect increasing attention to the physical, biological, and social contexts in which cognition occurs. CRUM is being expanded into CRUMBS, the Computational-Representational Understanding of Mind, Biological-Social. Perhaps even problems as difficult as the nature of consciousness will yield to an integrated, multidisciplinary assault.

## The Future of Human and Machine Intelligence

Is there a dark side to the continuing development of computational models of human and artificial intelligence? If you have seen the *Matrix* and *Terminator* movies, you are aware of the scenario in which intelligent machines eventually come to dominate and mistreat humans. This is not a crazy scenario. Some experts have estimated that increases in computer speed will make human-level intelligence in machines possible within a few decades (Kurzweil 1999; Moravec 1998). We might hope that machine intelligence would treat humans well, but there is no reason to expect that superintelligent computers could or would be programmed to hold paramount the interests of humans. Because a program that makes possible an extraordinarily intelligent computer would be too large and complex to be written by humans, it would have to be the result of generations of evolutionary self-improvement. Programs could easily evolve to further the goals of computers rather than people. Human ethical beliefs are closely tied in with emotional reactions such as empathy and compassion. I argued in chapter 10 and 11 that we should not expect artificial intelligences to have emotions and consciousness at all like ours. Hence, a future generation of intelligent machines could be a race of psychopaths, incapable of caring about the fate of the biological beings whose intelligence they have surpassed.

There are two reasons why I think the scenario in which humans are superseded by intelligent computers is much farther off than Kurzweil and Moravec predict: first, they underestimate the computational power of human brains and second, they overestimate the ease with which intelligent computers can be programmed. Their prediction is based on the exponential increase in processing speed of computer chips, which continues to double every 12–18 months as it has for decades. Kurzweil estimates the computing speed of the human brain at around 20 million billion calculations per second, based on 100 billion neurons, each with a thousand connections and the slow firing rate of 200 calculations per second. Assuming continued exponential increase in chip speed, digital computers will reach the 20 million billion ($10^{15}$) calculations per second mark around 2020.

However, the molecular chemistry of the brain suggests that this estimate of its computational power may be very misleading, both quantitatively and qualitatively. If we count the number of processors in the brain as not just the number of neurons in the brain, but the number of *proteins* in the brain, we get a figure of around a billion times 100 billion, or $10^{17}$. Even if it is not legitimate to count each protein as a processor all by itself, it is still evident that the number of computational elements in the brain is more than the $10^{11}$ or $10^{12}$ neurons. Moreover, the discussion of hormones in chapter 9 shows that the number of computationally relevant causal connections is far greater than the thousand or so synaptic connections per neuron. I do not know how to estimate the number of neurons with hormonal receptors that can be influenced by a single neuron that secretes hormones or that activates glands that secrete hormones, but the number must be huge. If it is a million, and if every brain protein is viewed as a miniprocessor, then the computational speed of the brain is on the order of $10^{23}$ calculations per second, far larger than the $10^{15}$ calculations per second that Kurzweil expects to be available by 2020, although less than where he expects computers to be by 2060. Thus, quantitatively it appears that digital computers are much farther away than Kurzweil and Moravec estimate from reaching the raw computational power of the human brain.

Furthermore, intelligence is not merely a matter of raw computational power, but requires that the computer have a sufficiently powerful program to produce the desired task. My Macintosh G4 laptop computer can calculate $2^{100,000}$ in a couple of seconds, the same amount of time in which I can only calculate $2^5$, but the computer lacks the programming to be able to understand language and solve complex problems. Kurzweil and Moravec are aware that it is a daunting task to write the billions or trillions of lines of software that would be needed to enable the superfast computers of the future to approach human cognitive capabilities, but they blithely assume that evolutionary algorithms will allow computers to develop their own intelligent software. Evolutionary computation, which uses algorithms modeled in part on human genetics, is indeed a powerful means of developing new software (Koza 1992), but it is currently limited by the need for humans to provide a criterion of fitness that the genetic algorithms serve to maximize. In humans, the evaluation of different states is usually provided by emotions, which direct us to what matters for our learning and problem solving. Computers currently lack such intrinsic, biologically provided motivation, and so can be expected to have difficulties directing their problem solving in nonroutine directions.

Perhaps software will be developed that does for computers what emotions do for us, but current computational research on emotions has yet to decipher the complexity of the human emotional system and its numerous neurotransmitters and neuromodulators. Although there is a current resurgence of interest in emotions, it is being treated by researchers as a symbolic or electrical phenomenon rather than a chemical one. The complexity of human emotions, based on looping interactions among neural, hormonal, and immune systems, may be too complex for people to figure out how to program and also too complex for a program created by humans to evolve. We can nevertheless get an approximate understanding of these systems by using computer simulations and other methods to sketch the mechanisms by which they operate.

Regardless of the challenges stated above, this does not mean that computers of great intelligence in special areas will not be developed. It may be quantitatively and qualitatively difficult for AI researchers to duplicate the human brain, but intelligent computers may be developed by other means, just as IBM managed to build the world's best chess player by combining clever software with extraordinarily fast computer chips. But we should not expect a computer developed in this way to have all the mental capacities of humans, and we certainly should not expect it to have anything like human consciousness, which may be intrinsically tied to human emotions and hence, to our peculiar brain chemistry (chapter 11).

In sum, I doubt that the present generation is in serious danger of becoming obsolete or subservient to intelligent machines. But it would be a tragedy to the human species if our children or grandchildren inhabit a world where intelligence is dominated by computers. There are more optimistic scenarios—for example, one in which people acquire a kind of immortality by virtue of the transfer of their neural structures to computer chips. However, this may turn out to be no more technologically feasible than transporting between space ships in *Star Trek*. Perhaps the most scientifically plausible scenario is not one in which people are dominated by machines or downloaded into them, but rather one in which people integrate machines more and more fully into their cognitive operations. For example, Brooks (2002) speculates that people may someday have a device implanted in their brains that provides direct mental access to the Internet and interpersonal communications.

**Your Future in Cognitive Science**

The challenges and prospects of cognitive science make it obvious that there are many promising frontiers of research. But undergraduates attracted to the study of mind face difficult decisions since the mind can be investigated from the perspectives and methods of many different disciplines. Undergraduates can shop around, finding relevant courses in cognitive psychology, artificial intelligence, philosophy of mind, cognitive anthropology, linguistics, and cognitive neuroscience. But graduate students are forced into greater specialization. Here are some straightforward suggestions for students facing choices about how to continue their study and research on the nature of mind:

1. *Pick an aspect of mind that excites you.* What aspects of thinking do you find most interesting?

2. *Pick a methodology.* What kind of investigation is best suited to your interests and talents? Do you find experimental design more or less interesting than computer programming? Do you like to collect linguistic examples, or do you prefer to think about normative aspects of thinking the way that philosophers often do? The choice of methodology will determine more than anything else the field in which you seek further training.

3. *Keep your eyes open to other fields.* Having chosen one of the disciplines of cognitive science, you are in danger of becoming so immersed in the substantial task of becoming competent in an established field that you will forget about all the interesting connections to other fields. Only a few universities currently have graduate programs in cognitive science (see the Web site listed below). Students in a typically narrow program will have to struggle to keep their interdisciplinary interests alive.

4. *Integrate and collaborate.* Avoid dogmatism: do not suppose that the theoretical and methodological approach dominant in your graduate department is the only way to study the mind. In addition to seeking theoretical integration, keep your mind open to combining methodologies—for example, doing both experiments and computer simulations. Since acquiring mastery of even one methodology is a demanding task that can consume an entire graduate career, try to find collaborators with similar interests and different skills. Much of the best work in cognitive science has been performed collaboratively by researchers who combine insights and methodologies.

Students not interested in getting involved in cognitive science research nevertheless can have substantial motivation for keeping up with the field, because of continuing practical applications. Law, medicine, engineering, business, the arts, and education are all domains to which an improved understanding of mind will have substantial relevance.

Chapter 1 concludes with six assumptions that governed the writing of this text, and I hope that all have been rendered plausible. Cognitive science is interesting and exciting, and involves multifarious, interdisciplinary approaches that center around the computational-representational understanding of mind, which is, however, in need of expansion and supplementation. Many exciting projects in cognitive science await new investigators.

## Summary

Cognitive science has had numerous achievements, both theoretical and applied, but there remains enormous scope for further theory and experiment. Progress in understanding the mind will not be confined within narrow fields, but will require cross-disciplinary, experimental, and theoretical integrations. The development of artificial intelligence that might surpass human intelligence raises difficult ethical issues. Students contemplating a future in cognitive science have a wealth of problems and approaches to choose from.

## Discussion Questions

1. What is more impressive, how much cognitive science has contributed to the nature of mind, or how much remains to be understood?
2. What are the impediments to developing further experimental and theoretical integrations in cognitive science?
3. What methods strike you as most interesting and fruitful for future work on the nature of mind?
4. Would a fully developed artificial intelligence likely be good, evil, or neutral?

## Further Reading

See the end of chapter 1 for suggestions about further general reading in cognitive science.

## Web Sites

Academic programs in cognitive science:
http://www.cognitivesciencesociety.org/graduate/
World Transhumanist Society: http://www.transhumanism.org/about.htm

## Appendix: Resources in Cognitive Science

Note: This list is not intended to be exhaustive, but merely to provide pointers to some of the most useful sources.

**Reference Works**

Interdisciplinary

*A Companion to Cognitive Science*

*Encyclopedia of Cognitive Science*

*MIT Encyclopedia of the Cognitive Sciences*

Disciplinary

*Dictionary of Psychology*

*Dictionary of Philosophy*

*Encyclopedia of Artificial Intelligence*

*Encyclopedia of Philosophy*

*Glossary of Cognitive Science*

*International Dictionary of Psychology*

*Routledge Encyclopedia of Philosophy*

**Journals**

Interdisciplinary

*Behavioral and Brain Sciences*

*Cognition*

*Cognitive Science*

*Cognitive Science Quarterly*

*Cognitive Systems Research*

*Journal of the Learning Sciences*

*Linguistics and Philosophy*

*Mind and Language*

*Trends in Cognitive Sciences*

Philosophy

*Journal of Philosophy*

*Mind*

*Minds and Machines*

*Philosophical Psychology*

Psychology

*Cognition and Emotions*

*Cognition and Instruction*

*Cognitive Psychology*

*Journal of Experimental Psychology: Learning, Memory, and Cognition*

*Psychological Review*

*Psychological Science*

Artificial Intelligence

*Artificial Intelligence*

*AI Magazine*

*Connection Science*

*Computational Intelligence*

*Journal of Experimental and Theoretical Artificial Intelligence*

*Machine Learning*

Neuroscience

*Cognitive Neuroscience*

*Neural Computation*

*Neural Networks*

*Trends in Neuroscience*

Linguistics

*Language*

*Foundations of Language*

*Linguistic Inquiry*

Anthropology and Sociology

*Current Anthropology*

*Social Studies of Science*

## Organizations

American Association for Artificial Intelligence

Cognitive Neuroscience Society

Cognitive Science Society

Society for Machines and Mentality

Society for Philosophy and Psychology

## Conference Proceedings

*Advances in Neural Information Processing Systems*, published by the MIT Press.

*Proceedings of the Cognitive Science Society Conference*, published by Erlbaum.

*Proceedings of the International Joint Conference on Artificial Intelligence,* published by Morgan Kaufmann.

*Proceedings of the National Conference on Artificial Intelligence*, published by AAAI Press.

## Publishers

Publishers who frequently produce books relevant to cognitive science include Basil Blackwell Ltd., Cambridge University Press, Harvard University Press, John Benjamins, Kluwer Academic Publishers, Erlbaum, the MIT Press, Morgan Kaufmann Publishers, Oxford University Press, and University of Chicago Press.

## Internet

See the numerous Web sites listed at the end of the preceding chapters. Links to all the Web sites mentioned in this book can be found at http://cogsci.uwaterloo.ca/courses/resources.html. My own Web site is http://cogsci.uwaterloo.ca.

# Glossary

Note: Words in italics have their own entries in the glossary.

**Abduction**  Reasoning that generates hypotheses to explain puzzling facts.

**ACT**  "Adaptive Control of Thought"—A computational theory of thinking developed by John Anderson.

**Affective computing**  Study of computing technology that relates to, arises from, or deliberately influences *emotions*.

**Algorithm**  A step-by-step procedure for solving a problem.

**Amygdala**  Almond-shaped part of the brain involved in *emotions* such as fear.

**Analogy**  Mental process that makes connections between relations in two sets of objects.

**Anthropology**  The study of the origins, distribution, social relations, and *culture* of human beings.

**Artificial intelligence**  The study of how computers can be programmed to perceive, reason, and act.

**Backprogagation**  Learning *algorithm* in *feedforward* networks that adjusts the strengths of the links between *neurons*.

**Bayesian network**  A directed graph that that can be used to reason with probabilistic information.

**Case-based reasoning**  Reasoning by *analogy*.

**Chaos**  Property of a *dynamic system* that it is highly sensitive to small changes.

**Cognitive grammar**  Approach to *linguistics* that rejects the traditional separation of syntax and semantics.

**Cognitive science**  The interdisciplinary study of mind and intelligence.

**Coma**   State of deep unconsciousness caused by disease or injury.

**Computation**   Physical process with states that represent states of another system and with transitions between states that amount to operations on the *representations*.

**Concept**   *Mental representation* of a class of objects or events that belong together, usually corresponding to a word.

**Conceptual change**   Process in which *concepts* acquire new *meaning*.

**Conceptual combination**   Process in which new *concepts* are constructed by joining or juxtaposing old ones.

**Connectionism**   Approach to *cognitive science* that models thinking by artificial *neural networks*.

**Consciousness**   Mental state involving attention, awareness, and qualitative experience.

**Cortex**   Outer layer of the brain, responsible for many higher cognitive functions.

**CRUM**   Computational-Representational Understanding of Mind: the hypothesis that thinking is performed by *computations* operating on *representations*.

**Culture**   The way of life of a society, including beliefs and behaviors.

**Data structure**   An organization of information in a computer program.

**Deduction**   Reasoning from premises to a conclusion such that if the premises are true then the conclusion must also be true.

**Distributed artificial intelligence**   Problem solving that requires communication among more than one computer, each of which possesses some intelligence.

**Distributed cognition**   Problem solving that requires communication among more than one thinker.

**Distributed representation**   *Neural networks* that use patterns of activity in multiple nodes or *neurons* to stand for objects or situations.

**Dopamine**   *Neurotransmitter* involved in reward pathways in the brain.

**Dualism**   Philosophical view that the mind consists of two separate substances, soul and body.

**Dynamic (dynamical) system**   Collection of interacting objects whose changes are describable by mathematical equations.

**Electroencephalogram (EEG)**   Recording of electrical activity in the brain.

**Embodiment**   Property of having a body and experiencing the world by means of it.

**Emotion**   Positive or negative mental state that combines physiological input with cognitive appraisal.

**Emotional intelligence**   Ability to deal effectively with the *emotions* of oneself and others.

**Empiricism**   The philosophical view that knowledge comes primarily from sensory experience.

**Explanation schema**   *Mental representation* of a pattern of causal connections.

**Feedforward network**   Artificial *neural network* in which the flow of activity is in one direction, from input *neurons* to output neurons.

**Frame**   Data structure that represents a *concept* or *schema*.

**Functionalism**   Version of *materialism* according to which mental states are defined by their functional relations, not by any particular kind of physical realization.

**Hebbian learning**   Process in *neural networks* that strengthens the association between two *neurons* that are simultaneously active.

**Hippocampus**   Brain region involved in the acquisition of memories.

**Image**   Mental structure that is similar to what it represents.

**Induction**   Reasoning that introduces uncertainty.

**Inheritance**   Form of inference in which information is transferred from a higher to a lower structure.

**Innate**   A *representation* or process that is genetic rather than learned.

**Insula (insular cortex)**   Brain region that integrates information from many bodily senses.

**Intentionality**   Property of a *representation* or mental state that it is about some aspect of the world.

**Lesion**   Abnormal change in an organ such as the brain.

**Linguistics**   The study of language.

**Link**   Connection between two artificial *neurons* that enables one to influence the activity of the other.

**Local representation**   Artificial *neural network* in which each node stands for a single concept or proposition.

**Logic**   The study of valid reasoning.

**Magnetic resonance imaging (MRI and fMRI)**   Technique that uses magnets to produce images of the structure and function of organs.

**Materialism**   Philosophical view that minds are purely physical.

**Meaning**   The content of a *representation* that results from its relations to other representations and the world.

**Mechanism**   System of interconnected parts that produces regular changes.

**Memory**   Storage of information, either temporary (short-term or working memory) or permanent (long-term).

**Mental model**   Mental structure that approximately stands for something in the world.

**Mental representation**   A structure or process in the mind that stands for something.

**Metaphor**   Use of language to understand and experience one kind of thing in terms of another.

**Model**   Structure that approximately represents some objects or events.

**Multiagent system**   Interacting collection of computers capable of intelligent action.

**Neural network**   Interconnected group of *neurons*.

**Neuron**   Nerve cell.

**Neuroscience**   Study of the structure and functioning of brains.

**Neurotransmitter**   Molecule that transmits nerve impulses across a *synapse*.

**Parallel**   Process in which more than one computation is performed at the same time.

**Parallel constraint satisfaction**   Process in which a problem is solved by using a parallel *algorithm* to find the best assignment of values to interconnected aspects of the problem.

**Parallel distributed processing**   Approach to *cognitive science* that models thinking by artificial *neural networks* with *distributed representations*.

**Philosophy**   Study of the fundamental nature of knowledge, existence, and morality.

**Positron emission tomography (PET)**   Technique that uses radioactive isotopes to produces images of the chemical function of organs such as blood flow in the brain.

**Prefrontal cortex**   Area of the brain at the front of the front of the *cortex*, responsible for the highest cognitive functions such as reasoning.

**Production rule**   a representation of the form IF something THEN something.

**Psychology**   Study of the minds of humans and other animals.

**Rationalism**   The philosophical view that knowledge comes primarily by reasoning that is independent of sensory experience.

**Recurrent network**   *Neural network* in which the output of some *neurons* feeds back via intervening connections to become input to them.

**Relaxation**   Process in which an artificial *neural network* reaches a state of stable activations.

**Representation**   A structure or activity that stands for something.

**Robot**   Machine capable of performing complex physical acts similar to ones done by humans.

**Rule**   A *mental representation* of the form IF something THEN something.

**Schema**   A *mental representation* of a class of objects, events, or practices.

**Search**   A computational process of looking for or carrying out a sequence of actions that lead to desired states.

**Situated action**   Action that results from being embedded in a physical or social world.

**SOAR**   "State, Operator, And Result"—A computational theory of thinking developed by Allen Newell and others.

**Social cognition**   Study of how people think about each other.

**Social epistemology**   Study of social practices that encourage or inhibit the development of knowledge.

**Somatic marker**   Brain signal corresponding to states of the body relevant to *emotions*.

**Source analog**   Set of objects, properties, and relations that suggests conclusions about a target analog.

**Spike train**   Firing pattern of a *neuron*, consisting of a sequence of firing episodes.

**Spreading activation**   Computational process in which the activity of one structure leads to the activity of an associated structure.

**Syllogism**   Kind of *deduction* in which the premises and conclusions have forms such as "All A are B" and "No A are B."

**Synapse**   Space in which a signal passes from one *neuron* to another.

**Target analog**   Set of objects, properties, and relations that can be learned about by comparison to a source analog.

**Theory**   Set of hypotheses that explain observations.

**Thought experiment**   Use of the imagination to investigate nature.

**Ventromedial prefrontal cortex**   The bottom-middle part of the *prefrontal cortex*.

**Whorf hypothesis**   Conjecture that language determines how we perceive and think about the world.

# References

Abraham, R. H., and C. D. Shaw. 1992. *Dynamics: The geometry of behavior.* 2nd ed. Redwood City, Calif.: Addison-Wesley.

Adams, M. J. 1990. *Beginning to read.* Cambridge, Mass.: The MIT Press.

Aitchison, J. 1987. *Words in the mind: An introduction to the mental lexicon.* Oxford: Basil Blackwell.

Akmajian, A., R. A. Demers, A. K. Farmer, and R. M. Harnish. 2001. *Linguistics: An introduction to language and communication.* 5th ed. Cambridge, Mass.: The MIT Press.

Allen, R. H., ed. 1992. *Expert systems for civil engineers: Knowledge representation.* New York: American Society of Civil Engineers.

Allman, J. M. 1999. *Evolving brains.* New York: Scientific American Library.

Anderson, J. A., and E. Rosenfeld, eds. 1988. *Neurocomputing.* Cambridge, Mass.: The MIT Press.

Anderson, J. A., and E. Rosenfeld, eds. 1998. *Talking nets: An oral history of neural networks.* Cambridge, Mass.: The MIT Press.

Anderson, J. R. 1983. *The architecture of cognition.* Cambridge, Mass.: Harvard University Press.

Anderson, J. R. 1993. *Rules of the mind.* Hillsdale, N.J.: Erlbaum.

Anderson, J. R. 2000. *Cognitive psychology and its implications.* 5th ed. New York: Worth.

Anderson, J. R., Y. Qin, V. A. Stenger, and C. S. Carter. Forthcoming. The relationship of three cortical regions to an information-processing model. *Cognitive Neuroscience* 16, 637–653.

Asada, M. et al. 2003. An overview of RoboCup-2002 Fukuoka/Busan. *AI Magazine* 24 (2, summer), 21–40.

Ashby, F. G., and E. Walrdron. 2000. The neuropsychological bases of category learning. *Current Directions in Psychological Science* 9, 10–14.

Barnes, A., and P. Thagard. 1997. Empathy and analogy. *Dialogue: Canadian Philosophical Review* 36, 705–720.

Barrett, R. A. 1991. *Culture and conduct: An excursion in anthropology.* 2nd ed. Belmont, Calif.: Wadsworth.

Barsalou, L. W. 1983. Ad hoc categories. *Memory and Cognition* 11, 211–227.

Barsalou, L. W., W. K. Simmons, A. K. Barbey, and C. D. Wilson. 2003. Grounding conceptual knowledge in modality-specific systems. *Trends in Cognitive Sciences* 7, 84–91.

Bartlett, F. C. 1932. *Remembering.* Cambridge: Cambridge University Press.

Barton, S. 1994. Chaos, self-organization, and psychology. *American Psychologist* 49, 5–14.

Bates, E. A., and J. L. Elman. 2002. Connectionism and the study of change. In M. H. Johnson, Y. Munakata, and R. O. Gilmore, eds., *Brain development and cognition,* 2nd ed., 420–440. Oxford: Blackwell.

Bechtel, W., and A. A. Abrahamsen. 2002. *Connectionism and the mind: Parallel processing, dynamics, and evolution in networks.* 2nd ed. Oxford: Basil Blackwell.

Bechtel, W., and G. Graham, eds. 1998. *A companion to cognitive science.* Malden, Mass.: Blackwell.

Bechtel, W., P. Mandik, J. Mundale, and R. S. Stufflebeam, eds. 2001. *Philosophy and the neurosciences: A reader.* Malden, Mass.: Blackwell.

Benington, J. H., and H. C. Heller. 1995. Restoration of brain energy metabolism as the function of sleep. *Progress in neurobiology* 45, 347–360.

Bergmann, M., J. H. Moor, and J. Nelson. 2003. *The logic book.* 4th ed. Columbus Ohio: McGraw-Hill.

Blackmore, S. 2004. *Consciousness: An introduction.* Oxford: Oxford University Press.

Block, N. 1978. Troubles with functionalism. In C. W. Savage, ed. *Perception and cognition.* Minneapolis, Minn.: University of Minnesota Press.

Block, N., O. Flanagan, and G. Güzeldere, eds. 1997. *The nature of consciousness: Philosophical debates.* Cambridge, Mass.: The MIT Press.

Boroditsky, L. 2003. Linguistic relativity. In L. Nadel, ed., *Encylopedia of cognitive science.* Vol. 2, 917–921. London: Nature Publishing Group.

Boroojerdi, B., M. Phipps, L. Kopylev, C. M. Wharton, L. G. Cohen, and J. Grafman. 2001. Enhancing analogic reasoning with rTMS over the left prefrontal cortex. *Neurology* 56, 526–528.

Braine, M. D. S. 1978. On the relation between the natural logic of reasoning and standard logic. *Psychological Review* 85, 1–21.

Braine, M. D. S., and D. P. O'Brien. 1998. *Mental logic*. Mahwah, N.J.: Erlbaum.

Brewer, W. F., and J. C. Treyens. 1981. Role of schemata in memory for places. *Cognitive Psychology* 13, 207–230.

Brooks, R. A. 1991. Intelligence without representation. *Artificial Intelligence* 47, 139–159.

Brooks, R. A. 2002. *Flesh and machines: How robots will change us*. New York: Pantheon.

Bruer, J. T. 1993. *Schools for thought: A science of learning in the classroom*. Cambridge, Mass.: The MIT Press.

Bruner, J. S. 1990. *Acts of meaning*. Cambridge, Mass.: Harvard University Press.

Bruner, J. S., J. J. Goodnow, and G. A. Austin. 1956. *A study of thinking*. New York: Wiley.

Buchanan, B., and E. Shortliffe, eds. 1984. *Rule-based expert systems*. Reading, Mass.: Addison-Wesley.

Busemeyer, J. R., and J. T. Townsend. 1993. Decision field theory: A dynamic-cognitive approach to decision making in an uncertain environment. *Psychological Revew* 100, 432–459.

Cacioppo, J. T. et al., eds. 2002. *Foundations in social neuroscience*. Cambridge, Mass.: The MIT Press.

Card, S. K., T. P. Moran, and A. Newell. 1983. *The psychology of computer-human interaction*. Hillsdale, N.J.: Erlbaum.

Carruthers, P. 2000. *Phenomenal consciousness: A naturalistic theory*. Cambridge: Cambridge University Press.

Chalmers, D. J. 1996. *The conscious mind*. Oxford: Oxford University Press.

Cheng, P. W., and K. J. Holyoak. 1985. Pragmatic reasoning schemas. In *Cognitive Psychology* 17, 391–416.

Chi, M. 1992. Conceptual change within and across ontological categories: Examples from learning and discovery in science. In R. Giere, ed., *Cognitive models of science*, 129–186. Minneapolis, Minn.: University of Minnesota Press.

Chomsky, N. 1957. *Syntactic structures*. The Hague: Mouton.

Chomksy, N. 1959. Review of *Verbal behavior*, by B. F. Skinner. *Language* 35, 26–58.

Chomsky, N. 1972. *Language and mind*. 2nd ed. New York: Harcourt Brace Jovanovich.

Chomsky, N. 1980. *Rules and representations*. New York: Columbia University Press.

Chomsky, N. 1988. *Language and problems of knowledge*. Cambridge, Mass.: The MIT Press.

Chomsky, N. 2002. *On nature and language*. Cambridge: Cambridge University Press.

Christoff, K., V. Pabhakaran, J. Dorfman, Z. Zhao, J. K. Kroger, K. J. Holyoak, and J. D. K. Gabrieli. 2001. Rostrolateral prefrontal cortex involvement in relational integration during reasoning. *NeuroImage* 14, 1136–1149.

Churchland, P. M. 1989. *A neurocomputational perspective*. Cambridge, Mass.: The MIT Press.

Churchland, P. M. 1995. *The engine of reason: The seat of the soul*. Cambridge, Mass.: The MIT Press.

Churchland, P. S. 1986. *Neurophilosophy*. Cambridge, Mass.: The MIT Press.

Churchland, P. S. 2002. *Brain-wise: Studies in neurophilosophy*. Cambridge, Mass.: The MIT Press.

Churchland, P. S., and T. Sejnowski. 1992. *The computational brain*. Cambridge, Mass.: The MIT Press.

Clark, A. 1997. *Being there: Putting brain, body, and world together again*. Cambridge, Mass.: The MIT Press.

Clark, A. 1999. An embodied cognitive science. *Trends in Cognitive Sciences* 3, 345–351.

Clark, A. 2001. *Mindware: An introduction to the philosophy of cognitive science*. New York: Oxford University Press.

Conati, C., A. Gertner, and K. Vanlehn. 2002. Using Bayesian networks to manage uncertainty in student modeling. *User Modeling and User-Adapted Instruction* 12, 317–417.

Cooper, L. A., and R. N. Shepard. 1973. Chronometric studies of the rotation of mental images. In W. G. Chase, ed., *Visual information processing*, 75–176. New York: Academic Press.

Cosmides, L., and J. Tooby. 1999. Evolutionary psychology. In R. A. Wilson and F. C. Keil, eds., *The MIT encyclopedia of the cognitive sciences*, 295–298. Cambridge, Mass.: The MIT Press.

Costello, F. J., and M. T. Keane. 2000. Efficient creativity: constraint-guided conceptual combination. *Cognitive Science* 24, 299–349.

Crick, F. 1994. *The astonishing hypothesis: The scientific search for the soul*. London: Simon and Schuster.

Crick, F., and C. Koch. 1998. Consciousness and neuroscience. *Cerebral Cortex* 8, 97–107.

Croft, D., and P. Thagard. 2002. Dynamic imagery: A computational model of motion and visual analogy. In L. Magnani, ed., *Model-based reasoning: Scientific discovery, technological innovation, values,* 259–274. New York: Kluwer/Plenum.

Crowley, K., and R. S. Siegler. 1993. Flexible strategy use in children's tic-tac-toe. *Cognitive Science* 17, 531–561.

Damasio, A. R. 1994. *Descartes' error.* New York: Putnam.

Damasio, A. R. 1999. *The feeling of what happens: Body and emotion in the making of consciousness.* New York: Harcourt Brace Jovanovich.

D'Andrade, R. G. 1995. *The development of cognitive anthropology.* Cambridge: Cambridge University Press.

Davidson, R. J., D. Pizzagalli, J. B. Nitschke, and K. Putnam. 2002. Depression: Perspectives from affective neuroscience. *Annual Review of Psychology* 53, 545–574.

Davidson, R. J., K. R. Scherer, and H. H. Goldsmith, eds. 2003. *Handbook of affective sciences.* New York: Oxford University Press.

Dawson, M. R. W. 1998. *Understanding cognitive science.* Oxford: Blackwell.

Dean, T. L., and M. P. Wellman. 1991. *Planning and control.* San Mateo, Calif.: Morgan Kaufmann.

Dehaene, S., E. Spelke, P. Pinel, R. Stanescu, and S. Tsivkin. 1999. Sources of mathematical thinking: Behavioral and brain-imaging evidence. *Science* 284, 970–974.

Dennett, D. 1991. *Consciousness explained.* Boston: Little, Brown.

Dietrich, E., ed. 1994. *Thinking computers and virtual persons: Essays on the intentionality of machines.* San Diego, Calif.: Academic Press.

Dourish, P. 2001. *Where the action is: The foundations of embodied interaction.* Cambridge, Mass.: The MIT Press.

Dreyfus, H. L. 1991. *Being-in-the-world.* Cambridge, Mass.: The MIT Press.

Dreyfus, H. L. 1992. *What computers still can't do* 3rd ed. Cambridge, Mass.: The MIT Press.

Dym, C. L., and R. E. Levitt. 1991. *Knowledge-based systems in engineering.* New York: McGraw-Hill.

Edelman, G. M., and G. Tononi. 2000. *A universe of consciousness: How matter becomes imagination.* New York: Basic Books.

Ekman, P. 2003. *Emotions revealed: Recognizing faces and feelings to improve communication and emotional life.* New York: Henry Holt.

Eliasmith, C. 2003. Moving beyond metaphors: Understanding the mind for what it is. *Journal of Philosophy* 100, 493–520.

Eliasmith, C., and C. H. Anderson. 2003. *Neural engineering: Computation, representation and dynamics in neurobiological systems.* Cambridge, Mass.: The MIT Press.

Eliasmith, C., and P. Thagard. 2001. Integrating structure and meaning: A distributed model of analogical mapping. *Cognitive Science* 25, 245–286.

Elman, J. L., E. A. Bates, M. H. Johnson, A. Karmiloff-Smith, D. Parisi, and K. Plunkett. 1996. *Rethinking innateness: A connectionist perspective on development.* Cambridge, Mass.: The MIT Press.

Evans, T. 1968. A program for the solution of a class of geometric analogy intelligence test questions. In M. Minsky, ed., *Semantic information processing*, 271–353. Cambridge Mass.: The MIT Press.

Fazio, R. H. 2001. On the automatic activation of associated evaluations: An overview. *Cognition and Emotion* 15, 115–141.

Feigenbaum, E., P. McCorduck, and H. Nii. 1988. *The rise of the expert company.* New York: Vintage.

Feldman Barrett, L., and J. A. Russell. 1998. Independence and bipolarity in the structure of affect. *Journal of Personality and Social Psychology* 74, 967–984.

Feldman, J. A. 1981. A connectionist model of visual memory. In G. E. Hinton and J. A. Anderson, eds., *Parallel models of associative memory*, 49–81. Hillsdale, N.J.: Erlbaum.

Fellbaum, C., ed. 1998. *WordNet: An electronic lexical database.* Cambridge, Mass.: The MIT Press.

Fikes, R., and N. Nilsson. 1971. STRIPS: A new approach to the application of theorem proving to problem solving. *Artificial Intelligence* 2, 189–208.

Fineman, S., ed. 2000. *Emotion in organizations.* London: Sage.

Finger, S. 1994. *Origins of neuroscience: A history of explorations into brain function.* New York: Oxford University Press.

Finke, R. 1989. *Principles of mental imagery.* Cambridge, Mass.: the MIT Press.

Finke, R., S. Pinker, and M. Farah. 1989. Reinterpreting visual patterns in mental imagery. *Cognitive Science* 13, 51–78.

Finke, R., T. B. Ward, and S. M. Smith. 1992. *Creative cognition: Theory, research and applications.* Cambridge, Mass.: The MIT Press/Bradford Books.

Finucane, M. L., E. Peters, and P. Slovic. 2003. Judgment and decision making: The dance of affect and reason. In S. L. Schneider and J. Shanteau, eds., *Emerging perspectives on judgment and decision research*, 327–364. Cambridge: Cambridge University Press.

Flanagan, O. 1992. *Consciousness reconsidered*. Cambridge, Mass.: The MIT Press.

Flanagan, O. J. 2000. *Dreaming souls: Sleep, dreams, and the evolution of the conscious mind*. Oxford: Oxford University Press.

Fodor, J. 1975. *The language of thought*. New York: Crowell.

Forbus, K. D., Gentner, and K. Law. 1995. MAC/FAC: A model of similarity-based retrieval. *Cognitive Science* 19, 144–205.

Forbus, K., P. Nielsen, and B. Faltings. 1991. Qualitative spatial reasoning: The CLOCK project. *Artifical Intelligence* 51, 417–472.

Forbus, K. 2001. Exploring analogy in the large. In D. Gentner, K. H. Holyoak, and B. K. Kokinov, eds., *The analogical mind: Perspectives from cognitive science*, 23–58. Cambridge, Mass.: The MIT Press.

Foss, J. E. 1995. Materialism, reduction, replacement, and the place of consciousness in science. *Journal of philosophy* 92, 401–429.

Frege, G. 1960. *Translations from the philosophical writings of Gottlob Frege*. Trans. by P. Geach and M. Black. Oxford: Basil Blackwell.

French, R. M. 2002. The computational modeling of analogy-making. *Trends in Cognitive Sciences* 6, 200–205.

Frijda, N. H. 1986. *The emotions*. Cambridge: Cambridge University Press.

Funt, B. 1980. Problem solving with diagrammatic representations. *Artificial Intelligence* 13, 201–230.

Galegher, J., R. E. Kraut, and C. Egido, eds. 1990. *Intellectual teamwork: Social and technological foundations of cooperative work*. Hillsdale, N.J.: Erlbaum.

Gardner, H. 1985. *The mind's new science*. New York: Basic Books.

Genesereth, M. R., and N. J. Nilsson. 1987. *Logical foundations of artificial intelligence*. Los Altos, Calif.: Morgan Kaufmann.

Gentner, D. 1983. Structure-mapping: A theoretical framework for analogy. *Cognitive Science* 7, 155–170.

Gentner, D. 1989. The mechanisms of analogical learning. In S. Vosniadou and A. Ortony, eds., *Similarity and analogical reasoning*, 199–241. Cambridge: Cambridge University Press.

Gentner, D., K. H. Holyoak, and B. K. Kokinov, eds. 2001. *The analogical mind: Perspectives from cognitive science*. Cambridge, Mass.: The MIT Press.

Gibson, J. J. 1979. *The ecological approach to visual perception*. Boston: Houghton-Mifflin.

Gick, M. L., and K. J. Holyoak. 1980. Analogical problem solving. *Cognitive Psychology* 12, 306–355.

Gick, M. L., and K. J. Holyoak. 1983. Schema induction and analogical transfer. *Cognitive Psychology* 15, 1–38.

Giere, R. 1988. *Explaining science: A cognitive approach*. Chicago: University of Chicago Press.

Gigerenzer, G. 2000. *Adaptive thinking: Rationality in the real world*. New York: Oxford University Press.

Gigerenzer, G., U. Hoffrage, and H. Kleinbölting. 1991. Probabilistic mental models: A Brunswikian theory of confidence. *Psychological Review* 98, 506–528.

Gilovich, T., D. Griffin, and D. Kahneman, eds. 2002. *Heuristics and biases: The psychology of intuitive judgment*. Cambridge: Cambridge University Press.

Glasgow, J. I., S. Fortier, and F. Allen. 1993. Molecular scene analysis: Crystal structure determination through imagery. In L. Hunter, ed., *Artificial intelligence and molecular biology*, 433–458. Cambridge, Mass.: The MIT Press.

Glasgow, J. I. 1993. The imagery debate revisited: A computational perspective. *Computational Intelligence* 9, 309–333.

Glasgow, J. I., and D. Papadias. 1992. Computational imagery. *Cognitive Science* 16, 355–394.

Gleick, J. 1987. *Chaos: Making a new science*. New York: Viking.

Glucksberg, S., and B. Keysar. 1990. Understanding metaphorical comparisons: Beyond similarity. *Psychological Review* 97, 3–18.

Glymour, C. 2001. *The mind's arrows: Bayes nets and graphical causal models in psychology*. Cambridge, Mass.: The MIT Press.

Goel, V. 2003. Evidence for dual neural pathways for syllogistic reasoning. *Psychologica* 32, 301–309.

Goel, V., B. Gold, S. Kapur, and S. Houle. 1998. Neuroanatomical correlates of human reasoning. *Journal Cognitive Neuroscience* 10, 293–302.

Goldman, A. I. 1999. *Knowledge in a social world*. Oxford: Oxford University Press.

Goldman, A. I. 2002. *Pathways to knowledge: Private and public*. Oxford: Oxford University Press.

Goldvarg, E., and P. N. Johnson-Laird. 2001. Naive causality: A mental model theory of causal reasoning and meaning. *Cognitive Science* 25, 565–610.

Goleman, D. 1995. *Emotional intelligence*. New York: Bantam.

Goss, S., C. Hall, E. Buckolz, and G. Fishburne. 1986. Imagery ability and the acquisition and retention of movements. *Memory and Cognition* 14, 469–477.

Gottesman, C. 1999. Neurophysiological support of consciousness during waking and sleep. *Progress in neurobiology* 59, 469–508.

Gottman, J. M., R. Tyson, K. R. Swanson, C. C. Swanson, and J. D. Murray. 2003. *The mathematics of marriage: Dynamic nonlinear models*. Cambridge, Mass.: The MIT Press.

Graham, G. 1998. *Philosophy of mind: An introduction*. 2nd ed. Oxford: Blackwell.

Griffiths, P. E. 1997. *What emotions really are: The problem of psychological categories*. Chicago: University of Chicago Press.

Groenewegen, H. J., and H. B. M. Uylings. 2000. The prefrontal cortex and the integration of sensory, limbic and autonomic information. In H. B. M. Uylings et al., eds. *Cognition, emotion, and autonomic responses*, 3–28. Amsterdam: Elsevier.

Hall, R. 1989. Computational approaches to analogical reasoning: A comparative analysis. *Artificial Intelligence* 39, 39–120.

Hameroff, S. R. 1998. Anesthesia, consciousness, and hydrophobic pockets: A unitary quantum hypothesis of anesthetic action. *Toxicology letters* 100/101, 31–39.

Hastings, J., K. Branting, and J. Lockwood. 2002. CARMA: A case-based rangeland management advisor. *AI Magazine* (2, summer) 49–62.

Hatfield, E., J. T. Cacioppo, and R. L. Rapson. 1994. *Emotional contagion*. Cambridge: Cambridge University Press.

Hebb, D. O. 1949. *The organization of behavior*. New York: Wiley.

Heidegger, M. 1962. *Being and time*. Trans. by J. Macquarrie and E. Robinson. New York: Harper & Row.

Hempel, C. G. 1965. *Aspects of scientific explanation*. New York: The Free Press.

Hesse, M. 1966. *Models and analogies in science*. Notre Dame, Ind.: Notre Dame University Press.

Hinkle, D., and C. N. Toomey. 1994. Clavier: Applying case-based reasoning in composite part fabrication. In *Proceedings of the Sixth Innovative Applications of Artificial Intelligence Conference*, 54–62. Menlo Park, Calif.: AAAI Press.

Hinton, G. E., and J. Anderson, eds. 1981. *Parallel models of associative memory*. Hillsdale, N.J.: Erlbaum.

Hinton, G. E., and T. J. Sejnowski, eds. 1999. *Unsupervised learning: foundations of neural computation*. Cambridge, Mass.: The MIT Press.

Hirschfeld, L. A., and S. A. Gelman, eds. 1994. *Mapping the mind: Domain specificity in cognition and culture.* Cambridge: Cambridge University Press.

Hoffman, M. L. 2000. *Empathy and moral development: Implications for caring and justice.* Cambridge: Cambridge University Press.

Hofstadter, D. 1995. *Fluid concepts and creative analogies: Computer models of the fundamental mechanisms of thought.* New York: Basic Books.

Hollan, J., E. Hutchins, and D. Kirsh. 2000. Distiributed cognition: Toward a new foundation for human-computer interaction. *ACM Transactions on Computer–Human Interaction 7,* 174–196.

Holland, J. H., K. J. Holyoak, R. E. Nisbett, and P. R. Thagard. 1986. *Induction: Processes of inference, learning, and discovery.* Cambridge, Mass.: The MIT Press.

Holtzman, S. 1989. *Intelligent decision systems.* Reading, Mass.: Addison-Wesley.

Holyoak, K. J., and P. Thagard. 1995. *Mental leaps: Analogy in creative thought.* Cambridge, Mass.: The MIT Press/Bradford Books.

Howson, C., and P. Urbach. 1989. *Scientific reasoning: The Bayesian tradition.* Lasalle, Ill.: Open Court.

Hummel, J. E., and K. J. Holyoak. 1997. Distributed representations of structure: A theory of analogical access and mapping. *Psychological Review 104,* 427–466.

Hummel, J. E., and K. J. Holyoak. 2003. A symbolic-connectionist theory of relational inference and generalization. *Psychological Review 110,* 220–264.

Hutchins, E. 1995. *Cognition in the wild.* Cambridge, Mass.: The MIT Press.

James, W. 1884. What is an emotion? *Mind 9,* 188–205.

Johnson, M. 1987. *The body in the mind.* Chicago: University of Chicago Press.

Johnson-Laird, P. N. 1983. *Mental models.* Cambridge, Mass.: Harvard University Press.

Johnson-Laird, P. N. 1988. *The computer and the mind.* Cambridge, Mass.: Harvard University Press.

Johnson-Laird, P. N., and R. M. Byrne. 1991. *Deduction.* Hillsdale, N.J.: Erlbaum.

Kahneman, D., P. Slovic, and A. Tversky. 1982. *Judgment under uncertainty: Heuristics and biases.* New York: Cambridge University Press.

Kandel, E. R., J. H. Schwartz, and T. M. Jessell. 2000. *Principles of neural science.* 4th ed. New York: McGraw-Hill.

Kant, I. 1965. *Critique of pure reason* Trans. by N. Kemp Smith. 2nd ed. London: MacMillan.

Keil, F. 1989. *Concepts, kinds, and cognitive development.* Cambridge, Mass.: The MIT Press/Bradford Books.

Keysar, B. 1990. On the functional equivalence of literal and metaphorical interpretations in discourse. *Journal of Memory and Language* 28, 375–385.

Kintsch, W. 1988. The role of knowledge in discourse comprehension: A construction-integration model. *Psychological Review* 95, 163–182.

Kintsch, W. 1998. *Comprehension: A paradigm for cognition.* Cambridge: Cambridge University Press.

Kintsch, W., D. Welsch, F. Schmalhofer, and S. Zimny. 1990. Sentence memory: A theoretical analysis. *Journal of memory and language* 29, 133–159.

Kirshner, D., and J. A. Whitson. 1997. *Situated cognition: social, semiotic, and psychological perspectives.* Mahwah, N.J.: Erlbaum.

Kitayama, S., and H. R. Markus, eds. 1994. *Emotion and culture: Empirical studies of mutual influence.* Hyattsville, Md.: American Psychological Association.

Kitcher, P. 1993. *The advancement of science.* Oxford: Oxford University Press.

Kolodner, J. 1993. *Case-based reasoning.* San Mateo, Calif.: Morgan Kaufmann.

Konolige, K. 1992. Abduction versus closure in causal theories. *Artificial Intelligence* 53, 255–272.

Kosslyn, S. M. 1980. *Image and mind.* Cambridge, Mass.: Harvard University Press.

Kosslyn, S. M. 1994a. *Elements of graph design.* New York: W. H. Freeman.

Kosslyn, S. M. 1994b. *Image and brain: The resolution of the imagery debate.* Cambridge, Mass.: The MIT Press.

Kosslyn, S. M., G. Ganis, and W. L. Thompson. 2001. Neural foundations of imagery. *Nature Reviews Neuroscience* 2, 635–642.

Kosslyn, S. M., G. Ganis, and W. L. Thompson. 2003. Mental imagery: Against the nihilistic hypothesis. *Trends in Cognitive Sciences* 7, 109–111.

Kosslyn, S. M., and O. Koenig. 1992. *Wet mind: The new cognitive neuroscience.* New York: Free Press.

Kosslyn, S. M., and S. P. Shwartz. 1977. A simulation of visual imagery. *Cognitive Science* 1, 265–295.

Koza, J. R. 1992. *Genetic programming.* Cambridge, Mass.: The MIT Press.

Kramer, P. D. 1993. *Listening to Prozac.* New York: Viking.

Krauss, L. M. 1996. *The physics of Star Trek.* New York: HarperPerennial.

Kroger, J. K., J. D. Cohen, and P. N. Johnson-Laird. Forthcoming. A double dissociation between logic and mathematics. *Cerebral Cortex*.

Kroger, J. K., F. W. Sabb, C. L. Fales, S. Y. Bookheimer, M. S. Cohen, and K. J. Holyoak. 2002. Recruitment in anterior dorsolateral prefrontal cortex in human reasoning: A parametric study of relational complexity. *Cerebral Cortex* 12, 477–485.

Kunda, Z. 1999. *Social cognition*. Cambridge, Mass.: The MIT Press.

Kunda, Z., D. Miller, and T. Claire. 1990. Combining social concepts: The role of causal reasoning. *Cognitive Science* 14, 551–577.

Kunda, Z., and P. Thagard. 1996. Forming impressions from stereotypes, traits, and behaviors: A parallel-constraint-satisfaction theory. *Psychological Review* 103, 284–308.

Kurzweil, R. 1999. *The age of spiritual machines*. New York: Viking.

Laird, J. E. 2001. Using a computer game to develop advanced AI. *Computer* 34 (7, July), 70–75.

Lakoff, G. 1987. *Women, fire, and dangerous things*. Chicago: University of Chicago Press.

Lakoff, G. 1994. What is metaphor? In J. A. Barnden and K. J. Holyoak, eds., *Advances in connectionist and neural computation theory*. Vol. 3, *Analogy, metaphor, and reminding*, 203–257. Norwood, N.J.: Ablex.

Lakoff, G., and M. Johnson. 1980. *Metaphors we live by*. Chicago: University of Chicago Press.

Lakoff, G., and M. Johnson. 1999. *Philosophy in the flesh: The embodied mind and its challenge to western thought*. New York: Basic Books.

Langacker, R. W. 1987. *Foundations of cognitive grammar*. Stanford, Calif.: Stanford University Press.

Langley, P. 1996. *Elements of machine learning*. San Francisco: Morgan Kaufmann.

Langley, P., and H. A. Simon. 1995. Applications of machine learning and rule induction. *Communications of the Association for Computing Machinery* 38, 55–64.

Larkin, J. H., and H. A. Simon. 1987. Why a diagram is (sometimes) worth ten thousand words. *Cognitive Science* 11, 65–100.

Latour, B., and S. Woolgar. 1986. *Laboratory life: The construction of scientific facts*. Princeton, N.J.: Princeton University Press.

Lave, J., and E. Wenger. 1991. *Situated learning: Legitimate peripheral participation*. Cambridge: Cambridge University Press.

Leake, D. B. 1992. *Evaluating explanations: A content theory*. Hillsdale, N.J.: Erlbaum.

Leake, D. B., ed. 1996. *Case-based reasoning: Experiences, lessons, and future directions.* Menlo Park, Calif.: AAAI Press/The MIT Press.

LeDoux, J. 1996. *The emotional brain.* New York: Simon and Schuster.

LeDoux, J. 2002. *The synaptic self.* New York: Viking.

Lenat, D., and R. Guha. 1990. *Building large knowledge-based systems.* Reading, Mass.: Addison-Wesley.

Levesque, H. J., R. Reiter, Y. Lespérance, F. Lin, and R. Scherl. 1997. GOLOG: A logic programming language for dynamic domanis. *Journal of Logic Programming* 31, 59–84.

Lewis, M., and J. M. Haviland-Jones, eds. 2000. *Handbook of emotions.* 2nd ed. New York: The Guilford Press.

Ling, C., and M. Marinov. 1993. Answering the connectionist challenge: A symbolic model of learning past tenses of English verbs. *Cognition* 49, 235–290.

Lodish, H., A. Berk, S. L. Zipursky, P. Matsudaira, D. Baltimore, and J. Darnell. 2000. *Molecular cell biology.* 4th ed. New York: W. H. Freeman.

Loewenstein, G. F., E. U. Weber, C. K. Hsee, and N. Welch. 2001. Risk as feelings. *Psychological Bulletin* 127, 267–286.

Lycan, W. G. 1996. *Consciousness and experience.* Cambridge, Mass.: MIT Press.

Maass, W., and C. M. Bishop, eds. 1999. *Pulsed neural networks.* Cambridge, Mass.: MIT Press.

MacGregor, D. G., P. Slovic, D. Dreman, and M. Berry. 2002. Imagery, affect, and financial judgment. *Journal of Psychology and Financial Markets* 1, 104–110.

Mackworth, A. 1993. On seeing robots. In A. Basu and X. Li, eds., *Computer vision: Systems, theory, and applications*, 1–13. Singapore: World Scientific.

MacWhinney, B., and J. Leinbach. 1991. Implementations are not conceptualizations: Revising the verb model. *Cognition* 40, 121–157.

Magnani, L., P. Nersessian, and P. Thagard, eds. 1999. *Model-based reasoning in scientific discovery.* New York: Kluwer/Plenum.

Maida, A. S. 1990. Frame theory. In S. C. Shapiro, ed., *Encyclopedia of artificial intelligence*, 302–312. New York: Wiley.

Mannes, S. M., and W. Kintsch. 1991. Routine computing tasks: Planning as understanding. *Cognitive Science* 15, 305–342.

Margolis, E., and S. Laurence, eds. 1999. *Concepts: Core readings.* Cambridge, Mass.: The MIT Press.

Marr, D. 1982. *Vision.* San Francisco: Freeman.

Marr, D., and T. Poggio. 1976. Cooperative computation of stereo disparity. *Science* 194, 283–287.

McCawley, J. D. 1993. *Everything that linguists have always wanted to know about logic—but were ashamed to ask.* 2nd ed. Chicago: University of Chicago Press.

McClelland, J. L., and J. L. Elman. 1986. The TRACE model of speech perception. *Cognitive Psychology* 18, 1–86.

McClelland, J. L., B. L. McNaughton, and R. C. O'Reilly. 1995. Why there are complementary learning systems in the hippocampus and neocortex: Insights from the successes and failures of connectionist models of learning and memory. *Psychological Review* 102, 419–457.

McClelland, J. L., and K. Patterson. 2002. Rules or connections in past-tense inflections: What does the evidence rule out? *Trends in Cognitive Sciences* 6, 465–472.

McClelland, J. L., and D. E. Rumelhart. 1981. An interactive activation model of context effects in letter perception. Part 1, An account of basic findings. *Psychological Review* 88, 375–407.

McClelland, J. L., and D. E. Rumelhart. 1989. *Explorations in parallel distributed processing.* Cambridge, Mass.: The MIT Press.

McCloskey, M., and N. J. Cohen. 1989. Catastrophic interference in connectionist networks: The sequential learning problem. In G. H. Bower, ed., *The psychology of learning and motivation.* Vol. 24, 109–165. New York: Academic Press.

McDermott, D. V. 2001. *Mind and mechanism.* Cambridge, Mass.: The MIT Press.

Medin, D. L., B. H. Ross, and A. Markman. 2001. *Cognitive psychology.* 3rd ed. Hoboken, N.J.: Wiley.

Merikle, P. M., and M. Daneman. 2000. Conscious vs. unconscious perception. In M. S. Gazzaniga, ed., *The new cognitive neurosciences,* 2nd ed., 1295–1303. Cambridge, Mass.: The MIT Press.

Metzinger, T., ed. 2000. *Neural correlates of consciousness.* Cambridge, Mass.: The MIT Press.

Mill, J. S. 1974. *A system of logic ratiocinative and inductive.* Toronto: University of Toronto Press.

Miller, G. A. 1956. The magical number seven, plus or minus two: Some limits on our capacity for processing information. *Psychological Review* 63, 81–97.

Miller, G. A. 1991. *The science of words.* New York: Scientific American Library.

Minsky, M. 1975. A framework for representing knowledge. In P. H. Winston, ed., *The psychology of computer vision,* 211–277. New York: McGraw-Hill.

Mitchell, M. 1993. *Analogy-making as perception.* Cambridge, Mass.: The MIT Press.

Montague, R. 1974. *Formal philosophy: Selected papers of Richard Montague*. New Haven, Conn.: Yale University Press.

Moody, E., and E. Skolnick, eds. 2001. *Molecular bases of anesthesia*. Boca Raton, Fla.: CRC Press.

Moravec, H. 1998. *Robot: Mere machine to transcendent mind*. Oxford: Oxford University Press.

Morris, J. S. 2002. How do you feel? *Trends in Cognitive Sciences* 6, 317–319.

Murphy, G. L. 2002. *The big book of concepts*. Cambridge, Mass.: The MIT Press.

Murphy, G. L., and D. Medin. 1985. The role of theories in conceptual coherence. *Psychological Review* 92, 289–316.

Nadel, L., ed. 2003. *Encyclopedia of cognitive science*. London: Nature Publishing Group.

Nagel, T. 1979. *Mortal questions*. Cambridge: Cambridge University Press.

Neapolitan, R. 1990. *Probabilistic reasoning in expert systems*. New York: Wiley.

Nelson, G., P. Thagard, and S. Hardy. 1994. Integrating analogies with rules and explanations. In K. J. Holyoak and J. A. Barnden, eds., *Advances in connectionist and neural computational theory*. Vol. 2, *Analogical connections*, 181–205. Norwood, N.J.: Ablex.

Nerb, J., and H. Spada. 2001. Evaluation of environmental problems: A coherence model of cognition and emotion. *Cognition and Emotion* 15, 521–551.

Nersessian, N. 1989. Conceptual change in science and in science education. *Synthese* 80, 163–183.

Newell, A. 1990. *Unified theories of cognition*. Cambridge, Mass.: Harvard University Press.

Newell, A., J. C. Shaw, and H. Simon. 1958. Elements of a theory of human problem solving. *Psychological Review* 65, 151–166.

Newell, A., and H. A. Simon. 1972. *Human problem solving*. Englewood Cliffs, N.J.: Prentice-Hall.

Nisbett, R. E. 2003. *The geography of thought: How Asians and Westerners think differently . . . and why*. New York: Free Press.

Nisbett, R. E., ed. 1993. *Rules for reasoning*. Hillsdale, N.J.: Erlbaum.

Norman, D. A. 1989. *The design of everyday things*. New York: Doubleday.

Norman, D. A. 2003. *Emotional design: Why we love (or hate) everyday things*. New York: Basic Books.

Nussbaum, M. 2001. *Upheavals of thought.* Cambridge: Cambridge University Press.

Oatley, K. 1992. *Best laid schemes: The psychology of emotions.* Cambridge: Cambridge University Press.

Oatley, K., and J. M. Jenkins. 1996. *Understanding emotions.* Oxford: Blackwell.

O'Brien, D. P., M. D. S. Braine, and Y. Yang. 1994. Propositional reasoning by mental models? Simple to refute in principle and in practice. *Psychological Review* 101, 711–724.

O'Hare, G. M. P., and N. Jennings, eds. 1996. *Foundations of distributed artificial intelligence.* New York: Wiley.

O'Reilly, R. C., and Y. Munakata. 2000. *Computational explorations in cognitive neuroscience.* Cambridge, Mass.: The MIT Press.

Paivio, A. 1971. *Imagery and verbal processes.* New York: Holt, Rinehart, and Winston.

Panksepp, J. 1998. *Affective neuroscience: The foundations of human and animal emotions.* Oxford: Oxford University Press.

Pearl, J. 1988. *Probabilistic reasoning in intelligent systems.* San Mateo, Calif.: Morgan Kaufman.

Pearl, J. 2000. *Causality: Models, reasoning, and inference.* Cambridge: Cambridge University Press.

Peirce, C. S. 1992. *Reasoning and the logic of things.* Cambridge, Mass.: Harvard University Press.

Penrose, R. 1994. *Shadows of the mind: A search for the missing science of consciousness.* Oxford: Oxford University Press.

Perry, E., H. Ashton, and A. Young, eds. 2002. *Neurochemistry of consciousness.* Amsterdam: John Benjamins.

Piaget, J., and B. Inhelder. 1969. *The psychology of the child.* Trans. by H. Weaver. New York: Basic Books.

Picard, R. W. 1997. *Affective computing.* Cambridge, Mass.: The MIT Press.

Pinker, S. 1994. *The language instinct: How the mind creates language.* New York: William Morrow.

Pinker, S. 1999. *Words and rules: The ingredients of language.* New York: HarperCollins.

Pinker, S. 2002. *The blank slate: The modern denial of human nature.* New York: Viking.

Pinker, S., and A. Prince. 1988. On language and connectionism: Analysis of a parallel distributed processing model of language acquisition. *Cognition* 28, 73–193.

Pinker, S., and M. T. Ullman. 2002. The past and future of the past tense. *Trends in Cognitive Sciences* 6, 456–464.

Polk, T. A., and C. M. Seifert, eds. 2002. *Cognitive modeling.* Cambridge, Mass.: The MIT Press.

Pollack, J. B. 1991. The induction of dynamical recognizers. *Machine Learning* 7, 227–252.

Pollock, J. L. 1995. *Cognitive carpentry: A blueprint for how to build a person.* Cambridge, Mass.: The MIT Press.

Port, R., and T. van Gelder, eds. 1995. *Mind as motion: Explorations in the dynamics of cognition.* Cambridge, Mass.: The MIT Press.

Posner, M. I., and S. W. Keele. 1970. Retention of abstract ideas. *Journal of Experimental Psychology* 83, 304–308.

Posner, M. I., and M. E. Raichle. 1994. *Images of mind.* New York: Freeman.

Prietula, M. J., K. M. Carley, and L. Gasser, eds. 1998. *Simulating organizations: Computational models of institutions and groups.* Menlo Park, Calif.: AAAI Press.

Prior, A. N. 1967. Logic, history of. In P. Edwards, ed., *Encyclopedia of philosophy,* vol. 4, 513–571. New York: Macmillan.

Putnam, H. 1975. *Mind, language, and reality.* Cambridge: Cambridge University Press.

Pylyshyn, Z. 1984. *Computation and cognition: Toward a foundation for cognitive science.* Cambridge, Mass.: The MIT Press.

Pylyshyn, Z. 2002. Mental imagery: In search of a theory. *Behavioral and Brain Sciences* 25, 157–237.

Quartz, S. R., and T. J. Sejnowski. 2002. *Liars, lovers, and heroes: What the new brain science reveals about how we become who we are.* New York: William Morrow.

Quinlan, J. R. 1983. Learning efficient classification procedures and their application to chess end games. In R. Michalski, J. Carbonell, and T. Mitchell, eds., *Machine learning: An artificial intelligence approach.* Palo Alto, Calif.: Tioga.

Read, S., and A. Marcus-Newhall. 1993. The role of explanatory coherence in the construction of social explanations. *Journal of Personality and Social Psychology* 65, 429–447.

Resnick, L., J. Levine, and S. Behrend, eds. 1991. *Socially shared cognitions.* Hillsdale, N.J.: Erlbaum.

Richards, D. 1990. Is strategic decision making chaotic? *Behavioral Science* 35, 219–232.

Rips, L. J. 1983. Cognitive processes in propositional reasoning. *Psychological Review* 90, 38–71.

Rips, L. J. 1986. Mental muddles. In M. Brand and R. M. Harnish, eds., *The representation of knowledge and belief*, 258–286. Tucson, Ariz.: University of Arizona Press.

Rips, L. J. 1994. *The psychology of proof: Deductive reasoning in human thinking.* Cambridge, Mass.: The MIT Press.

Rips, L. J., E. J. Shoben, and E. E. Smith. 1973. Semantic distance and the verification of semantic relations. *Journal of Verbal Learning and Verbal Behavior* 12, 120.

Rolls, E. T. 1999. *The brain and emotion.* Oxford: Oxford University Press.

Rosch, E. B. 1973. On the internal structure of perceptual and semantic categories. In T. E. Moore, ed., *Cognitive development and the acquisition of language*, 111–144. New York: Academic Press.

Rosch, E. B., and C. B. Mervis. 1975. Family resemblances: Studies in the internal structure of categories. *Cognitive Psychology* 7, 573–605.

Rosenbloom, P. S., J. E. Laird, and A. Newell, eds. 1993. *The Soar papers: Research on integrated intelligence.* Cambridge, Mass.: The MIT Press.

Rumelhart, D. E. 1980. Schemata: The building blocks of cognition. In R. Spiro, B. Bruce, and W. Brewer, eds., *Theoretical issues in reading comprehension*, 33–58. Hillsdale, N.J.: Erlbaum.

Rumelhart, D. E., and J. L. McClelland. 1982. An interactive activation model of context effects in letter perception. Part 2, The contextual enhancement effect and some tests and extensions of the model. *Psychological Review* 89, 60–94.

Rumelhart, D. E., and J. L. McClelland, eds. 1986. *Parallel distributed processing: Explorations in the microstructure of cognition.* Cambridge Mass.: The MIT Press.

Russell, S., and P. Norvig. 2003. *Artificial intelligence: A modern approach.* 2nd ed. Upper Saddle River, N.J.: Prentice-Hall.

Salomon, G., ed. 1993. *Distributed cognitions.* Cambridge: Cambridge University Press.

Savoy, R. L. 2001. History and future directions of human brain mapping and functional neuroimaging. *Acta Psychologica* 107, 9–42.

Schank, P., and M. Ranney. 1991. Modeling an experimental study of explanatory coherence. In *Proceedings of the Thirteenth Annual Conference of the Cognitive Science Society*, 892–897. Hillsdale, N.J.: Erlbaum.

Schank, P., and M. Ranney. 1992. Assessing explanatory coherence: A new method for integrating verbal data with models of on-line belief revision. In *Proceedings of the Fourteenth Annual Conference of the Cognitive Science Society*, 599–604. Hillsdale, N.J.: Erlbaum.

Schank, R. C. 1982. *Dynamic memory: A theory of reminding and learning in computers and people*. New York: Cambridge University Press.

Schank, R. C. 1986. *Explanation patterns: Understanding mechanically and creatively*. Hillsdale, N.J.: Erlbaum.

Schank, R. C., and R. P. Abelson. 1977. *Scripts, plans, goals, and understanding: An inquiry into human knowledge structures*. Hillsdale, N.J.: Erlbaum.

Scherer, K. R., A. Schorr, and T. Johnstone. 2001. *Appraisal processes in emotion*. New York: Oxford University Press.

Schmid, G. B. 1991. Chaos theory and schizophrenia: Elementary aspects. *Psychopathology* 24, 185–198.

Searle, J. 1992. *The rediscovery of the mind*. Cambridge, Mass.: The MIT Press.

Seidenberg, M. S., and J. L. McClelland. 1989. A distributed, developmental model of word recognition and naming. *Psychological Review* 96, 523–568.

Shanon, B. 1993. *The representational and the presentational*. New Yrok: Harvester Wheatsheaf.

Sharpley, A. L. 2002. Sleep: Slow wave and non-REM stages. In E. Perry, H. Ashton, and A. Young, eds., *Neurochemistry of consciousness*. Amsterdam: John Benjamins.

Shastri, L. 1999. Advances in SHRUTI—A neurally motivated model of relational knowledge representation and rapid inference using temporal synchrony. *Applied Intelligence* 11, 79–108.

Shastri, L., and V. Ajjanagadde. 1993. From simple associations to systematic reasoning: A connectionist representation of rules, variables, and dynamic bindings. *Behavioral and Brain Sciences* 16, 417–494.

Shelley, C. P. 1996. Visual abductive reasoning in archaeology. *Philosophy of Science* 63, 278–301.

Shepard, R. N., and J. Metzler. 1971. Mental rotation of three-dimensional objects. *Science* 171, 701–703.

Sinatra, G. M., and P. R. Pintrich, eds. 2003. *Intentional conceptual change*. Mahwah, N.J.: Erlbaum.

Skarda, C. A., and W. J. Freeman. 1987. How brains make chaos in order to make sense of the world. *Behavioral and Brain Sciences* 10, 161–195.

Smith, B. C. 1991. The owl and the electric encyclopedia. *Artificial Intelligence* 47, 251–288.

Smith, E., C. Langston, and R. E. Nisbett. 1992. The case for rules in reasoning. *Cognitive Science* 16, 1–40.

Smith, E. E., D. N. Osherson, L. J. Rips, and M. Keane. 1988. Combining prototypes: A selective modification model. *Cognitive Science* 12, 485–527.

Smolensky, P. 1990. Tensor product variable binding and the representation of symbolic structures in connectionist systems. *Artificial Intelligence* 46, 159–217.

Sobel, C. P. 2001. *The cognitive sciences: An interdisciplnary approach*. Mountain View, Calif.: Mayfield.

Solomon, M. 2001. *Social empiricism*. Cambridge, Mass.: The MIT Press.

Spellman, B. A., and K. J. Holyoak. 1993. An inhibitory mechanism for goal-directed analogical mapping. In *Proceedings of the Fifteenth Annual Conference of the Cognitive Science Society*, 947–952. Hillsdale, N.J.: Erlbaum.

Stabler, E. P. 1992. *The logical approach to syntax*. Cambridge, Mass.: The MIT Press.

Sternberg, R. J. 2003. *Cognitive Psychology*. 3rd ed. Belmont, Calif.: Wadsowrth.

Stillings, N. A., S. E. Weisler, C. H. Chase, M. H. Feinstein, J. L. Garfield, and E. L. Rissland. 1995. *Cognitive Science: An Introduction*. 2nd ed. Cambridge, Mass.: The MIT Press.

St. John, M. F. 1992. The story gestalt: A model of knowledge-intensive processes in text comprehension. *Cognitive Science* 16, 271–306.

Strauch, B. 2003. *The primal teen: What the new discoveries about the teenage brain tell us about our kids*. New York: Doubleday.

Suchman, L. 1987. *Plans and situated actions: The problem of human-machine communication*. Cambridge: Cambridge University Press.

Taatgen, N. A., and J. R. Anderson. 2002. Why do children learn to say "broke"? A model of learning the past tense without feedback. *Cognition* 86, 123–155.

Taylor, J. R. 2003. *Cognitive grammar*. Oxford: Oxford University Press.

Tesar, B., and P. Smolensky. 2000. *Learnability in optimality theory*. Cambridge, Mass.: The MIT Press.

Thagard, P. 1988. *Computational philosophy of science*. Cambridge, Mass.: The MIT Press.

Thagard, P. 1989. Explanatory coherence. *Behavioral and Brain Sciences* 12, 435–467.

Thagard, P. 1992. *Conceptual revolutions*. Princeton, N.J.: Princeton University Press.

Thagard, P. 1998. *Mind readings: Introductory selections in cognitive science*. Cambridge, Mass.: The MIT Press.

Thagard, P. 1999. *How scientists explain disease*. Princeton, N.J.: Princeton University Press.

Thagard, P. 2000. *Coherence in thought and action*. Cambridge, Mass.: The MIT Press.

Thagard, P. 2002. How molecules matter to mental computation. *Philosophy of Science* 69, 429–446.

Thagard, P. 2003. Why wasn't O. J. convicted? Emotional coherence in legal inference. *Cognition and Emotion* 17, 361–383.

Thagard, P., and E. Millgram. 1995. Inference to the best plan: A coherence theory of decision. In A. Ram and D. B. Leake, eds., *Goal-driven learning*, 439–454. Cambridge, Mass.: The MIT Press.

Thagard, P., and J. Nerb. 2002. Emotional gestalts: Appraisal, change, and emotional coherence. *Personality and Social Psychology Review* 6, 274–282.

Thagard, P., and C. P. Shelley. 2001. Emotional analogies and analogical inference. In D. Gentner, K. H. Holyoak, and B. K. Kokinov, eds., *The analogical mind: Perspectives from cognitive science*, 335–362. Cambridge, Mass.: The MIT Press.

Thelen, E., and L. B. Smith. 1994. *A dynamic systems approach to the development of cognition and action*. Cambridge, Mass.: The MIT Press.

Touretzky, D., and G. Hinton. 1988. A distributed production system. *Cognitive Science* 12, 423–466.

Towell, G. G., and J. W. Shavlik. 1994. Refining symbolic knowledge using neural networks. In R. Michalski and G. Tecuci, eds., *Machine learning: A multistrategy approach*. Vol. 4, 405–429. San Francisco: Morgan Kaufman.

Tversky, A., and D. Kahneman. 1983. Extensional versus intensional reasoning: The conjunction fallacy in probability judgments. *Psychological Review* 90, 293–315.

Tye, M. 1991. *The imagery debate*. Cambridge, Mass.: The MIT Press.

van Geert, P. 1991. A dynamic systems model of cognitive and language growth. *Psychological Review* 98, 3–53.

van Gelder, T., and R. Port. 1995. It's about time: An overview of the dynamical approach to cognition. In R. Port and R. van Gelder, eds., *Mind as motion: explorations in the dynamics of cognition*, 1–43. Cambridge, Mass.: The MIT Press.

von Eckardt, B. 1993. *What is cognitive science?* Cambridge, Mass.: The MIT Press.

Wagar, B. M., and P. Thagard. 2004. Spiking Phineas Gage: A neurocomputational theory of cognitive-affective integration in decision making. *Psychological Review* 111, 67–79.

Ward, L. M. 2002. *Dynamical cognitive science*. Cambridge, Mass.: The MIT Press.

Ward, T. B., S. M. Smith, and J. Vaid, eds. 1997. *Creative thought: An investigation of conceptual structures and processes.* Washington, D.C.: American Psychological Association.

Wason, P. C. 1966. Reasoning. In B. M. Foss, ed., *New horizons in psychology*, 1–43. Harmondsworth, Middlesex: Penguin.

Watson, J. 1913. Psychology as the behaviorist views it. *Psychological Review* 20, 158–177.

Wharton, C. M., and J. Grafman. 1998. Deductive reasoning and the brain. *Trends in Cognitive Sciences* 2, 54–59.

Wharton, C. M., K. J. Holyoak, P. E. Downing, T. E. Lange, T. D. Wickens, and E. R. Melz. 1994. Below the surface: Analogical similarity and retrieval competition in reminding. *Cognitive Psychology* 26, 64–101.

Whorf, B. 1956. *Language, thought, and reality.* Cambridge, Mass.: The MIT Press.

Widrow, B., D. E. Rumelhart, and M. A. Lehr. 1994. Neural networks: Applications in industry. *Communications of the ACM* 37 (March), 93–105.

Wierzbicka, A. 1999. *Emotions across languages and cultures: Diversity and universals.* Cambridge: Cambridge University Press.

Wilson, R. A., and F. C. Keil, eds. 1999. *The MIT encyclopedia of the cognitive sciences.* Cambridge, Mass.: The MIT Press.

Winograd, T., and F. Flores. 1986. *Understanding computers and cognition.* Reading, Mass.: Addison-Wesley.

Winston, P. 1993. *Artificial intelligence.* 3rd ed. Reading, Mass.: Addison-Wesley.

Wong, A. K. C., S. W. Lu, and M. Rioux. 1989. Recognition and shape synthesis of 3-D objects based on attributed hypergraphs. *IEEE Transactions on Pattern Analysis and Machine Intelligence II* (3), 279–289.

Wooldridge, M. 2002. *An introduction to multiagent systems.* Chichester: Wiley.

Wyngaarden, J. B., L. H. Smith, and J. C. Bennett, eds. 1992. *Cecil Textbook of Medicine.* 19th ed. Philadelphia: W. B. Saunders.

Zeman, A. 2002. *Consciousness: A user's guide.* New Haven, Conn.: Yale University Press.

# Index